HOOPS
STARS & STRIPES
THE ANDY LYNCH STORY

Best wishes

Andy Lynch

Celtic FC

Andy Lynch with Paul John Dykes

CQN BOOKS

Published by CQN Books, Scotland.

Copyright Paul John Dykes. All rights reserved.

First published in the United Kingdom in 2016 by CQN Books
ISBN 978-0-9934360-7-9

A catalogue for this book is available from the British Library
and the Irish Library in Dublin.

Cover & page design and typesetting
by Stephen Cameron for CQN Books.

Edited by Tom Campbell.
Publisher, David Faulds for CQN Books.

Printed by APS, Airdrie, North Lanarkshire

A special thank you to everyone in the
Celtic Quick News community and the wider Celtic family.

CQN has published books on Lisbon Lions Willie Wallace,
Tommy Gemmell, Charlie Gallagher and John Hughes
alongside Caesar & The Assassin
and The Winds of Change by Alex Gordon.

For the latest Celtic news and best Celtic conversation
visit www.celticquicknews.co.uk
and to shop online at www.cqnbookstore.com

ACKNOWLEDGEMENTS

My good friend, Paul John Dykes, has worked tirelessly to bring this book together. He has been patient and very helpful, and a big thank you goes out to him.

Writing my life story has made me appreciate a lot of things that I wouldn't have otherwise contemplated. My Mum and Dad gave me love and encouragement throughout their lives, and were always there for me and my brothers.

Both of my parents died from cancer, and I will be donating a percentage of any earnings made from this book to the Beatson West of Scotland Cancer Centre in Glasgow.

I also have to thank Mag, who was always there when things went wrong in my football career. She has been a great mother to our kids Nicola, Martin, Andrew, and Simon; and grandmother to Sophie, Erin, Ajay, Josh, Sean, Amelia and Maya.

I had great coaches who undoubtedly helped me believe in myself and strive to get better all the time. Harry Davis at Queen's Park, Jock Wallace at Hearts, and the great Jock Stein and Billy McNeill at Celtic. I also had so many coaches on my early journey in the game. Those dedicated men who ran the amateur and junior teams just for the love of football.

My partner Margaret wasn't around when I played football. However, she never ceases to be amazed at the number of people who come up to me and want to talk about Celtic. I try to explain that the people I speak to feel that they are part of a family - the Celtic family.

ABOUT THE AUTHOR

Paul John Dykes is the author of
The Quality Street Gang (2013) and
Celtic's Smiler: The Neilly Mochan Story (2015).

He was also the Executive Producer of the 2015
documentary adaptation of *Celtic's Smiler*.

All of these titles are available at:

www.cqnbookstore.com

Follow the author on Twitter @PaulDykes

AUTHOR ACKNOWLEDGEMENTS

I would like to dedicate my work on this book to my
father, Jimmy Dykes (AKA The Ginger Legend), who is
bravely fighting cancer. Keep The Faith!

The following people have supported me throughout
the writing of this book:

My wife, Lynsey (and WP), who stand by me through
every success and tribulation; My parents and siblings;
Tom Campbell for his expertise, advice and editing skills;
Stephen Murray, who introduced me to Andy;
Craig Brown Photography; Mikey Mlotkiewicz;
Steven Dow at 6 Yard Box; Jimmy Barker and all the
boys at Juno! and 7-a-sides records; John Murray;
David Faulds, Paul Brennan and everyone at CQN;
John Gerard Kelly (may he rest in peace).

And the man himself - Andy Lynch.

CONTENTS

ANDY LYNCH in conversation with the author, Paul John Dykes

CHAPTER ONE
ON THE ROAD

Let me take you on the road. On a remarkable journey that will span from Stenhousemuir to San Francisco, from Queen's Park to Queensland, the maniacal of a Glasgow derby to the Manic of Montreal... We will cover expansive stretches of open road, full of wonderment, while cruising along on auto-pilot with the sun in our eyes, sweet sounds in our ears, and not a care in the world... Other, more tumultuous areas of the trip are preceded by the ominously dark clouds that appear overhead. We will be taken off the beaten track on a bumpy ride over treacherous and winding paths and uneven surfaces, where anxiety lies before every bend. Negotiating this rough terrain is never easy and we will suffer a few blow-outs along the way before getting back on track. We will share the highs and the lows, the good and the bad, monumental success and debilitating disappointment.

I will take you on a guided tour of all the highways and byways of Scottish football throughout the late 60s to the early 80s: the great men that I have known, the talents wasted, the joys and pitfalls of life as a professional footballer, and how to come back stronger having sank to those depths of despair.

What about life after football? I'll tell you all about that as well. Is there such a thing as life after wearing the green-and-white hoops of Celtic? The club, its colours, the traditions, those unbelievable memories, the even more incredible supporters: those things have never left me, regardless of where I have ventured. I have been approached by Celtic fans all over the world from Kearney to Kilkenny and am always remembered for being 'Andy Lynch of Celtic'. I'm more than happy with that. I have been asked countless times about scoring the winner against Rangers in a Scottish Cup final, about winning 'the double' in 1977, and about 'the 4-2 game' in 1979. I will tell you all about these momentous occasions and more as we make our way through my long and meandering odyssey.

My football journey really began in April 1965 with a Charlie Gallagher corner-kick at Hampden Park. As a dramatic Scottish Cup final neared its conclusion, Celtic's towering and dominant centre-half, Billy McNeill, rose like a dove above the black-and-white jerseys of Dunfermline Athletic defenders to head the ball expertly into my path. As I stretched to make contact with my right foot, my so-called weaker foot, Celtic's captain had already turned away to celebrate one of the most important goals in the club's history.

That's true: from Gallagher's corner, to McNeill's head, to my foot. It felt like a dream. The national stadium was alive and buzzing; the green-and-white contingent among the 110,000 supporters had been success-starved for almost eight long years. As the winning goal registered, the Hoops' fans erupted into rapturous abandon as they shared in this momentous occasion. But could Celtic hold on for nine more gripping minutes to win the Scottish Cup?

I know what you're thinking. Surely Andy Lynch isn't old enough to have played in that cup final! And you'd be right. It took me another nine years before I could call goal-scorer Billy McNeill, and his fellow Celts Bobby Murdoch and Bobby Lennox my team-mates. Back then though, I was delighted to celebrate behind Dunfermline's goal as one of Hampden Park's ball-boys. Watch the old footage back (in colour) and you will see my red jersey which matched the number two on the back of Willie Callaghan's Pars' shirt as he dejectedly retrieved the match ball from the back of goalkeeper Jim Herriot's net, a ball poked in his direction by me.

That was the moment when the storm clouds dissipated for Celtic, and the resplendent heavens began to shine brightly. I was there as a 14-year-old ball-boy jumping up-and-down behind the goal to celebrate their 3-2 victory. I was so close to the Celtic players when this snapshot of glory was set in stone for the rest of time that I could make out their roars of elation. I could hear their breath, heavy with the reality of eight years without a trophy weighing down on their shoulders. I could see the beads of sweat on their brows, and the steam from their exhausted heads. And I couldn't hide my unbridled elation.

Billy McNeill was a hero of mine. With his brylcreem-shiny hair, side-combed to perfection, and his chest proudly sticking out, Billy was the archetypal leader of that burgeoning Celtic side. He had the stature of a head honcho even then and I've never seen anyone who could header a ball like he did. I would watch in awe as he sprang up and towered above all around him. He was a galactic figure and nobody had a chance against him in the air.

It wouldn't be long before I played against him, then alongside him, and then for him.

But for now, I had to endure the wrath of an irate Hampden Park official for having the nerve to celebrate this fantastic Celtic triumph while acting as an ambassador for the stadium's venerable tenants, Queen's Park Football Club. I was lambasted after the game for showing my true colours whilst representing the Spiders. By that time though I didn't care. My team had won their first trophy under a man who I would later call "Boss." Jock Stein, Scotland's greatest ever manager, had started his transformation of Celtic. Scottish football would never be the same again.

I had got involved at the national stadium through a childhood friend, Sandy West, who lived around the corner from my family in Cardonald in Glasgow's South Side. His dad was a Queen's Park Director and I was asked to help out on ball-boy duty. The down-side was that I had to attend Queen's Park home games, but the cup finals and international matches more than made up for that. By that age I was already football-daft and it meant that I could get close to the action and to some of my heroes.

The Ground Secretary, James Gillies, would write "to request my attendance" for each match and I recall a Scotland international where I was able to observe first hand the talents of Denis Law, Dave McKay, Ian St John and other stars of the time. They were practising in one of the vast areas behind Hampden's goals and I was transfixed by their immense ability as they volleyed the ball at pace to one another. The ball never hit the ground as they worked it around the group until one of them shouted and they switched direction and the foot they were using. The sequence lasted around ten minutes and I was amazed at their skill. They seemed superhuman and it was an inspiring experience. I decided that I would train and practice as much as I possibly could because I wanted to be as good as them. I wanted to play at Hampden Park.

If those players seemed other-worldly then it was nothing compared to watching Pele, the great Brazilian forward, in the flesh. I will never forget seeing the grandeur and fluidity of this genius in full flow when he graced the proud old Scottish turf with his brilliance on 25th June 1966.

But before I was lucky enough to see the Brazilian World Cup heroes up close, I had to negotiate a journey in the back of a police wagon. My dad's car wouldn't start that morning and so, true to form, my old man pulled a favour from his colleagues at Cardonald Police Station and I was given an escort to Hampden by the other boys in blue. I didn't relish being in the spotlight normally occupied by the city's criminal underworld and I slouched down in the back seat to hide from any onlookers. The shame of it all was too much. As well as my unorthodox travelling methods, Stevie Chalmers' goal in the 1-1 draw sticks in my mind, as does the sight of these South American masters, Garrincha and all, puffing away on cigarettes on the sidelines. How did they get away with behaving like that and still manage to be footballing gods?

Some 14 years earlier, Andrew Paul Lynch arrived into this world on 3rd March in the shadows of another famous Scottish football hotbed - Ibrox Stadium. I was born into the Catholic faith at St Francis Nursing Home in Govan as the third boy of four from the union of George Joseph Lynch and Jean Lynch nee Shearin. 59 Clifford Street in Ibrox was where my brothers and I called home. George and Matthew were my older brothers and Thomas is six years my junior.

As far back as I can recall, football was always part of my life. We were a working-class family from Glasgow, after all, and football was life itself to many of the city's inhabitants. My brothers and I had our own individual sets of friends and we rarely did things as a gang of four. Life seemed uncomplicated and innocent back then. Summers were gloriously golden and simple past-times became marvellous adventures for my friends and I. From climbing the chestnut trees of Bellahouston Park to plundering apples from the well-to-do, we made it up as we went along.

The high-levelled dykes of the tenement back-yards also became our playground. The kitchen window of my home overlooked the disused wartime air-raid shelters, and my mum could keep an eye on me as she scrubbed the dishes at the kitchen sink. I, in turn, would know when my dinner was ready.

My mother had been a 'Govan Queen' in her youth, which entailed her being trotted by horse and carriage in a carnival procession through the streets of Govan. My father had been nine years her senior when he asked for mum's 20-year-old hand in marriage. He was suitably grilled by my mother's family, and I am sure he always knew just how lucky he was to have married such a great woman.

When I was around 12, my mother was diagnosed with breast cancer. It devastated my father unlike anything I had ever witnessed, and we were all shocked as he struggled to come to terms with mum's illness. Thankfully for us all, she survived that early infliction and went on to live until she was 73.

Our family were like most of our neighbours in that we didn't have much money to throw about but my parents still managed to take us on holidays to such destinations as Millport, Rothesay and Fairlie. After a few years, as things got better, we widened our horizons to far-flung places like Bournemouth and Torquay.

Only one wage went into our house and there were six mouths to feed so my parents managed really well, and the four Lynch brothers were always grateful for what we got. I do recall my father having to buy me a sturdy pair of shoes at one point, as I was going through them too quickly by playing football every day in the school playground. He picked up a pair of huge brown brogues from the Barras for me, and I could only imagine the kind of abuse I was going to receive the next day at school when I wore them.

As expected, my class-mates dished out the ribbings about this awful-looking footwear but, much to my tormentors' intrigue, I calmly explained that they had been bought specifically as football shoes. At morning break my class-mates soon realised what I meant, as I ran around the playground and clattered them with these solid boats on my feet. Surprisingly, no-one mentioned my shoes again.

I also wore those shoes when fulfilling my role as an altar boy at Lourdes Chapel. There was a snooker hall next door to the chapel, and my elder brother, George (who is sadly no longer with us) would meet his friends for a few frames when he was meant to be at mass with me. He would then join me after the evening service and we'd walk home together. On our way home, I would have to explain what the sermon was about because our dad would inevitably question one of us about it. When he asked George, my brother would recite what I had told him and somehow managed to keep his nerve. It wouldn't surprise me, however, if our dad knew what his wayward son was up to.

My folks did everything they could to raise us well and they certainly succeeded. One Christmas morning I woke up to a gleaming red bike. It was a splendorous sight and felt like the most amazing gift I could ever have received. I cherished those wheels that allowed me to explore with even more zest and freedom. Looking back now I realise that it was a second-hand model, which my father had painstakingly painted, but I felt so lucky that my parents could give my brothers and I such seemingly lavish gifts. My dad was very good with his hands and I learned many years later from my mother that he would wait until we were all in bed before going up the loft to fetch his tools and materials to make and mend presents for us. One year he burned the midnight oil for weeks working on a model fort for me and I'm sure the smile on my face come Christmas morning would have made it all worthwhile for him.

My parents made huge sacrifices for my brothers and me and these realisations are often only appreciated when considered through the eyes of an adult years later. I may not have expressed it adequately then, but I was appreciative. The simplest of gifts I ever received was that of a football and I vividly remember getting a new plastic-coated one for my seventh birthday; at that time all-weather footballs were starting to take the place of the old, heavy leather ones. I treasured that ball and wouldn't take it out the house for days for fear of getting it dirty. After a week or so I started playing with it in the street or in the front close of our tenement building but I'd always wash it once I got back indoors. I was at my happiest with a ball at my feet and would also spend hours using a tennis ball to practice my early skills. Our next-door neighbours were the Hawthorn family and I'd employ their son, young Jimmy, as a goalkeeper when I needed one. Even at that age, I had made the decision that I wanted be a footballer and I dreamed of wearing the green-and-white hoops of Glasgow Celtic.

Celtic were always my team and, like many football fans, I inherited that allegiance from my father, who worked as a Constable for Glasgow Police. My dad was a real grafter and would work overtime when it was available to help raise his family. He would eventually progress to the position of Detective Sergeant and I am sure he witnessed some gruesome scenes on the mean streets of Glasgow throughout his lengthy career. On the occasions when he was off on a Saturday, he enjoyed nothing more than meeting a few pals for a couple of pints before heading to Celtic Park. I think that was the extent of his social life and he started taking me along to the games when I was about ten-years-old.

Life seemed a lot simpler in those days and there was a true community spirit in Ibrox where I lived. I recall going back and forth to neighbours' houses to borrow or drop off sugar or pick up some milk. Everyone seemed to help each other out and rallied around to make ends meet. The families who lived in our area shared a similar social standing and I certainly cannot remember any religious tension within the community back then. That's not to say that it didn't exist, and I'm sure it did to some extent, but this young soul was certainly never exposed to it in any harmful way.

Although I had burning ambitions to play for Celtic, geography meant that my first football wage would not be drawn from Celtic Park but from Ibrox Stadium, the home of my team's fiercest rivals. On match-days, the Rangers hoards would descend upon the South-Side of Glasgow in their tens-of-thousands and (as economic conditions improved) hundreds of cars would be parked on the streets surrounding my house. Rather than see this as a hindrance, I established a regular patch and politely asked the arriving motorists, "Can I watch your car, mister?" Anyone who has driven to a football game in Glasgow will be familiar with this ritual. A young ragamuffin will look after your motor while you enjoy the match and, at time up, your aspiring security guard will be rewarded with a few bob as a gesture of thanks. My entrepreneurial flair was evident even in my earliest years, as I secured business from around 20 vehicle owners for less than two hours of work. In saying that, I used to take a sneaky break with a few of the other boys when the main gates of the stadium opened for the last 20 minutes of the match and my friends and I would scurry up the terraces to catch the end of the game.

The first thing that hit me when I entered the vast expanses of Ibrox was the incredible atmosphere. The noise and thrilling excitement sent a shiver down my spine. I was immediately hooked on that feeling and, once I had tasted it, I wanted more. I was also engrossed as I watched all these giants playing at Ibrox. I used to stand at the Copeland Road end of the ground and studied the players' movement and positioning and was learning all the time. The skill of one player in particular left me mesmerised and it didn't matter to me that he wore the blue of Rangers. His name? Jim Baxter. His silky play, perfect passing and gliding movement as he effortlessly manoeuvred his lithe frame beyond the opposition left me enthralled. I also noticed that he was all left-footed, just like yours truly. Many years later I would have the pleasure of making Jim's acquaintance on more than one occasion but it wasn't on the field of play.

As soon as the full-time whistle blew, I would run back down to my patch to collect my earnings. As the drivers approached I would take an old hankie from my pocket and give their wind-screen a good clean for extra effect. It worked a treat and I still find it quite funny now when I think back to the Rangers' supporters paying a future Celtic player his early wages.

After a few months of 'car watching' I had my first taste of an Old Firm derby when my beloved team visited Ibrox and this was an experience that made a huge impression on me. I knew the two clubs were bitter rivals, of course I did, but I had never encountered anything quite like this. There was a tangible difference in the mood of the crowd that day. I could feel that the Ibrox atmosphere was far more intense than normal and the shouting and swearing was more vehemently aggressive and brutal. The noise increased to a completely different decibel level and there was a palpable undercurrent as the stadium became a bubbling cauldron. I was only ever interested in watching the football but what I felt around me that day made it pretty clear that this fixture was about more than just a game.

My father didn't know that I sneaked into Ibrox every fortnight and I'm pretty sure that he would have been more concerned about the safety aspect of it as much as anything else. When I look back and consider the age I was at that time, I realise that I had great freedom to explore the world without restraint. I suppose it helped me that there were three other children demanding the attention of my parents and I was able to slip away relatively unnoticed. Times have changed dramatically now though and I don't think many parents would be comfortable letting their kids mingle on their own with huge crowds like that. But I was fearless and I loved the excitement it gave me.

One thing that didn't overly excite me at that age was schoolwork and the Lynchs soon moved from Ibrox to a four-in-a-block at 62 Berwick Drive in Cardonald, where I started to attend Our Lady of Lourdes Primary School. My teacher, Miss Wilson, was terrific and dedicated her life to her class. Although I wasn't making great progress with the textbooks, at least I was making decent headway on the football front as an outside-left and I was selected to go to the Glasgow RC Schools' trials. Miss Wilson told me that I was to raise my hand at 3 p.m. on a Friday afternoon to remind her and she would allow me to leave school early to get a bus to Glasgow Green for the trials. On the first occasion that I did this, she acknowledged it and made a point of explaining to the rest of the class that I was representing the school at football. She then told me that they were all rooting for me. This made me feel like a million dollars and I also noticed that this extra attention seemed to impress the girls in the class and a young Frances McMenamin in particular. Frances and I had started school together at the age of five and she has gone on to achieve a wonderful level of success in the legal profession as one of the most respected Advocates in Scotland. It didn't go unnoticed to me that even that tiny bit of football stardom attracted female attention and this was an early indication (or warning) of one of the game's blessings (or vices) depending on which way you handle it.

Back to the football and all my practice and training paid off because I made the final cut. This meant that I would be playing games against other regions in Scotland and would be up against some of the finest young talents in the country. A young lad called Ronnie Glavin was also selected and we would later become team-mates at Celtic. Playing for Glasgow RC

Schools was an early challenge in my football career, as the competition was so fierce. It was a litmus test of capabilities and showed me exactly where I wanted to be. At primary school age, I was already given an indication of the levels I had to achieve and maintain if I wanted to carve out a career for myself as a professional footballer. The standards were unbelievably high but I was ready to do anything required to achieve my dream.

My schools football continued to progress as I made the step up to Our Lady of Lourdes Secondary and I also took part in coaching sessions at Lesser Hampden before playing matches for Queen's Park Victoria on school nights. Saturday afternoons were taken up with youth and amateur football and at different times I turned out for Mosspark, Eastercraigs and the much-lauded Glasgow United. My performances meant that I had become a much sought-after left-winger and a letter I received on 17th December 1966 from Jan Stevenson of Eastercraigs Amateur Football Club read:

"Jim Mullin has recommended you to us and if you are not committed to any club we would like very much to have you with us. I saw you playing against us at Lesser Hampden last year and was impressed. We are presently top of the under-16 league and are still in three cups.

"Good behaviour is expected on or off the field and any fines which are the result of trouble with the referee will not be met by the club.

"Finally, make sure your strip is clean, boots polished and hair combed. We may not be the best team in Britain but we can be the smartest."

As I said, the standards were set high for 15 and 16-year-olds but I think it is important to instil such values in players as soon as possible. These early lessons certainly made an impression on me and I carried on this disciplined approach throughout my career. As soon as I became associated with a club, be that amateur, junior or senior, I realised that I had to represent that side in the correct manner and always create a positive impression.

Glasgow United were a big name in youth football circles at that time and it was something of an honour to be asked to play for them. Many of their players were already earmarked to join professional clubs and Sam Beck, who ran the team, had an outstanding track record for developing young talent. One match in particular that stands out for me was played early in

1966 against a Celtic youth team. We beat them 3-2 and I set up a goal and played well on the left-wing. Celtic soon swooped for three of our players: a left-back called Freddie Pethard; Vic Davidson, who was a fabulous player and a stand-out at youth level; and a midfielder called Kenny Dalglish. The latter two would later be my team-mates at Celtic Park.

Even at that age, I could see that Kenny was a fantastic player who could turn a match on its head in an instant. He had that ability to win a game with one moment of magic. He was a decent young guy who just loved to play football like the rest of us. So what made him so special? Football historians and pundits will theorise about that until the end of time and it is difficult to point to one aspect of his make-up. He was an excellent player at that age but he was surrounded with players of a similar standard, and only one of them became 'the greatest Scottish footballer of all time'. Kenny lived his life the right way, he trained as hard as any other player I have ever known and of course he had natural, raw ability that he went on to develop and hone in emphatic fashion. When I think back to our time together at Celtic Park, I recall a player with an unquenchable thirst for playing in the bounce games at training. He had made it by then, he was a fully-fledged international, but he never wanted those games to end and he never wanted to lose. Kenny Dalglish had something that cannot be coached from a training manual. He was a winner and that is a character trait that is as powerful as any.

There were also a few promising players in Our Lady of Lourdes Secondary School team. Mr Martin Travers was a History teacher who coached our side and he was magnificent for us. He treated us like professionals and was a shining example himself, as he would often be seen playing tennis or running around the school perimeter. He was a dedicated athlete and demanded absolute commitment from his players, and he managed to get it. We won the Roseberry Shield after beating overwhelming favourites, St Mungo's, 4-2 in the final. My best friend from primary school, Gary Gallagher, was a clever jinking player who played left-half. I was outside-left and at inside-left was another great school friend of mine by the name of Tommy Craig. Tommy had a great football brain for one so young. Like me he was predominately left-footed and he would spray passes all over the field with precision. We had great synergy and often linked up to pick holes in defences and create goal-scoring opportunities.

It came as no surprise to me when Aberdeen signed Tommy at the tender age of 16. He went from strength to strength in the granite city and became the first Scottish teenager to be transferred for £100,000 when Sheffield Wednesday prized him away from Pittodrie Stadium in 1968. I was delighted for him when he got his move to the Dons and we used to write to each other after he moved into his digs up north. I did wonder when a club would come in for me though because I was at the right age and it was everything I had worked towards. When would it be my turn to sign the forms, fly the nest, and make another step up the football ladder? It never crossed my mind that I would be like the many other thousands of boys my age who had to find a job elsewhere and put their football dreams to bed.

School was finished for me at the earliest age possible (pupils were able to leave school at 16 then). While Tommy Craig was up at Aberdeen and my ex-Glasgow United team-mates Kenny Dalglish, Vic Davidson and Freddie Pethard had all been signed by Celtic, I went to sit my exam to become an apprentice compositor. It was obvious that I was never going to be a surgeon or a scientist and I left Our Lady of Lourdes Secondary before sitting my O-Level exams. School didn't appeal to me and, apart from playing football and the camaraderie I enjoyed with my team-mates, the only other aspect of attending school that interested me was chatting up the girls. So it was left to my dad to bail me out and he managed to arrange for me to sit the compositor exam at Glasgow College of Building and Printing. I started my two-year apprenticeship with Glasgow Corporation in Pollokshaws Road and I suppose that was something of a cross-roads in my early career. I had left school and had to get a job but I hadn't given up on my quest to become a professional footballer just yet.

I had been training with Queen's Park Victoria XI for a couple of years by that point. They were the amateur side's under-18s team and we used the Lesser Hampden pitch just adjacent to the national stadium. During this period I was lucky enough to be coached on several occasions by Queen's Park's first-team boss Harold Davis. Harold had played for Rangers as a defensive-midfielder for eight years and was seriously injured during his service in the Korean War. Despite being hospitalised for nearly two years following his tour of duty he was still as strong as an ox. He made a point of spending time with me one-to-one and would challenge me to get the ball off him as he shielded it like it was the Holy Grail. Try as I might, I was swept aside like leaves in the breeze; he was built like the side of a house and the most powerful man I had ever seen. Harold was the first great manager that I worked with in football. He made a huge impression on me and was one of life's finest motivators. I would go on to be coached by a few of Scottish football's greatest managers in the years that followed but there will always be a special place in my heart for Harold Davis, once of Rangers.

My compositor apprenticeship began on the work's van where the driver, Owen Travers, and I delivered printed materials all over Glasgow. I loved being out and about with Owen, who was an avid Celtic fan. He always had an infectious smile on his face, lived with his mother, and never married. Perhaps that was why he was always smiling? Owen was one of the thousands of supporters who travelled over to Lisbon on 25th May 1967 to watch that man Billy McNeill lift the European Cup. The change in fortunes for Celtic since I had seen them winning the Scottish Cup just two years earlier had been breathtaking.

I wasn't lucky enough to witness Jock Stein's football utopia of 1967 first hand but I did manage to watch it on the television thanks to my old boss, Malcolm Cameron. I recall going into his office on the Wednesday that week and sheepishly asking for the next day off. I think Owen Travers and I were about the only Celtic fans in the place so there weren't many workers on holiday.

"Do you have a doctor's appointment Andrew?" asked my gaffer without raising his head from the paperwork strewn all over his desk. "Yes, that's right Mr Cameron, a doctor's appointment," I responded whilst desperately trying to maintain my composure. To my surprise, he agreed to my request and I made my way to his office door with a spring in my step. "I hope your team wins, son," muttered Mr Cameron and I turned around briefly to catch the slightest hint of a smile on his face as I realised that he had double-bluffed me.

As much as I enjoyed the freedom of being out on the road with Owen, I had to prepare for a printing exam and my dad was determined that I wouldn't fail. After finishing his gruelling police shift he would join me in the kitchen and grill me on maths, English and general knowledge and even managed to get his hands on the previous year's exam paper to assist me with my revision. It was a tense time and on one occasion I found it so difficult to concentrate that my father lost his patience with me. What followed was a heart-to-heart discussion with my old man, who stressed the importance of getting a trade behind me. With tears in his eyes, my father explained that it was every young boy's dream to become a professional footballer and that I had to face up to the reality that it might not happen for me. This was a bombshell moment and I strongly opined that I could still make it as a footballer, I had no interest in a career in printing, and I didn't want to spend the rest of my life in a workshop. But my dad did have a point, as I was still on the vague periphery of the game while some of my contemporaries had made the step up. Despite this bite of reality being delivered from across the kitchen table, not making it as a footballer was still unthinkable to me.

I went into the exam at the College of Building and Printing with my dad's words ringing in my ears. I was only 16 and wanted to cling on to my dreams of following in the footsteps of the Scottish greats I had witnessed first-hand such as Jim Baxter and Billy McNeill. I still didn't want to let my old man down though; so I had to find an ally to help get me through this paper, someone who would assist me in my system of exam chicanery. Stevie Gaw was another young rabbit in the headlights who was working at the Govan Press at the time. I realised we were both in the same boat and we hit it off immediately. We quickly decided that we'd need to sit next to a couple of whizz-kids if we wanted to get through this academic torture. Stevie and I stationed ourselves next to the two brightest-looking students in the room and badgered them for the answers. Despite the exam monitor peering up from his Racing Post a couple of times, I think we just managed to get away with our ruse. The sense of relief as Stevie and I handed in our papers was palpable and we hoped we'd both be able to return to college for day-release with the requisite pass marks. Stevie Gaw has been a close friend of mine ever since that day but I never saw my clever-clogged partner in crime (whose paper I had more-or-less copied) ever again. When the results arrived in the post a few weeks later my dad was delighted and asked, "Well Andrew, was all that extra studying not worth it?" I just nodded and lied, "Yes, dad." If only my policeman father knew my crooked methods.

Meanwhile, I was enjoying my football with Queen's Park when I received a tip-off that Manchester United were sending Jimmy Murphy up to watch me playing one Saturday at Lesser Hampden. Murphy was the Assistant Manager to the legendary Matt Busby and had been influential in coaching and developing the Scotsman's ultimately tragic group of home-grown talents, 'The Busby Babes'. I began to dream of travelling down to Old Trafford to sign for one of England's greatest clubs.

Around about this time, I had decided to purchase a motor scooter to get me to and from work and training. As my wages wouldn't stretch to a Lambretta, I splashed out on a Vespa instead. One winter's night I was travelling home from training when a car in front of me turned right without signalling. This would-be mod was overtaking the offending vehicle at the very point that it turned unannounced and I careered into the motor and flew over its bonnet before coming to rest on the road in a daze. Talk about bad timing. The right side of my body and face was badly bruised and cut but I was lucky that my injuries weren't far more serious. This didn't stop me from attending training the following night, however, where I was approached by a concerned-looking Bert Cromar, who was our coach and a former Queen's Park player. Bert took one look at my battle scars and banished me from training. Worse still, he told me I wouldn't be playing on Saturday either. My dreams were going up in smoke just like my hapless scooter and I pleaded with him to at least let me sit on the bench as a sub. Credit to Bert, he was trying to look after my best interests but he was unaware that Manchester United were travelling up to watch me. He sent me home to lick my wounds and told me to report to Lesser Hampden on the Saturday where he would re-evaluate my fitness.

I don't think I slept for the next two nights as I worried that my opportunity to impress Manchester United was slipping away. When Saturday came, Bert Cromar still didn't want me to play and I think he only listed me as a substitute to pacify me. He told me to relax as I'd be back in the side the following week. Relax? Next week would be too late to keep my dream alive. During the match I deliberately jogged past the coach numerous times and tried to catch his eye so that he'd throw me into the action. About 15 minutes before the final whistle he finally relented and let me enter the field of play. I was out of the traps like a greyhound and frantically chased the ball to get involved and hopefully impress Matt Busby's right-hand man. My adrenaline got the better of me and the only thing I remember about the match was springing into the air for a high ball and getting a fair amount of force on to my header. Alas, the ball went in the wrong direction, and Jimmy Murphy headed back in the direction of Manchester without my signature. I was learning that football could be a cruel game and I decided that I perhaps needed a change of scene to revitalise my fortunes.

CHAPTER TWO
DOWN AMONG THE BIG BOYS

The spell between the ages of 16 and 18 is a vital period for all youngsters. Massive physical and mental changes take place and vital life decisions are made. Some of these choices can make or break your entire life especially if you are an aspiring athlete, and it can feel like a time of immense pressure and uncertainty. Around about this time, sometimes earlier, most of us are exposed to the temptation of alcohol and this can be a particular danger if your chosen path is in the world of sport. It's no secret that the tendency to indulge in the demon drink has destroyed and haunted many talented footballers for generations. I have witnessed this only too often in Scottish football and it is a vice that has squeezed the life out of countless players' promising careers over the years. I'm now going to describe my first bad experience of alcohol as a raw and innocent 16-year-old and it is one that should have put me off the stuff for life.

After crashing my scooter, I still used it for a while to get to and from work and I vividly recall that one of its final outings was the Friday before New Year's Eve in 1967. I was invited out by some of the men at lunch-time and told in no uncertain terms that it was a Glasgow Corporation tradition for everyone to have a festive drink. Not wishing to disappoint, I duly obliged and ordered a pint of lager like the rest of my work-mates. As the snow fell outside, the warm atmosphere within the confines of this Glasgow public house was intoxicating.

I was already aware that Queen's Park Victoria's match had fallen foul of the weather conditions and so I allowed myself the luxury of relaxing and enjoying the company of my fellow working man over a quiet pint. I hadn't really sampled much in the way of alcohol before this juncture (but

I am sure that any friends or family reading this will be thinking that I have certainly made up for it since then!) I slowly sipped my first pint and revelled in the welcoming ambience as all the lads had a good laugh and let their hair down. I felt better with every passing minute and soon consumed my second and then my third pint of this amber nectar as I thought to myself, "I could get used to this." It was New Year; so, somebody bought me a shot of whisky and some of the men had a couple more; and then it was back to the workshop where no further work would be done for the rest of the shift. The radios were blaring, Celtic were champions of Europe and everyone was on great form as the work-clock ticked rapidly towards clocking-off time when the weekend could really begin. Life was good.

And then, all of a sudden, it hit me. Maybe I didn't feel so good after all, as my head started to roll and the unmistakeable feeling of nausea began to take hold. I consoled myself a few times in the toilet cubicle but still felt lousy as I sat down in the workshop to take stock and hoped the dreadful feeling within my spinning head would subside. I had sowed the wind of the bevvy and, as I was reaping it's whirlwind, a lovely girl from the Bindery Department called Cathy took pity on me. As she laid my head against her chest and cooled my brow with dampened towels, I basked in the sweet scent of her perfume and wondered if I could just lie there until this abhorrent, debilitating condition disappeared. Cathy chatted away to her colleagues as if this was an everyday occurrence. "If only," I thought as I lay, the worse for drink, in the haven of her lap.

A few hours later, having wisely ditched my scooter, I made my way gingerly to the bus stop to take my pounding head homewards. I only made it as far as Bellahouston Park before alighting from the coach to be sick again. Why on earth had I allowed myself to fall foul of this most punishing of suitors? It had caused the death of a million dreams and been the scourge of a million scenes. Yet here I was under its dark spell and praying for mercy. The warm glow I felt in that Pollokshaws Road bar had long since passed. In its place was a burling wind and a gnawing fear of the wrath I would endure at the hands of my appalled and disappointed parents.

"I've been drinking... I don't feel that great... I don't have a game tomorrow... It's probably best that dad doesn't find out about this... I'm away off to bed..." I managed to explain all of this to my mother in one foul swoop on my way to my bedroom, where I suffered the spinning of the ceiling for a few hours more. Then I heard the sound I was dreading - the arrival home of my father. I could hear a muffled exchange between my parents in the kitchen and then the unmistakeable footsteps of my old man as he made his way along the lobby towards my alehouse-pungent bedroom. I braced myself for an absolute rollicking but, to my surprise, he sat himself down and explained that he understood why a boy my age would want to rub shoulders with my adult work-mates and have a few drinks after work. My dad told me to make no mistake, however, that if I had any aspirations to be a professional footballer then this must be a lesson learned. The penny well and truly dropped and my father didn't even have to raise his voice.

With a pounding headache and a sprinkling of self-pity, I awoke on the Saturday morning to the piercing ring-ring-ringing of our telephone. A few moments later my mother informed me that Mr. Harold Davis had been in touch and my heart began to sink to the bowels of my stomach. I was to report to Lesser Hampden at 1:30 p.m. to play for Queen's Park Hampden XI. This was a promotion, as the Hampden XI were Queen's Park's third team. I should have been over the moon but I felt as though I would have been better off hanging my head over the toilet. I couldn't hide my discontent from my mum, who showed me no sympathy as she curtly advised, "You'll be alright once you get up." It wasn't going to be that easy because I couldn't get up. My bones were rattling and I cursed myself for my previous night's ill-advised bacchanalia.

When I arrived at Lesser Hampden, I was delighted to see a layer of snow covering the pitch and I prayed that the falling flakes would get even heavier so that I could return home and seek refuge beneath my comfortable blanket. I have never been so relieved to hear a referee calling a game off but I wasn't out of the woods just yet. Harold Davis had called the office for an update and he wanted three of the Hampden XI squad to make their way to another venue. Queen's Park Strollers, their second team, still had a game to play and they were short of numbers. I felt numb when my coach gave me the nod and told me that Harold had selected me to make the step up. I had been promoted twice in one morning but could feel no elation whatsoever.

I am my greatest critic and I would rate my performance as average that day. Under the circumstances, mediocrity is the best I could ever have hoped for and I think the occasion and my adrenaline pulled me through the 90 minutes of my Queen's Park's reserves debut. Nobody at the club had been aware I was out the night before and I think I just got away with it on the day of the game. I knew that I could have performed far better, and I vowed never to put myself in such a predicament ever again. The following week, Harold Davis pulled me aside at training and congratulated me for a fine performance. He explained that the Strollers' coach was also highly impressed and that, if I kept up my hard work, then I'd be in the Queen's Park first-team soon enough. I felt ten-feet tall but there remained a sense of guilt that I had almost crashed-and-burned as a result of the excesses of a Friday night on Pollokshaws Road. I had missed out on the chance to woo Manchester United due to the slippery roads beneath my Vespa and I almost missed out on the opportunity to impress Queen's Park due to the slippery slopes of alcohol.

I just hoped that any future football career would include more trials and less tribulations.

Before I managed to secure the trial I was after, however, I made my third poor football decision six months later and moved into the junior ranks with Renfrew in June 1968. This meant that I had to cut my ties with Queen's Park, that fabulous old amateur club who live and breathe their motto, which translates to, "To play for the sake of playing." I owe a huge sense of gratitude to the oldest club in Scotland as they helped me just as they have helped countless other players over the years from Bobby Brown, Alex Ferguson, and Danny McGrain right up to the present day's international starlet, Andrew Robertson. Queen's Park truly are a Scottish football institution and should be celebrated for all that they do. I wrote to the club upon my departure and thanked them for setting me off on my quest to become a professional footballer. Characteristically, they replied and wished me their very best.

Almost as soon as the ink was dry on that correspondence, I realised that I had made a huge mistake. It was an error of judgment that almost resulted in me quitting the game altogether. In those days many senior clubs sent their young players to junior teams in a so-called effort to toughen them up and there was a mix of youth lads on the way up and grizzly old ex-pros playing out their last few years on tight, uneven, grassless pitches. I had decided to sign amateur forms with Renfrew Juniors, which meant that I didn't get paid but I had the option to sign for a senior club if I managed to impress one of their scouts. The term, 'junior,' may evoke visions of youth football but this league set-up in Scotland is a similar level to the non-league system in England. I was a ball-playing teenage winger and I soon realised that I was like a fish out of water in a Central League junior side. What won't kill you will make you stronger? Well, my time at Renfrew Juniors almost killed my football career.

As the winter months crept in, I remember one particular match that summed up my early experience of junior football. The temperature was below freezing and the layer of snow on the pitch colluded with the heavy leather ball to ensure that little in the way of attractive football would be played. My adversary for the afternoon was an overweight, 30-something right-back, who wanted to assault me through 90 minutes of one of his final pay-days so that he could get back to the boozer. I would have pitied this guy if he hadn't threatened me and my family at every opportunity but that kind of tactic only strengthened my indomitable spirit. I ran at him with pace every time I got the ball and, at one point, he shaped up to make a clearance and I opened my body up in an effort to block his cannon. His rifled volley crashed into my crown jewels and I collapsed into the foetal position in agony. Renfrew's 'physio' staggered on to the pitch with a cold sponge hanging from his kitbag and a fag-butt dangling from his mouth. I'm sure I was semi-comatose as he dragged me off the pitch so that the game could restart. "Just have a piss over there son and you'll be right as rain," suggested Renfrew Juniors' resident sports scientist.

I lasted until the end of the season but for the first time in my life I was having serious doubts that I would make it as a footballer. If the junior game was that tough then surely the senior competition would be even worse? I would later realise that this wasn't the case but as the 1968-69 season came to a close I refused to sign for another year and decided to take a break from the game altogether.

My old pal from primary school, Gary Gallagher, organised a summer jaunt to Blackpool with me and a couple of friends. I was looking forward to the break as I considered my future. A friend of my older brother, Matthew, kept asking me to go along to train with Kirkintilloch Rob Roy. 'The Rabs' had a decent set-up and had recently played in the Scottish Junior Cup final, where they lost to Cambuslang Rangers, but I was enjoying my break from football and I wasn't too keen to get back into the junior saddle. Matthew persisted however and told me that Rob Roy wanted to see me playing in an open trial match on the Sunday before I was due to head down to Blackpool. After much persuasion from my big brother I agreed to go along and took the bus out to Kirkintilloch. Unbeknownst to me, this was one of the best decisions of my football career and it kick-started a chain of events that would ultimately lead to me breaking into the senior ranks.

I had a field day during my trial match on the wide and lush greens of Adamslie Park and scored three of four goals in a 7-4 victory. It made a huge difference that I lined up alongside excellent players such as Joe Caven and Billy Walker. My break had done me the world of good and I realised that I had matured mentally and physically in the four or five months that I had been missing from the game. Joe Caven was an experienced ex-pro who had previously played with a host of clubs including Airdrie, Brighton, Raith Rovers and Morton and he gave me some important words of advice as we took a soak in the bath after the match. Joe figured that I wouldn't be in the junior picture for long and that the Rob Roy committee would offer me a signing-on fee of £20. He suggested that I should hold out for £30 because the club could recoup this ten-fold if, and when, I was to take the step-up to the seniors.

Sure enough, Club Chairman Mr Donald Graham, invited me into his office and explained in front of the committee that their normal signing-on fee was £20. He went on to reveal that Rob Roy were prepared to increase that by £5 because they could see that I had the potential to move on for a profit. Buoyed by my earlier bath-tub advice, I offered my signature for £40 and, as the committee members almost choked on their Bovril, Mr Graham recovered his composure to explain that no player had ever received such a monumental signing-on fee and that they would have to discuss the matter further. I went on to suggest that I fully intended to make the step up to senior football as soon as possible and that I would be a sound investment for them. I could see that Mr Graham was impressed with my negotiating skills and after some deliberation the committee agreed to my terms. I explained that I was visiting Blackpool later that week but that I was taking my boots and would train everyday while I was down there. I walked out of Mr Graham's office with my Blackpool holiday money in my back pocket and felt that my football career was finally back on track.

Although my trip to Blackpool was a lad's holiday and I would enjoy a few beers while I was down there, my football career was still my number one priority. As soon as my friends and I were settled into our seaside guest house, I told Gary I was off to find Bloomfield Road. My life-long friend was slightly bemused and wondered why I was visiting the local English Division Two side's stadium, so I explained that I was going to ask them for a trial. Sometimes in this life, a good old-fashioned Glaswegian gallus approach is the only way to make progress and I was brimming with confidence as I walked right up to Blackpool Football Club's front door and rang their bell. The old groundsman looked slightly bewildered as I explained that I had travelled down from Scotland and wanted a trial. As he raised his unruly eyebrows I went on to tell him that I was a decent left-winger and that I played for Kirkintilloch Rob Roy. With a shake of his head (and another twitch of his eyebrows) he instructed me to wait outside as he disappeared back within the bowels of the stadium. Ten minutes later and first-team Manager, Les Shannon, came out to see me. I was told to report back to the stadium at 10 a.m. for training.

Later that morning I trained with the Blackpool reserve and youth players and, although I noticed that the pace was a step-up from what I was used to, I felt that I equipped myself reasonably well. As I was getting myself ready to head back to the guest house, I was handed a letter by the Club Secretary, Mr Des McBain which read: *"You have been selected to play in a trial match. If available you should report at our training ground at Squires Gate with boots, towel and shin pads."* I was informed that the fixture would take place the following night against Coventry City and I immediately told them that I was available to take part. I ran all the way back to the guest house to tell Gary my phenomenal news and he couldn't believe that I had actually pulled this off. I had secured a training session and now a trial match while my friends were at the arcades chewing on Blackpool rock.

I played on the left side of midfield against Coventry City the following night and the coach felt that I played well. I was asked to take part in another game against Liverpool two nights later and I was only too happy to appear again as a trialist. The standard of the Liverpool side was the best I had ever come up against but I really got into my stride although the pace of passing was set at an extremely high tempo. I was doing well when I went into a crunching tackle in the second half and injured my ankle. The Blackpool physio strapped me up and assured me that it wasn't broken and that I should keep my weight off it and have it x-rayed once I returned to Scotland. Although I was disappointed to have picked up an injury, I felt that I had proven myself in highly-esteemed company. Coventry and Liverpool went on to secure top six league placings in England's Division One that season and I hadn't looked out of place going shoulder-to-shoulder with their reserve and youth players. I thanked all the staff and players at Blackpool and vowed to enjoy the rest of my holiday, whether I was injured or not.

A couple of days before we were due to return home, I went out for a few drinks with my travel companions to celebrate my successful trial matches with Blackpool F.C. I certainly didn't intend on heeding the physio's advice and laying low for the rest of the week in my room back at the guest house. We were all in high spirits as we walked past the famous Yates Wine Lodge Pub, but one of the guys we were with thought that it was a good idea to start shouting abuse at some of the English drinkers at the bar. This resulted in the predictable outcome and around a dozen booze-fuelled locals left their pub to give chase. With my ankle heavily strapped I had no option but to leg it and, after several lung-bursting minutes of sprinting, we split up like an ambush scene from Butch Cassidy and the Sundance Kid. Thankfully for us, and unlike Paul Newman and Robert Redford, we got out the other end relatively unscathed. Yet another evening was ruined by the nonsensical behaviour brought on by too much drink but on this occasion I was a blameless bystander.

Even this minor altercation with the restless natives couldn't take the shine off what was a fantastic holiday. Once we arrived back in Glasgow, Gary bought the *Evening Citizen* and we were amazed to read the headline on the back page which read, "Blackpool to sign Andy Lynch." I was gob-smacked and had a laugh at the fact that we had just been chased out of town and now they wanted me back. I could only deduce that The Seasiders had been in touch with Rob Roy about signing me after my two trial matches. The very mention of my name being associated with a big English club gave me a great sense of confidence. The football pendulum was beginning to swing in my favour and I wasn't about to rest on my laurels.

My ankle was back to full readiness by the time that I finally made my Rob Roy debut against Dunipace at Carronbank Park on 22nd August 1969. I scored one and set another up as we ran out 4-0 winners in front of a Blackpool scout and it seemed highly likely that I would be moving down to join the Tangerines full-time to finally pursue my dreams of football stardom. Blackpool made it known that they would watch me during my next few games but they had already been joined in the queue by Aberdeen, Coventry City, Dunfermline Athletic and Heart of Midlothian.

A few short weeks previously and I wasn't even playing football and now here I was with five senior teams on my trail. This was all a result of me taking a chance with the Rob Roy Juniors' trial match and then gate-crashing Blackpool's pre-season training; so, I had been the architect of my own destiny in many ways. I must admit, I was delighted that some Scottish clubs were interested in me because I didn't really fancy moving down to England just yet, although I would have done had that been my only option. I decided to concentrate on my performances and let the clubs make their move and it was Hearts who played their hand first.

Donald Graham approached me on the day of one of our games and advised that Hearts' Chief Scout, Dan Crawford, wanted to meet me afterwards. Our discussion took place in the Rob Roy boardroom, where I was met by Dan and another Hearts scout. They explained that I had been watched for several weeks and it was their belief that I could win a place in the Hearts first-team within a matter of months. That statement took me by surprise and I felt pretty humbled by it. At that time, many players my age were being signed by senior clubs and farmed him out to the junior leagues. I was delighted that Hearts wanted me in their first team so soon because they had a really strong side. Johnny Harvey was the man in charge of first-team affairs at Tynecastle and he wanted me to play as a trialist in a reserve game the following week. I was advised that the club had been searching the UK for a left-winger for some time and they believed that I was their ideal man. Talk about dangling a carrot in front of me. I was left with a firm hand-shake and the parting gambit, "Just come along to Tynecastle on Wednesday, enjoy the game and meet our Manager."

I respected Donald Graham and I was glad that we had a chance to discuss these developments once the Hearts representatives left Kirkintilloch. Mr Graham urged me to take my time before making a decision because there were plenty of clubs after me. I took his advice on board and hurried home to tell my dad the great news. The following Wednesday, we drove through to Tynecastle Stadium in Edinburgh with Mr Graham so that I could feature against Morton reserves. The playing surface was impeccable and, although I enjoyed the game, I still felt that I could have performed better.

Nobody ever had to tell me if I had played well or not. As I've mentioned before, I had been overly critical about my own performances for as far back as I can recall and I kept my very own 'Wee Red Book,' which included details of all my matches right back to 1966. This was my football diary and I collated every possible detail about each match that I had played in as I could including dates, opponents, venues, scores, positions played, goals scored, assists, and 'general comments'. The latter section included such observations as, *"Played average... Took too long to settle down... Right foot weakness... Slow in tackle... Taken off... Played terrible... Poor finishing shot..."* As these descriptions illustrate, perhaps I was slightly harsh on myself but it meant that I always strived for perfection and I was always looking to improve.

After my trial at Tynecastle, I showered and was taken into the Hearts boardroom with my dad and Mr Graham and we were introduced to the first-team Manager, Johnny Harvey. Mr Harvey was an ageing man with grey hair and a soft East Coast accent and he acknowledged that this had been the first time he had seen me playing in the flesh. Thankfully for me, he fully agreed with his scouts' reports and felt that I could fill the left-wing position in the first-team even though I was only 18-years-old. He spoke to me about the history of the club and asked me there and then to sign a contract and pledge my future to Heart of Midlothian Football Club. In return the club would give me first-team football. Mr Harvey also mentioned that the board would not stand in my way should an offer come in from a bigger club further down the line.

My mind was racing and I was given the opportunity to discuss the matter in private with my father and Mr Graham. There weren't many reasons why I shouldn't sign the contract but it did cross my mind that I should maybe wait a little longer in case Celtic came along. A few of my ex-team-mates were already in at Celtic Park but I had never been approached and I knew how rare these opportunities could be. I decided to sign on the dotted line that night for Hearts and the promise of first-team football was definitely the deciding factor. It was the right move for me at that point in my life and my starting wage was £35 per week. This would be supplemented with appearance money and win bonuses and I would remain a part-time player so that I could complete my apprenticeship as a compositor. It was decided that I would stay with my parents in Cardonald initially and travel to Edinburgh three nights a week for training. After a few months I would move to digs in Edinburgh and train full-time in the morning before being stationed at a printing firm in the afternoon to complete my trade. It was all a lot to take in but it was everything I had worked towards my whole life and, after the disappointments I had already suffered in football, I was ready to work as hard as it took to make a success of my Hearts career.

I hadn't realised it at the time but Johnny Harvey's insistence that I sign immediately may have been down to the fact that Coventry City had also been at the reserve match and were waiting in the wings. A newspaper report the following day read, *"Andy Lynch, who is regarding as one of Scotland's top juniors, completed a deal at Tynecastle after the teenager had impressed in a reserve team trial against Morton. Coventry, Blackpool and Dunfermline were all in for the Rob Roy starlet and Coventry's top Scottish representative, Dan Morris, had planned to rush young Lynch south today for signing talks with manager Noel Cantwell. But it was Hearts who got their man and Andy Lynch will turn out for the Edinburgh side on the left-wing."*

I travelled home from Edinburgh convinced that I had made the correct choice. All the years of training and practice had paid off and I was finally on the road to becoming a professional footballer. My father was delighted that I could still complete my apprenticeship and Rob Roy's Chairman, Mr Graham, had a cheque for £1000 in his suit pocket by way of a transfer fee. It was the perfect deal for all involved.

As we made our way back to Glasgow, I reminded Mr Graham that my monumental signing-on fee of £40, which paid for my trip to Blackpool and sparked off this chain of events, didn't seem so steep all of a sudden.

CHAPTER THREE
A JUNIOR JAMBOREE

It was on the ancient paving stones of Gorgie Road that I first met a man called Jock, who would be one of the finest coaches I ever had the pleasure of working with. His ability to motivate me and my team-mates was astonishing. Yes, he was an unstintingly hard task-master and one of the shrewdest one-to-one managers I ever encountered throughout my career. That hardness (and shrewdness) probably came from his upbringing in a Scottish mining village. Sure he was physically intimidating, and many witnessed this quality regularly in public, but at times he also had a sensitive (and intelligent) approach, reserved mainly for one-on-one situations. He was a genius at lifting his squad's spirits and his players would have ran through brick walls for him.

I first came into contact with him when I joined up with Hearts for training at Tynecastle, and he was the coach there. By now you will realise that this Jock was not the celebrated European Cup winner, Jock Stein, but rather Jock Wallace of Hearts.

This Jock had been instrumental in masterminding the shock 1967 Scottish Cup defeat of Rangers by their Berwick namesakes as player-manager, and he was now being groomed to take over Johnny Harvey's Tynecastle hot-seat by the time of my arrival in the capital. I immediately realised that Wallace's methods would be good for my development - and so it proved. It came as no surprise to me when he went on to accomplish domestic and European success in his coaching and managerial career after leaving Hearts.

I trained with the part-timers for the first few months of my career as a Jambo. The other coach who took the sessions was bonafide Tynecastle legend, John Cumming, who had been an absolute star in the great Hearts' sides of the '50s and '60s. His approach to the game could be exemplified by his famous quote, "Blood doesn't show on a maroon jersey," and I discovered early on that his nick-name had been 'The Iron Man' in his playing days on account of him playing on with a bloodstained bandage on his head, and inspiring his team to a 3-1 triumph over Celtic in the 1956 Scottish Cup final.

Coincidentally, I would team up with another decorated 'Jock and Iron Man' double-act later in my career once I left Edinburgh for pastures new.

The training was tough, just like Cumming, but I realised that the emphasis on hard-running was absolutely necessary due to the part-timers having had far less time to get into and stay in shape. We were all working during the day and it made for a hectic schedule. My own journey to Tynecastle started at clocking-off time (5 p.m.); I then got a bus from Pollokshaws Road to Queen Street Station, where I hopped on a train to Haymarket in Edinburgh; and then a brisk walk through Gorgie to Tynecastle. I did this three times a week and, when my Glasgow Corporation colleagues were spending time with friends and family during their holidays, I was travelling through to Edinburgh to train full-time. I didn't do this to solely impress Johnny Harvey but I think he was quietly pleased that I was showing a hunger to learn and improve.

The gaffer was full of praise when he spoke to the *Scottish Daily Express* at the time. *"I knew I had a good one when I signed him,"* explained Mr Harvey. *"He has loads of ability and is full of courage and enthusiasm. These few days of full-time training should help him immensely. He is just the kind of player we need in view of the injuries to our more experienced players."*

That spell of full-time football really paid off for me as my fitness levels benefited, and I was praying for a breakthrough so that I could play football for a living (and quit my day job). My father (always cautious) wouldn't have been enamoured with my outlook but I was clinging on to the promise I had been made upon signing for Hearts that I would soon taste top-flight action. Once that opportunity presented itself, I was ready to embrace it with open arms.

But first, reserve-team football beckoned and I was delighted, and a wee bit surprised, to find that it was far less harum-scarum than the junior game. I had more time on the ball and was surrounded by, as well as opposing, far more talented players. The pitches were in better condition and I wondered how much of a step-up in class and pace there would be when I made the transition to the first team.

It didn't take me long to find out, as Johnny Harvey kept his promise and I was thrown into my senior debut in the challenge match against the exotic-sounding Dallas Tornado at Tynecastle on 6th October 1969. The Texans were on an extended European tour as a build-up to their North American Soccer League (NASL) season and they boasted players from nine different countries in their ranks. Our party was comprised mainly of home-grown talents but we did have Norwegian internationalist Roald Jensen and the Dane Rene Moller to add some cosmopolitan flair to proceedings.

I started the match on the left wing and felt comfortable as we overcame the NASL side 4-1 in front of 5,500 floodlit home fans. Hearts' goals were scored by Jim Brown, Rene Moller and Neil Murray grabbed two from the bench. The line-up for my first ever senior game of football read:

HEARTS: *Jim Cruickshank, David Clunie, Peter Oliver, Jim Brown, Alan Anderson, Alan MacDonald, Roald Jensen (Neil Murray), Rene Moller (Jim Townsend), Donald Ford, George Fleming, Andy Lynch.*

Only 40 days after signing as a professional footballer and I was off and running at 18 years of age. Ironically, my nascent football journey saw me up against NASL opposition and it would be in that same league that it all-but-ended just 14 short years later.

Looking back now, I sometimes feel disappointed that my professional playing and coaching career can be gift-wrapped into a relatively short period. The reasons for this will become clear as we manoeuvre our way through this tale, but I certainly wasn't concerning myself with such bleak impulses on the night I made my first appearance. The old adage that a footballer's career is fleeting can be exemplified by my own story but, when I was in my late teens and early 20s (and everything was going well), I thought the dream would never end.

Mark my words - it's over in a flash.

Was I nervous as the team was read out in the Tynecastle changing room that night and I was named as number 11? Not really, but I was full of naïve abandon and not cockiness. I was excited that I was finally getting my big break and I felt ready for it. Reporters at the match may have called me, "An overnight success," but the truth was that I had worked for years to pull on that maroon jersey against these American cracks and I was hungry to make it count. I had already suffered some setbacks and I wasn't about to use this as a dress rehearsal. It was my intention to hold on to that first-team jersey.

As I was still part-time, I didn't really know the first-team squad all that well. Jock Wallace had made his mark on the side and they were a tough and organised unit. Credit is due to the senior professionals, who all welcomed me into the hub of the first-team dressing room and helped me to feel at ease. This is something I never forgot later on in my career when the shoe was on the other foot and I was the old head taking youngsters under my wing and offering them words of advice and encouragement.

Goalkeeper, Jim Cruickshank, was Scotland's Number One and he was the most ungainly-looking footballer I have even seen. He lived in Rutherglen and would meet me and the rest of the West of Scotland boys at Glasgow Queen Street to travel through to Edinburgh Haymarket. Jim would saunter up at the station with a cigarette dangling from his mouth and a Glasgow Herald tucked under his arm. He looked, walked and talked like an old man and his shoulders were always hunched over. His clothes were never the smartest and commuters would walk past Scotland's international goalkeeper without giving him a second glance.

Jim enjoyed a drink after training and after a match and a few in the squad were also in the habit of doing that. It was part of the culture back then but it didn't affect Jim's performances. He despised training and exerted as little effort as possible during the sessions but what a goalkeeper he was. This seemingly old, decrepit figure came alive on match day, and (like many stars) he seemed to reserve his finest performance for the most important fixtures. 'Cruiky' made save after save with lightning-quick reflexes, was nimble on his feet, and (loike every great 'keeper) was very brave. He wasn't particularly tall for a goalie (5' 11") and he never failed to amaze me with the athleticism he displayed during a game of football; after the match, he reverted back to the dishevelled Cruiky we all knew.

Our two first-choice centre-halves were Eddie Thomson and Alan Anderson, who had forged a solid partnership under the tutelage of Jock Wallace, incidentally a former goalkeeper. I don't think that today's forwards would relish the challenge of playing against these two, hard-as-nails defenders. Cruickshank, Thomson and Anderson had developed a solid defensive triangle at the back and I still believe that this is the first aspect of any side that needs to be established before success can even be considered.

Both Dave Cluny and Peter Oliver were versatile full-backs whose distribution was first-class. We had some quality players in midfield with the likes of Jim Brown, Tommy Veitch, George Fleming and big Alan MacDonald.

Back in the 1960s Scottish football relied heavily on home-grown players and we were able to develop enough talent to compete at the very highest levels in Europe. The national side were also a force to be reckoned with, having narrowly missed out on qualification for the 1966 World Cup finals. A feature of the Hearts side that I entered, however, was that we had a couple of overseas players in our ranks. Roald Jensen could be a match-winner when he was on song and Rene Moller was a moody guy who spent a couple of years in Edinburgh before returning to his native Denmark. Our two Scandinavians gave me an early taste of dealing with a multi-cultural changing room, which was something of a pre-requisite by the time I became a coach myself some years later.

The main striker was Donald Ford, another Scotland internationalist and one who also seemed to be an unlikely footballer. A refined character, Donald was a qualified accountant who in his spare time advised players with any financial issues they may have encountered such as filing income tax returns. Hailing from Linlithgow, Donald would walk around Tynecastle singing *Carpenters'* songs and I got on really well with him (despite that musical eccentricity). Despite his financial acumen and intelligence, he didn't have a great first touch, wasn't strong in the air, and his striking could be suspect. In and around the box, though, and Donald Ford was a deadly finisher. There are so many forwards out there who bring a lot to their teams by injecting pace, strength and aerial prowess to the game. Many of them lack that one obvious attribute of the genuine striker, however, - the knack of putting the ball in the net. Donald was a master at it and always seemed to be in the right place at the right time.

Hearts had some excellent players but there was no doubt in my mind that midfielder Jim Townsend was the cream of the crop. Jim had fantastic vision and orchestrated the pace for the entire side. His composure on the ball was immense but he could suffer the odd moment when the red mist would take over; inevitably this resulted in the stretchering-off of a hapless opponent, and a card for Jim.

I must have done enough to impress Johnny Harvey and Jock Wallace against Dallas Tornado, as I kept my first-team jersey for the league match at home to Motherwell five days later. We went into this encounter sitting a lowly 11th in the 18-team Scottish First Division and we faced a Motherwell side who were perched four places above us.

Hearts had been one of Scotland's top sides in the 1950s and 1960s: in the 14 years between 1954 and 1968, they had won the league twice and finished runners-up on four occasions; the Scottish Cup had been won in 1956 and lost in 1968; and the League Cup was added to the trophy cabinet four times, with another lost final in 1961. It had been the club's greatest purple (or maroon) patch in their history and I came into the side on the back of that halcyon era. The disappointment of the 1968 Scottish Cup final loss to Dunfermline was compounded by a poor 1968-69 campaign, where an eighth place league finish was matched by limp exits from the second round of the Scottish Cup and the sectional stages of the League Cup. The natives, so used to recent success, were becoming restless and yearned for new Hearts heroes to take them into the 1970s. Was I about to be one such terrace icon? I certainly hoped so.

According to the 13th October 1969 edition of the *Scottish Daily Express* I was a, "Great new find," as their football correspondent waxed lyrical about my maiden performance. "Hearts manager, John Harvey, has come up with a top find in talented young outside-left Andy Lynch," they continued. "Lynch is the most natural Tynecastle discovery since the golden days of Alex Young. He is fast proving to be Tynecastle's best number 11 since Ian Crawford. In the 2-2 draw with Motherwell on

Saturday, Lynch provided entertainment with his runs down the wing and showed a cool head in 10 minutes with a goal on his league debut."

The headline was reminiscent of the Friday night dream I had on the eve of the match, and my Hearts career was well and truly up-and-running. I remember being told by Johnny Harvey to just go out and play my normal game. What was my normal game? I hadn't given that much thought up until then. In the months that followed, Johnny Harvey and Jock Wallace always had a thorough dossier on our opponents and every player (except me) was briefed on exactly what was expected of him. After a few games I realised that they didn't want to over-complicate my game and I was given simple instructions such as, "Make yourself available... Try and get up the wing... And get in some crosses."

Surely football couldn't be that simple? Well, it seemed to work because after 10 minutes of my competitive debut I had scored my first senior goal.

Just six weeks previously I had been playing junior football and now here I was competing at Scotland's top level. Everything was vastly more vocal and seemed to rage on at a frantic velocity. The crowds seemed huge (10,307 for this encounter) but I was thriving on the pressure and atmosphere that surrounded me.

I instantly noticed that I had more time on the ball than I had been used to at junior and reserve level and I think players were largely wary of lunging in, as they wanted to avoid being caught out. We had gone behind to a seventh minute Jim Muir goal, but a wayward pass was then sent across the Motherwell six-yard box. I suppose it was a bit of a lost cause and would have gone out for a Hearts throw but, full of youthful exuberance, I stepped up a gear and gave chase. I managed to reach the ball as it trundled to the wide left of Peter McCloy's goal and I decided to take the 'keeper by surprise and struck it from a tight angle first time. It flew past McCloy at his near post and the maroon-and-white side of Midlothian erupted. That goal really boosted my confidence and I felt that the Hearts' crowd were right behind me from the very start.

There is a real affinity between football supporters and young players who break through into the first team and this is because every fan in those stands has dreamed of playing for their club. When they see a young boy coming into the side and doing well they are delighted for them because they are living the dream; they are fulfilling the supporter's dreams. I really felt that they were willing me on to do well.

When a new player is bought in then the jury is out and the newcomer has everything to prove. Football fans can be an unforgiving breed (and rightly so because they work all week to pay good money to watch their team) but I was delighted and relieved to have their full backing.

Buoyed by my perfect introduction, I was flying and thoroughly enjoyed the experience of my first 90 minutes of first-team football. I remember making a few more direct runs and wasn't afraid to try my luck out on goal again as the game ended 2-2. Fellow 19-year-old Jim Brown equalised with ten minutes to go after John McInally had put Motherwell 2-1 up at half-time.

My Monday shift at Glasgow Corporation couldn't end quickly enough as I was so keen to get back in to train at Tynecastle that night. When I arrived in the city I purchased the *Edinburgh Evening News* at the station to be faced by another bold headline: "A Star Is Born." The journalist responsible for this rhetoric was none other than Jimmy Wardhaugh, who had been part of the Hearts' 1950s vintage that featured the elder Alfie Conn and Willie Bauld. Striker-turned-writer Wardhaugh was referring to me as he paid a marvellous testimonial to my first outing as a Jambo. Expectations were cranked up a few notches after such a lofty headline was scribed by this Hearts goal-scoring legend but it didn't faze me and it didn't go to my head - there is no way my folks would allow that to happen!

Ayr United, Partick Thistle & Raith Rovers now stood between me and the fixture I had my eye on next - Celtic away. I got a hold of the Hearts fixture list immediately after the Motherwell game to check when we were playing my heroes. All I had to do was keep impressing for three more matches and my dream of playing at Celtic Park would come true. We drew with Ayr United at Somerset Park (0-0) and with Partick Thistle at home (1-1) before overcoming Raith Rovers at Tynecastle 3-2. John Harvey and Jock Wallace thought I did enough to keep my place in the side, and so I played my first match in Paradise on 8th November 1969.

It is a day I will never forget. I vividly recall my father offering to drive me to Celtic Park but, as much as I appreciated the gesture, I needed some time alone in the lead up to this match to take in the enormity of the occasion and to get my head into the right zone. My dad would have been immensely proud to chaperone me up to the front door of the stadium but I really had to deal with this on my own.

My white shirt and dark flannels were neatly pressed, my shoes were gleaming and, as I looked into the mirror to put on my Hearts' club tie, I considered just how quickly my life had turned around. Just two-and-a-half months previously I had made my debut for Rob Roy juniors and now I was standing getting myself composed to face Jock Stein's Celtic.

I felt ready for this monumental challenge.

I put on my Hearts blazer and a neat white trench coat, which hid the embroidered crest of Celtic's opponents from public scrutiny, before leaving my parents' house in Cardonald to get a bus into town. Early as ever, I arrived in the city and walked to London Road before catching another bus heading for the stadium. I made my way upstairs where there was a group of Celtic fans also making their way to the match. They were in great spirits and enjoying the moment as they burst into a rousing rendition of The Celtic Song. Even if I had removed my white trench coat to reveal my Hearts' blazer and introduced myself, these Celtic fans would have no idea who I was.

I was hoping that they would maybe know my name after the game was over.

I left those Saturday afternoon revellers to make their way to their pre-match bar of choice as I departed the bus and walked up to 95 Kerrydale Street, where lies a stadium in which my father and I had spent many memorable matches together. This day was different though, as my dad would be sitting in the stand courtesy of a complimentary ticket and I would be on the hallowed turf of Celtic Park.

I was met by the doorman, who stood firm until I explained that I was playing for Hearts that afternoon and that I had to get into the stadium to prepare for the game. As I approached the front door, I'm certain he already realised that I wasn't dressed for a day out in the Jungle but he kept a straight face and tested my nerve in any case.

Once inside the ground, I was pointed in the general direction of the away dressing room, and I had a quick look around before sitting alone in the cold and eerily quiet changing area. After a while I took a walk through the tunnel and ventured a few steps on to the lush, green stage.

From my earliest days kicking a ball around the streets of Govan I had dreamed of this moment. My imagination began to run wild as I found myself walking towards the left-wing area of the pitch. I took a few moments to visualise what I was going to do when the referee's whistle finally blew, and the history and traditions of this great football club washed over me like a tidal wave. The proud old building, admittedly a bit gritty, may have been empty but I felt a shiver down my spine as I pictured myself taking on Celtic's right-back and firing in a cross. Would I be tenacious enough to take on the Lisbon Lions' number two in front of the Jungle?

I couldn't wait to try.

It is a myth that any professional footballer would fail to put in 100% effort against the team they support. If anything, the occasion propels you to a greater level of performance. I wanted to win that match against Celtic more than any other game I had ever played in up to that point. All sorts of thoughts flitted across my mind: this was my bread-and-butter, my living, and I wanted my win bonus; I would also take great delight in impressing that big, imposing figure in the Celtic dug-out. Jock Stein was a notoriously difficult man to please and he would go on to lead his side to their second European Cup final that season.

My dream sequence was interrupted by voices and laughter as my team-mates made an appearance down the tunnel to join me. I had enjoyed my few moments of private reflection and it was an important part of my preparation that day but I was also delighted to see my comrades. I was the youngest member of the squad, and the more experiences guys helped to settle everyone down by keeping things light-hearted before a game.

As we were getting our kit on in the dressing room, I heard the rasping Wallyford growl of Jock Wallace: "We need to get into these fenian bastards the day," and he turned towards me. "What do you say Lynchy? What do you say Townie? Let's get into them."

Now Jock Wallace knew perfectly well that Jim Townsend (Townie) and I were Roman Catholics, and that was why he singled us out for his own brand of ribbing. He had a wry grin on his face when he said it, and I could hardly pull him up about his turn of phrase a mere four matches into my senior career. Incidentally, when we played Rangers at Ibrox a few months later, Jock was shouting at his players before the match: "Let's sort out these orange bastards."

These offensive and unacceptable slurs can get you jailed nowadays but they were used more freely in the far less enlightened times of my early career.

This type of attitude has been a blight on Scottish football for decades but this attitude didn't just exist on the football field. Religious prejudice was also rife in the printing trade back in the '60s and I was lucky to get my foot in the door, as it was a predominately closed shop for Catholics. In actual fact, I was one of the first Catholics to be given an apprenticeship and I am certain that this was mainly down to my father's intervention and persuasion. I heard my fair share of sectarian remarks from my fellow employees but the majority of them, regardless of their religion, were decent, hard-working people.

I was able to shrug off Jock's comments as I heard my name being called out as number 11 from the Hearts team sheet. Mission accomplished. An hour earlier and I had strolled through the tunnel at Celtic Park accompanied only by the sound of a few seagulls in the distance. Just before 3 p.m. on 8th November 1969 and the scene was a world away from my earlier period of contemplation as 35,000 fans erupted at the sight of Celtic and Hearts emerging from beneath the main stand. The home side lined up with five Lisbon Lions in their ranks, as the team read:

CELTIC: *Fallon; Craig, Gemmell; Murdoch, McNeill, Brogan; Johnstone, Dalglish, Hughes, Macari and Callaghan.*

Their teenager in Celtic's number eight shorts was already known to me from my Glasgow United days but this was to be Kenny Dalglish's fourth and final match for Celtic that season as the 'Quality Street Kid' struggled to find his feet. I was not concerning myself unduly with anyone else, though, as I lined up on my favoured left-wing in a Hearts side comprising of:

HEARTS: *Cruickshank; Clunie, Oliver; MacDonald, Anderson, Thomson; Jensen, Miller, Ford, Brown, Lynch.*

As I was warming up I couldn't help but glance over the half-way line to see my heroes. Four years earlier, I was a ball-boy at Hampden Park whilst half-a-dozen of these Celts played in the Scottish Cup final (John Fallon, Tommy Gemmell, Bobby Murdoch, Billy McNeill, John Hughes and Tommy Callaghan, who lined up for Dunfermline that unforgettable day).

If I ever wanted to play alongside these magnificent players then I had to impress the members of their incredible boot room, who were taking their seats in the Celtic dug out: Sean Fallon, Neilly Mochan, Bob Rooney, and that man Jock Stein. I was up against my boyhood idols but I didn't feel overawed. I held a composure and focus that belied my tender years.

Jim Craig was my direct opponent and I knew all about him. I didn't have to do my homework on any of those players because I had been watching them all for years. Jim hadn't made the 1965 Scottish Cup final side but had been part of that iconic clash in Lisbon a couple of years later and he played an important part in the opening two goals of the European Cup final (the first being for Inter Milan as he gave away a penalty!). He was quick and liked to get up the right flank to help his genius winger, Jimmy Johnstone. But I was fearless and fancied my chances against him. I was intent on pinning him deep in his own half and snuffing out his service to wee Jinky. Go past Jim and get the cross in. That would be my mantra for the afternoon.

The pace and atmosphere was breathtaking and I couldn't hear my team-mates as they shouted instructions and guidance from a few yards away.

I played on instinct and, incredibly, we destroyed this great Celtic side in the first 45 minutes. We went in at half-time two goals up through Roald Jensen and Donald Ford and Celtic failed to reply in the second period. Many years later, Jim Craig extracted a few of my teeth in his other career as a dentist. I think it was payback for the pain I inflicted on him that day.

The quality of that Celtic side could not be under-estimated. Jock Stein's men went on to win the league that season (their fifth in a then world-record sequence of nine championships in-a-row) and they had already won the League Cup two weeks' earlier when they defeated Saint Johnstone 1-0 with a Bertie Auld strike. They were just two victories away from a memorable quadruple that season: Aberdeen defeated them 3-1 amid controversy in the Scottish Cup final, and Feyenoord won the European Cup final 2-1 after extra time. So this was one Hearts victory we were all extremely proud of, as it came against one of the greatest Celtic sides of all time.

With all my friends and family being Celtic to the core, you can imagine the light-hearted abuse I got after this tremendous and unexpected win. Deep down, they were all delighted for me and I knew how well I had played. I had stopped updating my wee red book, where I critiqued every aspect of my performance on a game-by-game basis, but I still went through the entire match in my head to identify any flaws in my play. I couldn't identify many after this match however, as it was a vintage display of fast, attacking football and I was delighted with my contribution.

That sweet taste of success was something that consumed me and it motivated me to strive for even more of the same. After that win, I knew I could play and perform well at the highest level and against the very best, and I felt that anything was possible. If I continued to progress as I had done since my move from junior football, then there was no reason why I couldn't perform alongside Celtic-class players on a weekly basis.

Before I could do that however, I knew that changes had to be made. I positively had to go full-time at Tynecastle and leave my apprenticeship behind. The euphoric aftermath of a win against Celtic was as good a time as any to break this news to the man who had got me my start in the world of printing - my father. He had been watching me from Celtic's main stand, and I am sure that he didn't mind seeing his team being turned over that day. I knew that he wanted me to finish my apprenticeship so that I had my trade to fall back on but I had pushed my way into Johnny Harvey and Jock Wallace's plans and I was flying in their first team.

The prospect of entering the lion's den of Celtic Park was far more appealing than going home to tell my old man that I was about to quit my day job at Glasgow Corporation. Looking back now, it was a bold move and I must have been one head-strong teenager, but I felt it was definitely the right thing to do. The step-up to full-time training would undoubtedly improve my fitness and my performance, and it would allow me to cement myself in this up-and-coming Hearts side.

It was time for another heart-to-heart with my father across the kitchen table.

CHAPTER FOUR
THE JOCK OF HEARTS

My fellow workers were hurrying through the huge, clanking metal gates of the Glasgow Corporation building this Friday evening, and were making their way into the unbridled freedom that every weekend seemed to promise. Some would be heading home to the welcoming sight of their wives and children, while others had chosen to drop in at their favourite hostelries for a liberating pint or two. Those pints would serve as a quiet prelude to the unknown pleasures (or sufferings) typically offered by a Glaswegian weekend on the lash.

Whichever way we decided to spend our free time, the sound of that five o' clock bell was something that most of us had waited all week for. We knew that, whatever happened, we would at least be unconstrained by the tedium of work for a couple of days. And how we thanked God for such small mercies!

On this particular Friday night, however, the bell sounded like a death knell to my ears.

A heavy two-foot plank of wood was hidden inside my jacket as I stood a few yards from the main exit like a teenage vagabond awaiting my nemesis. I knew that, without my tool of choice, I had no chance against the brute I was about to encounter. It had all started with a friendly game of three card brag...

Earlier that afternoon, I was involved in a lunch-time card school, and I played like a hustler. I promise you, it was beginner's luck! Most of the lads (who were all much older than me) took my performance in good spirits, but there is always one bad loser and on this occasion he decided to take his frustrations out on the easy target.

The joker in the pack was a big guy, who must have been in his 30s (which seemed quite old to me back then). I had seen him around the workshops wearing a red, white and blue scarf, and he had never taken to me for some reason.

One of the other players shouted, "Last six hands," as the cards were dealt and we neared the end of our lunch break. The stakes kept getting higher and higher and I continued on my winning streak. I could sense a bad vibe coming from the Rangers fan as I scooped up more of his wages. I noticed his anger perpetuating through the claret of his bulbous cheeks, and I hoped I would lose the final game and relieve some of this tension. I didn't - cometh the trouble.

"You!" My new enemy shouted. He stood up and pointed at me as I stuffed my winnings into my pockets. "Why are you even playing with us? You're not part of our card school. You're at it."

"Don't be a bad loser big man. I won fair and square," came my defiant reply, as I had no intention of suffering the ignominy of standing down in front of my colleagues.

"Bad loser? I'll show you who's a bad loser. Any more of your lip and you're getting it," roared my would-be assassin as the veins in his neck protruded with rage.

I stood my ground and aimed a few expletives back at him, as I certainly wasn't about to let him bully me. It only fuelled his fire.

A moment of silence was broken by the lunch-time bell. Were we back at school? It felt like it.

"I'll deal with you at five o' clock," threatened this adult miscreant who should have known better.

"I'll see you then," came my reply, filled with a false bravado as I attempted in vain to stand up for myself. I had no other choice, because the rest of the men had left me to it, and offered me no support as they dispersed and made their way to their various departments a few shekels lighter.

What do I do now? I thought about making up an excuse to my gaffer and heading home early. I even considered locking myself in the cubicle of the toilet and staying there all weekend, but 10,000 Hearts fans, Johnny Harvey and Jock Wallace might have wondered where I was. Filled with indignation, I decided to meet this problem head on.

My old van-driving mate, Owen Travers, gave me the idea of getting tooled up, and explained that the bully wouldn't be so keen to try and give me a leathering if I were to suddenly produce a suitable defensive weapon. Owen was a diamond of a guy and I got on really well with him. Bizarrely, his suggestion made perfect sense and I decided on my weapon of choice - a big plank of wood!

I had no real plan in mind as the last of the workers finally disappeared from view, but I waited on my aggressor alone, with the anxiety of battle filling every ounce of my body. I stood there sweating, but clutching the plank. After about half-an-hour there was still no sign of my challenger and so I decided to go home, as it was obvious that the main attraction wasn't going to show up.

I had been more than prepared to stand my ground with a grown man, and wait on my moment of reckoning with a weapon hidden in my jacket. If necessary, I would have produced that weapon to engage in bloody battle in the shadow of my work gates. I had to stand up to that bully to prove a point to myself that I was no shirker and that I wouldn't be pushed around. I felt vindicated as I made my way home and discarded my (thankfully unused) club in some bushes.

My Hearts career had got off to the best possible start, but I felt that having an apprenticeship and only training part-time at Tynecastle would eventually hold me back. I would sit at my tea-break on a Monday morning and read the sports-pages of the newspapers lying around the tea-room. My full-time team-mates would be pictured enjoying bonding days off on golf outings while I was stuck at Glasgow Corporation, working to gain a trade that I had absolutely no interest in, and would probably never work at.

Something had to give.

After a couple of months (as agreed at the time of me signing my professional contract) I visited a small printers and some prospective digs in Edinburgh. This was with a view to moving to the capital to be closer to my club, and to complete my apprenticeship. The tiny printing shop was like something from a Dickensian tale. It was dark and dusty, and I half-expected Fagin to jump out from the workshop shadows at any moment to try and pick my pocket. I thanked the kind, old business-owner for his time in showing me around his workshop, and made my way to see where I would be living. As I looked around the cramped and vapid digs on the outskirts of town, I thought to myself, "This is not for me."

I had already faced the Lions of Lisbon at Celtic Park, and the bully-boy of Glasgow Corporation in his work-place; so, surely I would have no problems with breaking this news to my dad? Later that night, after we had finished dinner and were sitting around the kitchen table relaxing for the evening, I explained my master plan. As expected, my father strenuously objected to my proposal. He explained how worried he was that things might not work out with my football career and that a bad injury could end it all in a heartbeat. He desperately wanted me to finish my apprenticeship as my brothers had done before me - Matt was a journalist and George an electrician - and I fully understood where my dad was coming from. I stood my ground and explained to him that printing wasn't for me, the new workshop wasn't for me, and the digs weren't for me.

In summing up my case, I explained how much I would benefit from full-time training. If he thought I had done well at Celtic Park during Hearts' 2-0 victory then just imagine what I could achieve as a full-time footballer. I stressed that football was my game, not printing or anything else for that matter, and I would dedicate my life to making myself a success as a footballer. My dad looked at me with an unimpressed gaze, before letting out a defeated sigh, and then he reluctantly agreed to let me chase my dreams.

After getting clearance from the powers-that-be at Tynecastle, I went into work at Glasgow Corporation for the final time to say my goodbyes. My old boss, Malcolm Cameron, had always been decent with me. When I broke the news to him, he wished me well and recalled the time he had let me away from my shift early to watch Celtic's victory in the European Cup final on television. I thanked Owen Travers for his friendship and advice and he told me to go easy on Celtic the next time I faced them. Plenty of Rangers fans were there to give me their best wishes in my new career (I hadn't yet signed for Celtic right enough). Just as he had done for our battle of Pollokshaws Road, the bully boy who I'd beaten at cards failed to show up as I was waved off into the distance.

I never looked back.

Johnny Harvey and Jock Wallace were delighted that I had started training full-time. I felt that I was a more established part of the team and big Jock would take us all for extra physical afternoon sessions. He was always striving for perfection and would literally boot you up the backside if he thought for a minute that you were slacking. He had also found the perfect place to take us when the weather was good - Gullane Sands - and it wasn't to sunbathe with an ice-cream. He would make this training circuit infamous in Scottish football circles some years later by taking his successful Rangers team there, but the Hearts squad were unfortunate enough to sample the killer sand dunes first.

The players were made to ascend the steep sandy braes in two lines. There was no hiding place from Jock, and many of the players were physically sick during these gruelling sessions. I prided myself on being one of the fittest at the club, and I enjoyed the tough full-time training regime. On one occasion, however, I collapsed to my knees with exhaustion halfway through a circuit and began to retch. With his stop-watch on a lace around his neck and a whistle in his hand, Jock made his way up to me and asked, "Are you finished being sick, Lynchy?" I meekly nodded, to which he bellowed, "Well, get up and get it finished!" He could be such a gentle soul at times.

This mercurial and belligerent image was one which Jock became synonymous with as he went on to craft out a highly successful career in management. But there was another side to him that was equally as effective. After our glorious victory over Celtic, we won just two of our next eight games and my own performances began to dip slightly. I had gone off the boil, as all young players tend to do at some stage, and I wasn't sure why.

After training one day, Jock asked me to join him out on the Tynecastle pitch because he wanted a word. There was no-one else around as we walked along the half-way line, and the imposing Hearts' Coach asked me, "Are you getting enough rest in between training and games, son?" I assured him that I was doing everything possible to keep myself in top shape, to which Jock retorted, "Well, I hope you're behaving yourself back in Glesga!" I let out a nervous half-laugh as I told him I was staying out of trouble. "It's no' funny son. I'm deadly serious," came the response from a stony-faced Jock as we continued on our way across the half-way line.

"You're losing a wee bit of form just now Lynchy, and that's normal," explained Jock, as we walked up the pitch together. "We would have preferred to have rested you before now but we don't have another outside-left and so we're going to keep playing you. You see where we're standing just now?" I suddenly realised that we were out on the left-wing of the Tynecastle pitch, about 35 yards from goal, facing the Gorgie Road end of the stadium. "There are only two players in Scotland who are better than you in this area of a football pitch: Jimmy Johnstone and Willie Henderson. But, if you keep improving, you'll be up there with them. So, get your head down and keep working hard Lynchy, and you'll get back to your best, son. That's it, away you go."

As I seemingly floated out of the stadium on cloud nine, Jock's words of wisdom were ringing in my ears. Jock Wallace had just mentioned me in the same breath as two world-class players and, as I sat on the train back to Glasgow with a renewed vigour, I realised that my confidence had instantly returned. Jock's words had a similar effect on me as spinach did for Popeye, and our next game couldn't arrive quickly enough.

Coaches can learn everything about the science of tactics, performance and man-management from books, but the latter is very much a natural attribute that separates the good from the great in this business. The two finest managers I ever played under were both called Jock (and, strangely, they were the only two Jocks I've ever known) and they both had man-management ability in abundance. They could lift you up as easy as knock you down if and when it was necessary and they were the two most influential figures in my football career.

With my confidence fully restored, I felt ready to enter the cauldron of Easter Road for my first Edinburgh derby on 1st January 1970. The two sides that lined up in front of 36,421 New Year revellers were:

HIBERNIAN: *Marshall; Shevlane, Schaedler; Blackley, Black, Stanton; Graham, O'Rourke, McBride, Cormack, Stevenson.*

HEARTS: *Cruikshank; Clunie, Oliver; Brown, Anderson, Thomson; Moller, Townsend, Ford, Fleming, Lynch.*

The most memorable thing about this scoreless draw for me was that I shared a pitch for the first time with the great Joe McBride. This fellow Govan man had always been a hero of mine, and as a fan I had marvelled at him at his very peak with Celtic. For me, he was the complete striker, and could score with either foot as well as his head. He also had a fantastic temperament and showed a true grit and determination to come back from a serious knee injury that robbed him of a starting place in Jock Stein's triumphant Lisbon line-up. Many onlookers may have thought that Joe's finest years were behind him when Celtic sold him to Hibs, but he went on to forge an emphatic strike-force with the ex-Liverpool forward Peter Cormack. By the time that I faced one of my all-time footballing heroes, Joe McBride was 31 years-of-age, but he was still an outstanding goalscorer.

That transition from being a fan to rubbing shoulders with footballing icons overnight was something I had to get used to. I remember being in at Tynecastle one afternoon when all the other players had left and John Cumming was in the boot-room having a cup of tea with a visitor. I heard them catching up and sharing a laugh before John emerged from his room and told me to get ready and head into the gym because he wanted to introduce me to a friend of his.

After a few minutes, John's friend walked into the gym and introduced himself with a firm shake of the hand. It was none other than the great Dave MacKay, who had played alongside John Cumming in the 1950s and captained the side to the League Championship in 1958. That same year, Dave had also played for Scotland in the World Cup finals. By that point, he had already won a Scottish Cup in 1956 and a League Cup in 1955 before adding a second in 1959 prior to a big-money transfer to Tottenham Hotspur. This was like meeting Hearts' royalty.

"How are you getting on, son?" asked possibly the greatest Hearts player of all time.

"I'm enjoying it Mr MacKay," answered the young pretender.

"Good," said the man who featured in double and European-winning Spurs sides. "Nice to meet you. I know you're travelling over from Glasgow but this is a great club. So you give it your all and you might be following in my footsteps before you know it. In the meantime, let's have a wee kick about."

For many football fans, the lasting image of Dave MacKay is of him towering over Leeds United's Billy Bremner, with his fellow Scotsman's shirt gripped in his vice-like fist. This was a photograph that Dave himself loathed, due to the fact that it portrayed him as something of a bully. The truth of the matter was that he had recovered from a double leg-break and was unhappy that the fiery Bremner had taken a nibble at his recovering limb. A hard man Dave MacKay may have been but he was a perfectly polite gentleman on that unforgettable afternoon that I met him.

He was still playing professionally at that point and was built like an ox. We set ourselves up and started to fire balls back and forward to one another. His touch, poise and flexibility were magnificent, as he stroked the ball to me two-footed. I knew I was in the presence of greatness. The sweat was lashing off me as this legend gave me an impromptu workout. I thought back to the time I had watched as a ball-boy behind Hampden Park's goals. Back then Dave MacKay had practiced a similar routine with his Scotland team-mates and I had been transfixed by their incredible skills. Now here I was testing myself against the man himself.

He was a sensational player and he took it upon himself to spend a couple of hours with me. Perhaps his old Hearts team-mate, John Cumming, had told him I had potential and was willing to learn and that was why he decided to take some time out with me? Whatever the reasons behind it, I felt privileged to spend one-to-one time with this football icon. I think that I must have been sensitive to all of these learning opportunities. I took it all in, whereas some players may have let it go right over their heads. Even now when I think back to the late, great Dave MacKay I always appreciate the humility of the man. He gave me a couple of hours of his time and it meant the world to me.

The Ne'erday derby draw was part of an outstanding 17-game league sequence where we went on to lose only three matches in the run-in to a fourth-place finish in the Scottish First Division. We sat behind champions Celtic, Rangers and our Edinburgh rivals Hibs, in what was a vastly improved league campaign compared to finishing eighth the previous year. Unfortunately our endeavours in the domestic cup tournaments mirrored the season before as we bowed out of the Scottish Cup in round two (virtue of a 2-0 defeat to Kilmarnock) and failed to get out of our League Cup section.

I was delighted to make 14 competitive starts for the first-team in my debut season, and I managed to chip in with two goals, the second being the winner in a pulsating 3-2 win at Tannadice on 10th January 1970.

The one match I was disappointed to miss, however, was the return game against Celtic on 28th March 1970. We drew 0-0 at Tynecastle as Jock Stein's men clinched their fifth league championship in-a-row in front of an impressive 27,690 fans. That draw meant that the European Cup finalists failed to beat us all season, which was an accomplishment not to be scoffed at.

The whole squad were really positive and looking forward to building on a solid season when we received the news that hit us like a hammer-blow: Jock Wallace was leaving Tynecastle for pastures new. It shouldn't really have come as a surprise because Jock had been the main reason for our success the previous year. His influence had been noticed by Rangers and he had accepted the role of first-team Coach at Ibrox.

I spoke to my father about the situation and explained how disappointed I was to be losing such a huge figure from the club. I told him that I wanted to thank Jock for all the help he had given me, but I wasn't sure how to go about it. My dad advised me that it would be the decent thing to do and that I should just speak to Jock after our final training session. The following day, I nervously waited outside the changing-room area to try and catch a few seconds with Jock. A few of the other players were hanging around, and I wanted them to disappear as I was planning on having a private chat with my departing mentor.

"Mr. Wallace," I muttered, as he made his way to leave the dressing-room. "Can I have a quick word with you?"

"Aye son, what is it?" answered Jock in typically forthright fashion.

"I'd like to thank you for all the help you've given me, and wish you well in your new job," I recited, as I had practiced the previous night.

Big Jock just looked at me, ruffled my hair and barked loud for the whole squad to hear, "Lynchy, it's just a pity that you and Towny (Jim Townsend) are a couple of Tims. Because if you weren't, you would definitely both be coming with me to Ibrox."

So, I had said my goodbyes to the Jock of Hearts, and, as he walked away to the loud and over-zealous guffaws of the Tynecastle changing-room, I lamented his departure from Hearts and from my career. I knew that, back in those times, Rangers would never have signed me because of my religion, and I realised that we were unlikely to ever work together again.

Looking back to some of those early newspaper headlines now, my introduction to Scottish football prompted scribes to profess that, "A Star Is Born." A lot of that was down to the guidance of Jock Wallace and, if he had stayed, I am sure that I would have enjoyed plenty more success in Edinburgh. As it happened, I had to go elsewhere to achieve the glories that my "Star" billing had promised.

I can imagine that there are a lot of Celtic fans out there who don't like the man but he was terrific for me and a huge reason behind my early success. There is no doubt in my mind that my progress as a player was hampered by his departure and I am sure that I was not alone. There was no way that Hearts could find another man like Jock Wallace.

Our paths would cross again seven years later in the Scottish Cup final, and I'm sure a friendly ruffle of my hair was the last thing that Jock Wallace wanted to do to me that afternoon.

CHAPTER FIVE
THE ACE OF HEARTS

"We players of the Heart of Midlothian FC who took part in the two matches played recently against Burnley in the Texaco Cup have today officially requested to be placed on the open to transfer list of the club.

"There is no question of a rebellion by the players against the club or against the club rules. But the move has been made as being the only apparent one available as a protest against a decision of the Board of Directors concerning the games mentioned.

"The players tried earnestly to arrange a meeting with the Board to discuss the point at issue, but the Board declined to meet, and the players are thus left, apparently, no alternative to the step taken."

My signature appeared underneath this collective statement on Wednesday 14th October 1970, alongside my team-mates Jim Brown (21-years-old), David Clunie (22), George Fleming (22), Donald Ford (27), Peter Oliver (22), Kevin Hegarty (21), Eddie Thomson (23) and Jim Townsend (25). I was only 19 at the time and had been asked to sign the statement by some of the more experienced players, as a form of mutiny raged within the Tynecastle camp.

The written request was handed to the Hearts' board by captain, Eddie Thomson, and this action prompted the *Daily Mail* to pronounce that it was a "Soccer sensation," and that the move, "Was one of the saddest, yet one of the most significant moments in the entire history of one of Scotland's greatest clubs."

The argument was centred on a bonus, which had been promised by the Hearts' board, for the Texaco Cup first round tie against Burnley. This short-lived but lucrative tournament had been dubbed 'The British Cup' by the press and we had been promised a decent bonus if we were able to turn around a 3-1 deficit, after being outplayed down at Turf Moor in the first leg. Perhaps the directors did not expect to pay such a bonus but a healthy crowd of 15,861 turned up for the return match in Edinburgh, and I scored the fourth (and winning) goal as we ran out 4-1 victors on the night, going through to the next round 5-4 on aggregate. The following morning, the *Daily Record* had called me, "A wonder winger for Hearts," as I turned it on against English opposition.

We still hadn't received our bonus a fortnight later and then, to add insult to injury, we were offered £30-a-man less than we had been promised by the thrifty blazers of the boardroom. The players knew that the tournament had generated huge sponsorship revenue from Texaco, and the club had received hefty gate receipts as the English opposition seemed to capture the imagination of Scottish football fans at the turnstiles. Yet, the board were holding out on us. It was a hugely regrettable situation that spilled out on to back-page headlines all over the country, and it was very unsettling for the entire team.

Johnny Harvey was handed the unenviable task of reading out a response from the board to the players, which stated that the £30 would not be paid and the board would not meet the squad to discuss the matter. Captain Eddie Thomson was in disbelief as he spoke on behalf of the team, "What does it matter if it's £30 or 30 shillings? We are all Hearts-daft, but we are still professionals. This is our living. Are we asking for the moon or something? We are only asking for what we were promised."

As you can imagine, this type of infighting was the last thing the club needed, but it was a point of principle and we felt the board had conducted themselves dreadfully.

The effect was being seen on the pitch. The gaping wound left by Jock Wallace's departure hadn't just failed to heal, it was beginning to fester. As a result, our performances were a world apart from the impressive showings at the tail-end of the previous campaign. The Burnley victory was just our fourth of 1970-71 and our seven defeats and two draws had meant we were again out of the early-season League Cup at the sectional stage and struggling in the league as early as October.

I had got off to a decent start and performed well in our first win of the season away to Clyde, where I scored a brace in an impressive 5-1 victory. The Scottish Daily Express were singing my praises when they reported, "Leading the assault on the poor Shawfield team were Johnny Harvey's brilliant babes Kevin Hegarty and Andy Lynch." Quotes of such a positive tone were always welcome and it felt like a great personal triumph when I could read them the morning after a match, but I was concerned at the lack of consistency we had shown as a unit since big Jock's departure.

Our stand-out performance the previous season had undoubtedly been at Celtic Park but we weren't so lucky at my boyhood haunt this time around. We had drawn them in the League Cup sections and I faced the one-and-only Jimmy Johnstone on both occasions. I was never normally asked to track back but the gaffer made an exception when we were up against this genius, and accordingly I was expected to help out my left-back Peter Oliver.

I recall being out on the Jungle side of the field and wee Jinky was on top form. It was an absolute privilege to be on the same pitch as the European Cup winner, but I couldn't just stand there in awe of him. He could go past players like they weren't there and if he was in the mood (as he was that day), he would come back to take you on again and again. I'm sure this was all great fun for Jimmy and the Jungle punters but Peter Oliver and I were having a torrid time of it.

On one occasion he was twisting and turning past Peter at will, and I was in full flight to try and offer some back up and close down Celtic's number seven. Just as I approached Jimmy (in front of his most adoring fans), my aluminium studs lost their grip on the heavy pitch and I slipped backwards. At that very moment, wee Jimmy turned around and the studs of my boot swiped upwards and flicked the wee man's face.

I landed in a heap on the Parkhead turf beside him, and Jimmy looked down at me in shock as the game raged on elsewhere on the pitch. I had come close to assaulting one of my all-time heroes, and I was full of apologies as I struggled back to my feet. "I didn't mean that Jimmy," I protested. "I slipped… I'm sorry…"

"That's alright, son; don't worry about it," replied the pocket dynamo, apparently unruffled.

I was genuinely concerned that he would think ill of me. As much as I wanted to win the game there was no way that I wanted anything to happen to Jimmy Johnstone. He was a national treasure!

I know it has been said before, and well documented too, but wee Jimmy was deceptively strong. I mean, he was nearly impossible to push off the ball. His wee legs were so powerful. When you look back at some of the treatment the wee man got on the football field, I doubt that anyone else suffered so much physical abuse. There was little protection from the referees, so what would wee Jimmy do? His answer was typical of the man… Refuse to wear shin-guards, roll his socks to his ankles, and dare his opponents to try and thwart him. Jimmy Johnstone was a magician with that football and there were plenty of full-backs who weren't even capable of kicking him, never mind getting the ball off him.

If that had been a close shave for Jimmy, then I wasn't to be so lucky a few weeks later in the first Edinburgh derby of the season at Easter Road. Another healthy crowd of 23,225 turned out on 5th September 1970 but they were not to be thrilled with much goal-mouth action as the game again ended in a scoreless draw.

My own participation in the capital's showpiece fixture was short-lived. I lasted only half-an-hour before a sickening clash of heads with Hibs' defender Eric Schaedler resulted in me being stretchered from the field of play and rushed to hospital. I was severely concussed and had to be hospitalised for a few days with facial and shoulder injuries; Johnny Harvey was said to be "very concerned" as he paid me a visit in hospital. I felt really guilty as my ever-supportive parents were forced to cancel their holiday in order to nurse me back to full fitness at home.

Young players can bounce back quickly, however, and a few weeks later I was back to my best, as we destroyed the surprising league leaders Airdrie 5-2, and I scored another couple of goals. This match was followed by our Burnley victory and the bonus debacle it sparked. With nine first-team players on the transfer list, and dissent in the dressing room, we lost six of our next seven matches.

Clearly all was not well on Gorgie Road.

The one match we did manage to win was in the first leg of the Texaco Cup quarter final. Our 5-0 victory set us up to see off the challenge of Airdrie (who had knocked out Nottingham Forest in the earlier round). The Broomfield men edged us in the second leg but our 7-3 aggregate advantage was just as convincing as the score-line suggested.

During the first half of my second season, I started to realise that the atmosphere around Tynecastle wasn't the same as I had enjoyed in my introductory campaign. As I've mentioned already, the biggest reason for this was the absence of Jock Wallace, but the players had definitely lost further faith in the board after the bonus row, and our form stuttered from one week to the next. All I wanted to do was play and enjoy my football but there was to be even more upheaval before the season was out.

Being a full-time player meant that I had more leisure time on my hands, and I enjoyed playing golf and snooker when I had the chance. As was the norm back then, some of the more senior players enjoyed going for a few pints after training. It may be frowned upon nowadays, but it was accepted and enjoyed when I played.

Fair play to the older guys, they looked upon me as being too young to be joining them on their drinking exploits around town. I think they looked after me and were quite protective of me in that respect. Jim Townsend and Jim Cruickshank in particular would make a point of telling me to get on the Glasgow train home and go and play golf. They were perhaps of the opinion that I could achieve more in the game, and they didn't want such bad choices to creep into my makeup on their watch.

The lads who enjoyed their pint would come into training the following day and really hammer the running. Back then, they thought that they could balance out the damage that the alcohol was doing with hard training, but how wrong they were! They were fooling themselves.

Our form actually began to pick up in November as we defeated St Mirren (1-0), Dundee United (1-0), and Ayr United (2-1); drew with Falkirk (1-1); and lost 1-0 to Aberdeen at Pittodrie.

I vividly recall the Falkirk goal-scorer was a tenacious forward from Govan by the name of Alex Ferguson (now known universally as 'Sir Alex'). Like myself, Fergie started his football career off at Queen's Park and he went on to become the most famous of Govan's footballing sons. He is world-renowned as a football manager and this has inevitably minimised the focus on his playing career. However, I remember him as a strong striker and prolific goal-scorer who always gave opposition's defences a torrid time of it. His playing career was winding down by the time I faced him but he had played with distinction for Saint Johnstone, Dunfermline Athletic and Rangers in his prime. In fact, on the day I celebrated Celtic's 1965 Scottish Cup win, Fergie had been a Pars player, but to his disappointment he was left out of the side that day following a loss of form.

Hearts' own loss of form seemed to be thwarted somewhat with a change of management in December. As Johnny Harvey moved upstairs at Tynecastle to become General Manager, he was replaced by former Dundee player and Scotland Youth Coach, Bobby Seith.

Perhaps initially buoyed by the managerial change, we embarked on a ten-game run in which we lost just one match (2-1 away to Saint Johnstone) and I chipped in with another three goals from the left wing, as we climbed up to seventh place in the First Division by the end of January 1971.

I was delighted to continue my run of first-team games, but I was always looking to improve and I started putting in extra training shifts when my team-mates had afternoons off. One of the aspects of my play that I wanted to work on was getting my 'standing only' right foot on to more productive action, as I explained to The Weekly News:

"I'm the first to admit that my right foot's only a swinger but it's never bothered me until now. With Hearts' new style of forward play, interchanging much of the time, I now find myself as much on the right as on the left. Of course, I still bring the ball to my left foot even when I'm away from my normal beat, and maybe it looks awkward. But it's just the same as, say, George Fleming, our outside-right, taking to his right foot when he's on the left wing. However, I've always maintained that a right-footed player can get away with it more easily, for most folk are right-footed and it perhaps looks more natural to them.

"Still, I must admit I've missed a few chances recently through teeing the ball up for my left foot, and that's not good enough when the side as a whole have a goal-scoring problem. Against Hibs on New Year's Day I missed one from quite close in on the right when I hitch-kicked with my left instead of hooking with my right. I wasn't even on the target. Believe me, the lads didn't miss me. And I can't say I blamed them. For every missed chance could mean money thrown away. Hence my decision to go on overtime."

My new gaffer, Bobby Seith, seemed impressed with my focus and drive as he explained, "Left-footers are often more one-footed than other players but as far as I'm concerned, Andy's better with his one foot than most players are with two. He is playing so well that I see no reason for concern. Besides, I know just how much work he's putting in on our shooting practice sessions. Day after day I see him persevering with his right foot. And although he's far from perfect, I'm sure his dedication to improve his game will yet show dividends."

Although I was an established first-team member by that stage, my extra training sessions were designed to keep me in that starting line-up. I took nothing for granted and was particularly hard on myself, as I had always been from my earliest years. On the occasions where I allowed myself an afternoon off, I would occasionally meet up with my old Glasgow United team-mates, Kenny Dalglish and Vic Davidson, for a game of snooker back in Glasgow.

Both of these guys were fabulous footballers and seemed destined for great things in their early careers at Celtic. With first-team opportunities at a premium, both of them were struggling to get into Jock Stein's first team and they were getting a bit frustrated with reserve team football. By this stage, I had played around 40 first-team games for Hearts.

I remember them telling me that some top English clubs had been trying to entice them down south with promises of first-team football. More worryingly was the fact that they were seriously considering their options. I couldn't envisage them leaving Celtic and, although I was dedicated to Hearts, deep down I still adored the Hoops and knew even then that Kenny was a special talent. I gave them my advice for what it was worth and advised them to stay put and that their chance would come soon enough. I'm sure Kenny was glad that he did because it wasn't long before he burst on to the scene at Celtic Park.

A muscular injury meant that I played in only three of Hearts' final 17 games of the season and this run saw us losing eight matches in a lacklustre finale to what was a difficult campaign. I was disappointed to miss the two-legged Texaco Cup final against Wolverhampton Wanderers, following our extra time defeat of Motherwell in the semi-final. Wolves beat us over two legs and the final appearance was undoubtedly the high point of our season, as we finished a lowly 11th in the league and were knocked out of the Scottish Cup by Hibs (of all teams) in the fourth round. Once again, we failed to get out of our League Cup section, which seemed to be coming an annual occurrence.

We did have an end-of-season North American tour to look forward to, however, and the experience of travelling to the States at a relatively early stage of my career undoubtedly made a huge impact on my later football and life choices.

Our tour ran from 4th May to 31st May 1971 and we played a lung-bursting 10 matches in that short period. The whole experience was fantastic and I will never forget boarding the plane in London and discovering that it was on two levels. Once we had taken off, the players all made their way to explore what was upstairs and we discovered that there were roulette wheels and poker tables to keep us occupied on our long-haul flight. It was like something from a James Bond movie!

We should have got used to things being different because that is what our American trip continually provided us with. The heat and humidity was unlike anything I had ever experienced, and many of the stadiums that we played in were laid with Astro Turf (which was unheard of in the UK back then). There were also football and baseball lines marked permanently on the field of play, which took a bit of getting used to.

Everything seemed to be bigger, louder and more colourful, and it was a bit like a dream world. But I really did take to my new surroundings, and I think a seed was planted in my own mind during that tour.

I felt lucky to have experienced the fantastic set up of 1970s soccer in America. Back then, the football world probably viewed the American game as being of a poor standard, but they were still in their infancy and were learning at that point. Even in those early tour games in which Hearts participated, the American sides were physical and competitive; it was far from a walk in the park.

I was really impressed with the way the authorities went about their business. They were decades ahead of the British game in terms of broadcasting, sponsorship and importing players and they knew the importance of providing customers with entertainment. I still watch the American game now, 40-odd years later, and I am not surprised that many of their fixtures have started to attract capacity crowds in modern stadiums.

I always felt that there was a real possibility that 'soccer' would end up as the number one sport in North America. The implications of that would be huge when you consider the amount of kids who are involved in and play American football, baseball, ice hockey and basketball. But parents and schools have come to realise that it is one of the least dangerous sports compared with the others mentioned, and they know it is enjoyed throughout the rest of the world; so, why not in America?

Hearts kicked off our tour in New York ,and eventually finished in Montreal, a city I was to get to know much more intimately some years later. Coincidentally, our first match was against the team I had made my Hearts debut against, Dallas Tornado, but I think all our long-distance travelling had tired us out, as we were flat throughout our scoreless draw.

Even the teams had exotic, box-office-sounding names like the St Louis All Stars, Atlanta Chiefs, Washington Darts, Philadelphia Spartans, Toronto Metros, Rochester Lancers and the world famous New York Cosmos, who we beat 4-2 at the Yankee Stadium. Whatever happened to being called United, Albion, City or Rovers? Perhaps such typically British monikers wouldn't have been glitzy enough for the American audience.

For our second game, we were based in Atlanta, Georgia to play the Atlanta Chiefs, who had embarked on a special recruitment drive in preparation for our visit and had signed several players from England and Europe to boost their chances of victory.

All the Hearts' tour games counted as league points as far as our American opponents were concerned because each NASL club had to play four visiting teams as part of their schedule. A novel scheme was also introduced whereby six points were awarded for a win and a special bonus point was added for every goal scored. As I said, the Americans liked to do things their own way.

Our prolific goal-scorer Donald Ford said to the Scottish press on the eve of the match in Atlanta, "No matter what the result tonight, we won't be sorry to see the back of this town. We have no complaints about the hotel or the hospitality but there is a terribly tense atmosphere because of the political problems in the area. Some of the lads found this out for themselves when they went sight-seeing. The reception they got from some of the locals was not too pleasant."

Our highly-rated striker had been in touch with his cousin, who was based near to our hotel, and he had kindly invited us out for a drive around the city one evening. I noticed that Donald's cousin seemed nervous any time we stopped at traffic lights, and he explained that he didn't like going out at night on account of the amount of shootings and robberies that regularly took place in the area. He told us that he always had to have his wits about him and, when he stopped at traffic lights, he had to be prepared to pull his gun if he saw anyone approaching his vehicle. He then produced a big revolver from under his seat to illustrate how he would combat his concerns. As we all stared wide-eyed for a moment or two, I started revising the pros and cons of living in America.

We were kept well informed throughout the tour by NASL Executive Director Phil Woosnam, who had been an international striker for Wales in his playing days. The other official who was responsible for organising the tour itinerary was none other than Clive Toye, who at that time was the NASL's Director of Administration and Information. Clive was a true progenitor of the game in America and was the man responsible for enticing the great Pele over to the States to play for the last three years of his career. With the New York Cosmos.

When we arrived in Washington D.C. (District of Columbia), the Mayor, Walter E. Washington, welcomed us as "The Hearts of Scotland Soccer Team," as 'Heart of Midlothian' was clearly not razzamatazz enough. We were then serenaded on to the field of play with the familiar sound of the bagpipes.

Although we went down 1-0 to the Atlanta Chiefs, we overcame the Washington Darts 3-0 four days later in what was the Washington side's first defeat at home in two years. I scored twice against the Darts with my first coming directly from a corner kick and my second with my right foot. All that extra training on my standing foot was finally paying off.

I scored further goals against Philadelphia Spartans (4-0) and Toronto Metros (3-0) as I really came on to my game. Our next fixture was christened "The Battle of Rochester" by the *Daily Express*, as we drew 0-0 against the Lancers in a bad-tempered encounter where the 5,500 crowd booed and jeered every Hearts move. There was a near riot at the end of the match when Rochester's Italian fans invaded the pitch to attack the 'Hearts of Scotland'. This resulted in The Iron Man, John Cumming, being felled by a series of kicks, Donald Ford suffering a gash above his eye after being punched, and yours truly having my eye poked! We managed to get off the pitch and had to flee back to the hotel, still wearing our strips, and get changed in our rooms.

Another interesting feature of our tour matches was that the organisers analysed the performance of each and every player and provided a statistical breakdown after the games. In our 4-2 defeat of the New York Cosmos, their statistics revealed that: "The best performer in New York was Andy Lynch, who had no fouls against his name; one goal, two assists, and 12 corners to his credit. According to the sheet he never put a foot wrong and I must say he really did have a stormer."

I was again on the score-sheet against the local Newton club in a 1-1 draw before we destroyed Montreal Olympic 7-0 at the Autostade. I would play and coach in Montreal a decade later and am delighted to say that their local side (by then called the Manic) had improved considerably compared to this showing.

Our American tour was a real eye-opener for me. I enjoyed being 'on the road' and travelling from city to city. The schedule was gruelling but the environment suited me and I played well and scored a few goals. As I flew home to Prestwick Airport from Montreal I knew that I had developed a real affinity with the place, and I am certain that my time there in the early 70s played a huge role in me returning when I left Scotland nearly ten years later.

My first term as a professional footballer had been rocked by the end-of-season departure of Jock Wallace; my second was hampered by transfer requests and a change of manager. I had also encountered some niggling injury problems throughout that campaign, and I truly hoped that, after our successful tour of North America, 1971-72 would be my best season yet in the maroon of Hearts.

After my end-of-season injury I had been ordered to rest completely and was banned from training for four months until the middle of July 1971, as I explained to the *Sunday Post* at the time, "It all started when I broke down with a muscle strain in the middle of last season. In an effort to hold my place in the team I kept quiet about it. But as the weeks went on I went from bad to worse. I went to see two specialists when I got to the stage where I couldn't play at all. I felt sure they'd know the answer. But I'd contracted an injury they knew nothing about. Just as I was having my best season, it looked as if I'd be out for months. One thing they did say was that the only cure was long and absolute rest. That might have been alright for some people but not for me. I kept turning up for training but inevitably broke down again. Then Mr Seith solved the problem the only way he could - by banning me from the ground on training days."

Despite playing fairly well in my third season at Tynecastle, I felt there was something missing in my football. The change of manager probably had a lot to do with it, and I knew that some of the other players weren't particularly enjoying the direction in which the club was heading.

Don't get me wrong; Bobby Seith was a respected man around the club. He had been a huge success at Dens Park as a player and was part of the 1962 championship-winning side, who went on to make the European Cup semi-finals the following year. Eventual winners A.C. Milan ended their run at the penultimate stage before defeating Eusebio's Benfica for their first tournament victory. His exploits as a player were more than well regarded but it was obvious that things weren't working out for him at Hearts. We still had a decent squad and some other promising youngsters had broken through in the past few seasons in the shape of Roy Kay and Kevin Hegarty, but the team somehow didn't seem to be going anywhere.

I had noted that I always seemed to enjoy playing against English opposition in the Texaco Cup. The style of play of our English counterparts suited me and I wondered if my future perhaps lay down south. I began to reconsider my future options...

It was round about this period of contemplation that I spotted a small snippet in the Evening News of 30th August 1971 that really got my attention: "Celtic manager Jock Stein has spoken favourably of winger Andy Lynch in the past and might be interested in the Glasgow-born player."

Was it just paper talk? Perhaps it was but the plot thickened as the *Times* followed up this story the following day: "Bobby Seith would not comment on reports of a player switch involving Andy Lynch of Hearts, and Willie Wallace of Celtic. With youngsters Kenny Dalglish, Lou Macari and Vic Davidson all coming into the plan now, Celtic could perhaps be persuaded to allow Wallace to go back to Tynecastle."

Talk of a transfer to Celtic was exciting, but it failed to unsettle me. In actual fact, it spurred me on to try even harder to impress Jock Stein. True to form, I scored my sixth goal of the season - and the winner - against Newcastle United in the Texaco Cup, first round, first leg at Tynecastle in front of 18,000.

£180,000 man, Malcolm McDonald, was playing upfront for the Magpies and I managed to outshine him during our 1-0 win, which prompted The People to suggest that Spurs were ready to swoop for my signature. I had shown up well against the Londoners in our 2-1 friendly win over them in August where we came up against a fantastic side comprising of such talents as Pat Jennings, Cyril Knowles, Alan Mullery, Martin Chivers, Martin Peters and Alan Gilzean. An 18-year-old Edinburgh native called Graeme Souness had also kept the bench warm for Spurs that afternoon.

A 2-1 victory over Souness' future employers Rangers (our first against the Glasgow side at Tynecastle in 12 years) on 2nd October 1971 kept my name in the headlines, and the *Evening Times* reported further on goings-on at Parkhead: "John Hughes can go for cash or for a swap-plus-cash deal. Stein has always liked Andy Lynch of Hearts."

Whether it was Willie Wallace, John Hughes, or anyone else for that matter, I just wanted to find out if Jock Stein really wanted to take me to Paradise, because I would have walked through to Celtic Park from Tynecastle to sign the contract. Back in my playing days, managers had solid links to certain journalists and there was a mutual respect in many cases. If a story appeared in one of the newspapers back then, it normally carried some substance and was not the foolish gossip that is too-often churned out as an 'exclusive' these days.

While this transfer saga rumbled on, I again suffered my reoccurring pelvic injury and spent another three months on the sidelines. I later deduced that I could have avoided these career-long injury problems had I been given complete rest when they were first discovered. After just a few first-team games with Hearts, I had noticed pains in my groins and I alerted our physio and John Cumming, who would give me two pain killers to ease the discomfort.

From my late teens, I was playing top-flight competitive football, training flat out and still physically growing but I was supplied with more and more painkillers when I even felt as much as a twinge. I didn't understand what these pills were doing to me and my body eventually became immune to them. It was the beginning of a long and frustrating injury problem that would nearly drive me mad when I finally made it to Celtic Park. I hold no grudges towards John Cumming or the Hearts physio for providing me with these painkilling pills. This type of treatment was widespread when I played and they were only doing what they thought was right for me and the side back then. Although every professional club had a physiotherapist, there were precious few resources, and players would often have to go elsewhere to have their long-term conditions treated. When my injury problems later reoccurred during my early months with Celtic, they threatened to wreck my entire career.

Having recuperated over the festive period, I returned to the bench at Ibrox on 22nd January 1972 to watch Rangers destroying us 6-0. A Derek Johnstone hat-trick was added to by Willie Johnston, John Greig and my future Celtic team-mate Alfie Conn. The humiliation of such a landslide victory by Rangers, whom we had defeated at Tynecastle in the corresponding fixture just before my injury, fuelled my determination to get back into my number 11 jersey as soon as possible.

This only took me seven days, as I signalled my return to first-team duty by scoring a venomous 20-yard strike with my right foot in a 2-0 victory against Clyde. This win sparked a much-improved run of 16 games and just two defeats as the 1971/72 season drew to a close.

One of those defeats was inflicted by Celtic, who knocked us out of the Scottish Cup after luckily gaining a replay in the fifth round. Around that time, Lou Macari had really began to shine for Jock Stein, and it was the bhoy from Largs who scored the solitary goal on our home patch to do the damage. He went on to score against Kilmarnock in the semi-final (3-1) before netting a brace in an emphatic 6-1 defeat of Hibs, as the Celtic mean machine wrapped up another double-winning campaign.

Having already secured their seventh championship in-a-row two weeks previously, Celtic were applauded on to the Tynecastle field on 29th April 1972 by my Hearts team-mates, me included. We followed up this respectful gesture by handing the Scottish champs a soccer lesson as we came back from a goal down to record a stylish 4-1 win. It could have been more, as we had a goal disallowed and missed a penalty in front of a ground exclusively filled with home fans due to a Celtic fans' boycott over increased ticket prices.

The man largely responsible for Celtic's ongoing domestic success - Jock Stein - was also missing from Tynecastle that day, as he was in London to watch the European Championship semi-final encounter between England and West Germany. His absence meant that I was unable to impress him further, which was a pity as I approached somewhere near my top form again.

Hearts' impressive end-of-season run clawed us up to a sixth-placed finish in the table, just five points behind third-placed Rangers. Despite this vast improvement at the season's tail-end (and our undoubted ability to beat any other Scottish team on our day), it all appeared bitter-sweet as I seriously doubted that the club were going to improve any further.

Tommy Docherty called me up for the Scotland under-23 squad the following season, and we played the Scottish Professional Youth Team at Easter Road on 20th November 1972. I lined up alongside the likes of Joe Craig (Partick Thistle), Johnny Doyle (Ayr United), Dom Sullivan (Clyde) and Tom McAdam (Dumbarton) and it was a decent personal reward for my own performances in the first half of 1972/73.

This call-up was further proof that my ability was being noticed from other quarters of the game but there was no way that I would have left Tynecastle for just any Scottish club. It was either the team of my dreams or a move down south for my wife and me. I thought it was a distinct possibility: I had always shown up well against Celtic, scored fairly regularly for Hearts from the wing, had a habit of performing well against English opposition (in the Texaco Cup and friendlies), and now I had an international honour to my name.

What else would it take for the newspaper reports to become reality and for Jock Stein to make his move?

The missing part of the jigsaw was just about to fall into place.

READY FOR ADVENTURE: This was the 8th October 1969, and I'd just made my first-team debut for Hearts

THE HOOPS: I always liked the look of that kit, but I wasn't sure about the colour-scheme of first club Mosspark United.

THE ACE OF HEARTS: I relished playing against English opposition. Here I am firing in a shot against Spurs.

THE STRIPES: I picked up some great experience at Tynecastle, and starred alongside some top-notch players.

THE AULD FIRM: I loved playing in these unique fixtures. This 1978 League Cup final ended in a 2-1 extra-time defeat.

THE HOLY TRINITY: It's the 1977 Scottish Cup final and I'm in possession of the hooped jersey, the number three shorts, and the ball.

HOOPS ON PATROL: Lining up alongside Ronnie Glavin, Roy Aitken, Pat Stanton and Johnny Doyle.

LEADING BY EXAMPLE: I clear from Frank McGarvey, as we defeat Saint Mirren 2-1 on 30th September 1978.

HITTING THE SPOT: I've just scored the winning goal from a penalty against Rangers in the 1977 Scottish Cup final.

WHEN TEN MEN WON THE LEAGUE: Celebrating one of the greatest results in Celtic's long and distinguished history.

WE'VE WON THE LEAGUE AGAIN: That 1979 team had a strong bond and unflinching spirit. It was a great dressing-room to be part of.

NO FOOTBALL: That was how it felt during my lengthy lay-off through injury.

AGAINST ALL THE ODDS: I celebrate with Billy McNeill and John Clark as we snatch the 1979 League Championship from under Rangers' noses.

FLY THE FLAG: I am proud to have been part of the 1978/79 league-winning side.

THE LYNCH MOB: The four Lynch bhoys, who enjoyed nothing more than playing football in the back yard, and kicking lumps out of one another.

TO KERRYDALE STREET VIA QUEEN STREET

75

CHAPTER SIX
TO KERRYDALE STREET VIA QUEEN STREET

My transfer to Celtic was engineered by a Glasgow Queen Street newspaper salesman called Jimmy Flaherty, who was known to everyone as 'Flax'. It seems inconceivable now that a football club who had won the European Cup just six years previously would instigate a big money transfer with a rival team through such an unlikely and everyday punter as Flax, but that is exactly what happened.

I used to get the train to Edinburgh every morning with the other west of Scotland boys who played with Hearts at the time (guys like Jim Cruikshank and Jim Townsend), and I'd see Flax as we boarded from Glasgow. He would just bark things out at you when you were talking to him but everybody knew him, including Jock Stein. Big Jock wanted to know everything that was going on and he could utilise and trust a guy like Flax because he would keep everything to himself; he wasn't a loose tongue. This newspaper salesman was in the know with big Jock and I can say for a fact that he was a middle-man for a lot of potential Celtic signings who were going through Queen Street every morning. Jock Stein had trusted lieutenants planted all over Glasgow. He knew when players were out having a drink and where their favourite haunts were. Everything would get back to Jock and you had to get out of bed early in the morning to get one over on him, if you ever dared.

Things had not been the same at Tynecastle since Jock Wallace left and I started to think that I would maybe try and get away and find myself a new team. We still had a decent bunch of players but without Wallace getting an extra 10% out of them it just wasn't working out. When a massive presence like Jock Wallace is removed from any club it leaves a huge void. He kept the morale high on the training pitch and in the dressing room and that had all been lost. I respected Bobby Seith as a man and previously as a player but there was no way he could fill Wallace's boots as a character or as a manager.

I had also suffered a niggling groin injury that would come and go and I didn't feel that I was getting any real treatment from the Hearts physiotherapist. In saying that, it had been a fantastic few years for me at Hearts and I knew that some big teams in England had been watching my progress. I had matured since my trial with Blackpool and would not have been averse to a move down south at that point in my career. I was 21 and would have fancied going down to Tottenham Hotspur, who had shown an interest, but of course my ideal destination would have been Celtic Park. In fact, Celtic were the only other Scottish side I would have joined. It was difficult because there were no agents in those days to put the word out for you and source you a new club.

That's where Flax stepped in.

It was a morning at the train station like any other. I had travelled through to Edinburgh from Glasgow Queen Street since I was 18 and I had seen Flax there every morning selling his newspapers. This guy was very matter-of-fact and he would just tell you like it was without any airs and graces. However, on this particular morning he called me to one side and dropped a bombshell in my ear that reverberated throughout my entire system:

"Don't utter a word to anybody but big Jock's interested in signing you. He'll take you to Celtic Park."

I could not believe this. Jock Stein? Celtic? This was my dream but I didn't have a clue what to do next. My middle-man kept me right though, "You do nothing. Don't rock the boat or ask for a transfer".

As I left Flax to catch my carriage to the capital, I felt ten feet tall. I'm not sure what Jock Stein's train of thought was but there seemed like a huge delay in anything happening after that. I started to become restless and I'd ask my link to Celtic Park every now and again if there was any movement imminent, and he'd say, "Don't worry, just keep your head down and don't do anything". Days moved into weeks and then into months and my initial excitement began to turn into frustration as I heard nothing more about Celtic's supposed interest. I wasn't sure if Stein realised that if things dragged on then I would become unsettled and it might affect my performances with Hearts. Perhaps if I wasn't playing at Tynecastle then my stock would drop and big Jock could get me for the figure that suited him.

During the months where I was left hanging on by Jock Stein, I would often speak to my dad and he offered me advice like any good father would. We both dearly wanted the Celtic deal to go through but I had to consider my own personal situation (I had recently got married, and I couldn't wait on the call indefinitely), and I couldn't wait on the call indefinitely. I had to consider the prospect of Celtic not making Hearts an offer and where that would leave my football career.

Following deep discussions with my dad, and after months of deliberation, I took the bull by the horns and decided to ask for a transfer. My father and I wrote a respectful letter to the Board of Directors at Heart of Midlothian Football Club and, as we placed the handwritten note into an envelope, I wondered if my fate would be sealed like the transfer request contained within.

Bobby Seith was not best pleased the following day when I handed him my written intentions. It was his job to pass it onto the Hearts board but I ensured him that I would continue to give everything I could for the Gorgie Road club until I got my move. Overall, things had gone well at Tynecastle and I had really developed as a player since joining them as a raw 18-year-old. I would never forget that Hearts gave me my big break and I had a couple of good years there but it was time to move on. In any case, I wanted to impress any scouts who might come and see me once my desire to move became public knowledge. That particular process took about 24 hours to materialise.

If I thought Bobby Seith was angry with me then he had nothing on Flax. As I walked towards Glasgow's very own town crier the following day I could see the headlines on his newspaper stand: "Lynch seeks transfer from Hearts". Flax scowled at me and signalled for me to go over to him before growling, "What did I tell you? The big man is going off his rocker." After months of waiting on Jock Stein's call, I was in no mood to justify my decision, "Listen Flax, I've done what I've done and Jock can take it or leave it." After all, I had a mortgage to pay like every other working man and football is an extremely short career. I really had hoped that Celtic would have made their approach several months before but I decided that I couldn't wait any longer and it now seemed probable that I would go down south.

Meanwhile, I continued to dedicate myself during training and games with Hearts and hoped that my dream of signing for Celtic may still come true. It felt like a risk at the time but putting in my transfer request seemed to spark Celtic back into life and before I knew it the deal was back on.

The *Evening Times* of 11th October 1972 reported: "Hearts will consider offers or any suitable propositions for left-winger Andy Lynch. Lynch asked for a transfer this week because he felt he needed a change of club to 'recharge his batteries.' He is an orthodox winger, still only 21, and has played over a hundred games and scored some 30 goals. Manager Bobby Seith said, 'We will consider a cash bid, or a player exchange, or any other deal that may be satisfactory to the parties concerned.' Some time ago it was understood that Celtic were interested in Andy Lynch."

Soon after making headlines and getting a rollicking from Jock Stein via Flax, I was given the nod to go and see Bobby Seith in his office after a training session at Tynecastle. I thought, "Here we go," as Jock Stein's masterplan started to fall perfectly into place. Bobby told me that Hearts had accepted an offer from Celtic and that the transfer would happen the next day. The next day I would be a Celtic player - Andy Lynch of Celtic Football Club. I liked the sound of that. I had imagined and dreamt and fantasised about this day my whole life and, after the opportunity seemed to have passed me by, it made this experience all the sweeter. I was ready for this; ready to sign for my boyhood heroes. I couldn't wait to get back on the train home to Glasgow and tell my family and close pals this unbelievable news. They were all massive Celtic fans and I knew they would be ecstatic for me. My father would be so proud that I was signing for his team; signing for our team.

The following day, Wednesday 7th February 1973, I travelled to Tynecastle to bid my farewells to the Hearts men I had played, battled, trained, won, lost and showered with for over three years. You create and build a unique bond with your team-mates at a football club but I was soon to realise that, when you move on, you leave them all behind. I was swapping the maroon of Edinburgh's Hearts for the green-and-white hoops of Glasgow's world-famous Celtic.

As I climbed into the Rolls Royce owned by the Hearts Chairman, Mr William Lindsay, the realisation began to hit me that I was a short drive away from fulfilling everything I had toiled so tirelessly to achieve. All the training, hard work and social sacrifice was leading me to a hotel in Bathgate where I would meet the great Jock Stein and sign for the seven-in-a-row Scottish champions, Celtic Football Club. Mr Lindsay was a decent man, he had been excellent with me when I first signed for Hearts and he realised that this was a momentous day for me and my family, as I was joining the club I had always supported. He wished me well as we made the short drive to meet Jock Stein at a halfway house.

I started visualising myself pulling that green-and-white jersey over my head for the first time. The famous green-and-white hoops that meant so much to so many people all over the world, and I was going to be representing all those people as an ambassador of this unique football institution. I really could not believe what was happening. I was still trying to stay calm and not let my imagination run wild as we arrived at the hotel and waited in the lounge for this giant of European football to arrive.

Mr Stein arrived alone in his big, square, dark green Mercedes and, as we shook hands, the buyer and seller exchanged pleasantries before producing some paperwork that required signatures. This was business and I was the commodity. A document had been forgotten and I could see that this slightly annoyed Jock Stein but his irritation did not last too long and we were soon in his big Mercedes heading through to Glasgow. I sat in the passenger's seat of this imposing man's car and never said a word. I just sat there like a five-year-old on his first day at school; I was completely awestruck.

Sinking back into the spotless leather upholstery of this German automobile, I allowed myself a few moments of reflection. I reminisced about Charlie Gallagher's cross meeting the head of Billy McNeill in that Scottish Cup final of 1965, and me jumping around behind the goals as a Hampden Park ball-boy. Billy McNeill would now be my team-mate, colleague and captain. That victory eight years previously had heralded a new beginning for Celtic and now I was part of the journey. In that time the iconic figure, whom the Celtic fans now called 'Cesar', had held aloft both the national trophy and the League Cup on five occasions and had won the league championship seven times in-a-row. The Holy Grail, the big cup, had of course been won just two years into this fantastical odyssey.

Jock Stein was in the driving seat in more ways than one as he turned and told me that I would be signing a two-year contract with a three-year option and that I would be getting paid £60-per-week. He casually informed me that when my contract was up after two years I could discuss my terms with him and, if I had done well, he would look at giving me a rise on my basic wage. Finally, he advised that the contract was not negotiable. I just nodded in agreement. If Jock Stein had told me to sign a contract where I was to pay Celtic £10 a week I would have agreed the terms just as willingly. That was the magnitude of me signing for this club. This was not about the money, it was about me pulling that Celtic jersey on and representing this great club.

On our way to Parkhead, we headed for the city centre as Jock wanted to register my signing forms with the Scottish Football Association. As we approached Bridgeton Cross we were struggling for time (as the SFA offices were due to close) and, with heavy traffic building up, a policeman was on a traffic point allowing a few cars at a time to go through. With one car in front of us, the cop signalled to stop our lane and big Jock immediately blasted the horn at him. The hapless officer looked around and, when he realised who was driving the dark green Mercedes, he unceremoniously halted the other lines of traffic and waved us through as if he was in the presence of the King and ruler of all. Come to think of it, maybe he was.

The complex mind of Jock Stein has intrigued players, global reporters, coaches and legions of Celtic supporters for generations and its successful exploration would provide the ultimate blueprint for untold sporting riches. It is the question I have been asked more often than any other, "What was big Jock really like?" Yet I had my own private audience with him the day I signed for Celtic and I could barely utter a word to him.

Over the years that I worked with Jock, I realised that there were many sides to this man's character. Let me say right away that my everlasting memory of him is one of great respect and admiration. His football achievements were astounding, and not just with Celtic. There were many faces to big Jock and I don't mean that as a slight because he had to employ that approach to be a success. He dedicated his life to the club and had led them to two European Cup finals by the time that I had joined. We were on our way to nine championships in-a-row, so his workload and responsibilities were monumental. He had his trusted assistant Sean Fallon, trainer Neilly Mochan, and physio Bob Rooney to help him implement his football operation. In the office were Irene and former Celt Jim Kennedy but there were very few other members of staff employed at the stadium. It is unimaginable when you look at the sheer scale of the business operation now.

Jock could be a very intimidating man, especially when he felt that players were not giving their all. He didn't spare anyone, and if you were a Lisbon Lion or a player who had only played a handful of first-team games the message was the same, "Do the job or you're out." I admired that approach because everyone knew where they stood. Jock Stein's job was to win games for Celtic and, although he could be a very ruthless man in this pursuit, I believe that he could also be a very caring person. He had a lovely smile and enjoyed a laugh like everyone else and if Jock was happy then we were all happy. His leadership skills second-to-none and he was very articulate and knowledgeable with the political agendas of the time. He was a former miner (and miner's son) after all, and his working-class sensibilities gave him a core set of values that he used to maximum effect in managing his own team of men.

Jock Stein told *The Daily Record* at the time of my signing, "Although Andy hasn't been in the Hearts top team for some time, we have been watching him closely. We had a look at him in a reserve game on Saturday. I will have to see him training before I decide how quickly he can come into our side. He is a good player and that is why I have gone for him."

"Every transfer is a gamble," said Stein to *The Daily Mail*. "We gambled with Joe McBride, Tommy Callaghan, Harry Hood and Willie Wallace. They all paid off. We are betting now on the potential of Lynch. He's only 21 after all. We believe he could fit in well here at Parkhead. I have seen him several times and was impressed by his natural left foot and the way he can carry the ball. Natural left-wingers are few and far between these days. By next season, prices will be higher than ever, Lynch might have been at a prohibitive figure by then. And we are always looking to the future. Jimmy Johnstone is coming back and we want as much as possible on both wings. I don't think that Lynch is sure himself of what is his best position but he looked good in training and we'll decide on Friday whether to include him in the first-team pool."

"I am absolutely delighted that I have joined Celtic," I told *The Daily Express*. "It has always been my ambition to play for them. Now I have got my chance. Since I asked Hearts for a transfer last October, I have been out of the first team with a leg injury. Now I hope my luck has turned."

The day I signed for Celtic truly was the greatest day of my football career, and probably the greatest day of my life. The realisation that I was a Celtic player was breathtaking and there was great joy in the Lynch household when it finally happened. My family, extended family members and everyone who knew me were thrilled that I had signed for our team; so, the achievement was not just for me to enjoy, it was for my family and my dad in particular. He was a very proud man and I know it meant the world to him. I made sure that I shared any success I later enjoyed at Celtic with my dad. I nearly always made a point of going to spend some time with him when I won leagues and cups and we'd have a few pints and savour those special moments. I think he took more pleasure in us winning than I did. There wasn't too much celebrating for me upon signing for Celtic however, as I knew that this was only the beginning and the real hard work was about to start. Jock Stein told me that he would give me time to get "Celtic fit" and at the time I didn't quite grasp what he meant. I was soon to learn that I would need to work harder than I had ever done before, as the training instantly intensified with extra afternoon sessions.

I remember making front-page headlines in the following week's Valentine's Day *Celtic View*. In other news, the club paper had started reporting that Celtic had encountered a "hoodoo left-back problem" on account of the sheer raft of injuries to those deployed in the number three shorts. Davie Hay, Jimmy Quinn, Jim Brogan and young Donald Watt had all spent time on the treatment table which meant that Pat McCluskey and even Tommy Callaghan had to play as makeshift left-backs. I wondered who would be playing behind me as I vowed that I'd be happy to play in any role for Celtic. Little did I know that circumstances would result in Andy Lynch being

Celtic's number three for years to come but only after I had been tested to my absolute limit after more than a year in the football wilderness.

I would say at that point of my career, being a Celtic supporter steeped in the traditions of the club from a young age could sometimes be a handicap for me as a player. I did not realise at the time but I put a tremendous amount of added pressure on myself to succeed in what had been a lifetime's ambition, and it is only now that I can appreciate what I should have done differently in my early days at Celtic Park.

With hindsight I can also understand why there was such a delay in me finally signing for Celtic after getting the initial tip-off from Flax months before. Lou Macari had been a huge success after coming through the ranks with the rest of his Quality Street Gang crop and the club sold him for a Scottish record fee of £200,000 to Manchester United in the middle of January 1973. This transfer undoubtedly freed up some funds for Jock Stein as he moved the following week to sign the Kilmarnock goalkeeper, Ally Hunter, for £60,000. I then came in from Hearts at the beginning of February for £35,000 and we later signed Stevie Murray from Aberdeen for £50,000. In turn, Hearts used the £35,000 bounty they received for me to purchase the prolific Drew Busby from Airdrieonians.

I remember meeting wee Louie Macari a few weeks after I signed. He came back up from Manchester to take in a game and we were both sitting in the main stand at Celtic Park. He came up to me to see how I was doing and asked, "So, what's it like to play for Celtic?" and I remember replying, "Brilliant. I can't wait to get into it". I really appreciated that Louie took the time to wish me well. It also showed me that Celtic never leaves you, even if you leave them.

The day after I signed, my daily route to work changed, as I no longer had to travel into the capital haze to ply my trade as a footballer. As I made my way into Kerrydale Street for the first time as a Celtic player I knew that this was where I belonged. I was shown into the first-team dressing room to meet my new team-mates and, even though I had played against many of them for a few seasons, I was still slightly in awe of these players I would now be training alongside. I actually found it quite intimidating at first. It was all a bit much because I was a Celtic supporter and I couldn't believe that I was now getting changed next to four Lisbon Lions and a host of other supreme talents. Let me take you beyond the changing room door and introduce you to those Celtic stars I called my team-mates:

The leader, of course, was Billy McNeill who was now regarded as the club's iconic captain on account of his continental endeavours. Billy was a good bit older than me and I still rated him as one of the finest defenders in European football at that stage of his career. I had worshiped him as a fan and now I could learn from him as a player.

Billy had always captained the more experienced Celts in our squad and he was in that position when the rest of us arrived at Celtic Park so he had that stature and seemed to carry it very naturally. He also had some of the more unenviable responsibilities as part of his leadership role but that came with the territory. I doubt that many outside of a football changing room would ever appreciate that side of his job. For example, other players in the team would want Billy to be a spokesperson for the squad in relation to asking big Jock for wage rises and bonuses and I certainly didn't envy him with that one. He couldn't win because there was no way that he would get what the players wanted and then some of them maybe slightly resented him for it.

I felt that Billy managed to balance his relationship with the boss and his team-mates perfectly and I will never forget how welcome he made me feel at the club. I immediately took a liking to Billy and had a huge level of respect for him, both professionally and on a personal level. It is fitting that there is now a statue of the man at the foot of The Celtic Way.

Bobby Murdoch was a magnificent player and a lovely guy. He was very down-to-earth and humble despite having achieved so much in the game. Bobby had terrific balance and vision and knew exactly where he was playing the ball as soon as he received it. His range of passing was incredible and he could put the ball on the toes of Jimmy Johnstone and Bobby Lennox from distance. Although he was to leave Celtic fairly soon after I joined, I was hugely impressed by him in our short spell together.

Jimmy Johnstone and Bobby Lennox could not make me feel more welcome when I came in. They were best buddies and thick as thieves. Wee Jimmy was so full of fun and very passionate about his beloved Celtic.

His ability in training was a thing to behold and I felt privileged to share a pitch with him. When wee Jinky was on song, he was unstoppable and an absolute pleasure to watch.

Jimmy's partner in crime, Bobby Lennox, always had a smile on his face. He had such a lengthy career at Celtic Park and managed to maintain an incredibly high standard of fitness and performance throughout. Jock Stein (and later Billy McNeill) knew the value of having such a personality in the dressing-room.

We also had the younger raft of players that the press had called 'The Quality Street Gang' and they were well named. The cream of the crop was Kenny Dalglish, whom I had known from our earlier days at amateur side Glasgow United and he made me feel very welcome. I always knew that Kenny would reach a higher level than the rest of the Glasgow United boys and he was well on his way to becoming the most celebrated Scottish footballer of all time when I arrived at Celtic Park. I didn't remind him of our snooker hall conversation a few years previously when he was seriously considering a move away from Celtic Park. Kenny had an insatiable appetite for the game and was a dedicated trainer. He always seemed to be a step ahead of his opponent and was certainly in a different class to most. I still have a photo of Kenny shaking my hand the day I signed and, although our dress-sense and waist lines may have altered slightly since then, we haven't changed all that much.

Vic Davidson was the other boy I played with at Glasgow United and he was still close to Kenny in the early '70s, although his progress had not been as meteoric as many had expected. There was no doubting Vic's ability but the sheer competition for places made it difficult for him to make the breakthrough. Like so many others, he had to move on to make a career for himself.

Jimmy Quinn was the fastest player I ever encountered during my football career and he had started off as a striker like his legendary grandfather of the same name. Due to the left-back "hoodoo" that Celtic were encountering, Jock Stein had converted Jimmy to left-back, where he could overlap at will. Playing a centre-forward at left-back seemed like a desperate measure, and it was clear that the gaffer was finding it increasingly difficult to fill the departed Tommy Gemmell's number three shorts.

Another difficulty that Jock Stein was struggling to manage was the derailing career of the great George Connelly. George was Scotland's Player of the Year when I joined him in the Parkhead squad but it was clear that all was not well as he began to drift away from the game at a time when he should have been nearing his prime. I really liked big George and we got on well. What can I say about his ability? He was something of a phenomenon who was equally effective in midfield or at sweeper. The big man had it all.

Davie Hay was very close to George. They had a tight friendship and I think Davie looked out for his big pal. He was a power-house of a player and it was no surprise to me that he was nicknamed 'The Quiet Assassin'. He seemed to have effortless fitness and could work from one penalty box to another for 90 minutes.

Full-back Danny McGrain was the model of consistency and another outstanding professional. On a Saturday, Danny made the game look easy but it took a lot of effort all week to make it look so effortless. The strength of character shown by him in overcoming serious injury and illness was inspirational to me as a fellow professional.

Paul Wilson was another Quality Street Kid who went on to win full Scottish international honours. Paul could play through the middle or on the wing and he never seemed to score ordinary goals. His were normally spectacular efforts and he had the ability to go on mazy runs, where he would dribble past a host of defenders before slotting the ball away. His vintage season (1974/75) came in the year I made my 'comeback' but more of that later.

Brian McLaughlin came through the youth ranks with Tommy Burns but broke into the first-team at just 16 years of age. To have done that under the watchful gaze of Jock Stein was an incredible achievement and that feat was a measure of Brian's ability. Jock had designs on playing us both as wingers, and that was something I would have relished. Brian was one of the finest strikers of a ball I ever witnessed and with either foot too. A dreadful injury hampered what would have been a glorious career from this Grangemouth youngster.

Sweeper Pat McCluskey was a real character with a great sense of humour. The likeable defender was also a very talented singer like his father before him. Pat would have been a stalwart for any other team in the country but the competition for places meant that he did not enjoy the longevity at Celtic that his talent probably deserved.

Jim Brogan was another wholehearted defender who could play anywhere across the back. His versatility maybe meant that he didn't establish himself as a first choice but he was an extremely popular figure in the dressing room. Jim owned a garage and tried in vain to pass himself off as an honest businessman. Thankfully I never purchased a vehicle from him but many of the other boys did and the motors were all fit for the scrap-yard as soon as they rolled out of Jim's show-room. The affable second-hand salesman pleaded his innocence of course and would often appease his dissatisfied customers on the way back from away matches by producing a cheeky bottle of Sherry for the bus ride home.

Tommy Callaghan was nick-named 'Tid' and he claimed that it was a Fife term that roughly translated to 'Pele'. We both resided in Bishopbriggs and so travelled through to the Park together. Tid was a popular member of the squad and we became good friends. I always felt that he didn't get the credit he deserved and I remember him as being one of those players who always made himself available for a pass. Like Jim Brogan, Tid had a penchant for a glass or two of Sherry.

Striker Harry Hood had been a revelation in his younger days with Clyde and he was an immensely skilful player, who could create a chance and score a goal out of nothing. Harry was one of the few players from our squad, like Tommy Callaghan and myself, who never won a full Scotland cap.

Another outstanding goal-scorer was fan's favourite, Dixie Deans. The word 'gallus' sums Dixie up to a tee. Let's just say that he was far from being the shy and retiring type and he often had our dressing room in fits of laughter with his antics. I always thought that his partnership with Kenny Dalglish was deadly and he had the uncanny ability to linger in the air for crossed balls. He was a terrific threat in the box and he reminded me in many ways of one of my favourite players of years gone by, Joe McBride.

Goalkeepers Ally Hunter and Evan Williams made up an incredible first-team pool of over 20 players and they were all a genuinely down-to-earth group. Upon arriving at Celtic Park, I immediately noticed that the players were all very humble and there were no bad eggs in the camp. They all had their feet very firmly on the ground and I put that down to Jock Stein and his trusted backroom team. There were men in Stein's boot room, namely Sean Fallon and Neilly Mochan, who could bring anyone back down to earth if they ever got carried away with themselves.

One of big Jock's trusted backroom unit was his old team-mate from the 1950s, Neilly Mochan, who was the trainer and kitman by the time that I arrived at Celtic Park. You would always see Neilly with a straight face but you knew he was ready to just burst out laughing at the next prank he was working on. He was an important cog in Stein's well-oiled machine and he was the man responsible for our training kit. He had a boot room and a store room and the latter was full of tracksuits and all sorts of other kit but he would never give us them. He would just tell us that we didn't need tracksuits to train as they would make us soft. "We didn't get tracksuits in our day, son, and we beat Rangers 7-1," would be one of his favourite quips. It would be minus three degrees and Neilly would give us a t-shirt, shorts and a slightly heavier jumper and that was our lot. I remember wee Jimmy was freezing one morning and he was saying to Neilly, "Come on, get the finger out, open that store room and give us some tracksuits," and Neilly replied, "They're for the pansy boys, you don't need them. The boss says that they stay in there and that's that."

Once you finally got your training gear from Neilly, you'd leave Celtic Park with all the other players to jog along London Road to our Barrowfield training complex (to call it a complex is perhaps pushing it slightly). Barrowfield was where the Lisbon Lions had trained and it was basically a couple of run-down pitches where shoots of grass were at a premium in the quagmire of boggy mud.

I noticed that there were no nets in the goals as Sean Fallon sent us for a few laps around Barrowfield to get warmed up. As assistant manager, the charming Sligo man was the ideal foil for big Jock. Another ex-team mate of Stein's, Sean was a genuinely lovely human being who fulfilled his role to perfection. Whereas Jock Stein kept his personality fairly private, Fallon was a very open and outgoing gentleman whose shrewd influence at Celtic Park was not to be underestimated.

Sean didn't allow us to train on the pitches on my first day due to torrential rain so he asked some of the players to remove their jerseys to make goals at the side of the pitch and we went straight into a 13-a-side bounce match. This was my first test as a Celtic player and I realised that the ever-watchful Sean Fallon would be keeping an eye on the new boy's performance during this 40-minute encounter. I scored two long-range efforts as my team won 2-1 and things couldn't have gone any better. Here I was, training with the Celtic players I had watched as a supporter and showing up well as I aimed to secure a first-team berth in Jock Stein's side. Big Jock was revered all over Europe and it was pretty overwhelming to consider that he had identified me as a player he wanted at this magnificent football club. My first day at training had gone incredibly well and I went home hoping that I would be in the first-team pool for Saturday's league encounter at Celtic Park against Partick Thistle.

So Flax, the Queen Street newspaper salesman, turned out to be a very reliable, if unlikely, football source for yours truly. This was during a time in Scottish football where agents were unheard of and Jock Stein managed to operate by utilising a select number of trusted aides, and Flax was certainly in that bracket. Once I finally got my move I would see him regularly up at Celtic Park in the late afternoon as I was leaving training and he was going up to the stadium to meet with big Jock. He would be at every Celtic match and when we got off the coach for an away game you would see him waiting on us. He was there to help Jock Stein and he did it with pride. I know that he came from a large Celtic-supporting family and I will always appreciate the small part that Flax played in getting me my dream move to Paradise.

CHAPTER SEVEN
JUST ANOTHER SATURDAY?

There is no doubt that Hearts were the perfect club for me when I signed in 1969. The management and directors had promised me first-team football, and they were true to their word. I fitted in well enough with the other professionals, and played well enough to be noticed, and talked about. The supporters also got behind me from the very beginning and this helped me substantially, especially in my earliest days at Tynecastle.

But, as I developed as a player, I had my eyes fixed on distant horizons; I felt that Hearts became a stepping stone for a move either to Celtic or the English top flight. There is no disrespect intended towards Hearts in me making that assertion. I was a young but very ambitious professional, and I felt that Hearts had stagnated after Jock Wallace left, and were failing to move forward.

As a wise man once said, "Be careful what you wish for."

I got the move of my dreams when I signed for Jock Stein and Celtic. But that dream soon turned into a near nightmare, partly due to my reoccurring groin injury.

"There wasn't the scope for me to play the game in my own way," I explained to the Celtic View upon signing for my beloved Hoops. "Soon I found I wasn't enjoying my football and I knew that I would have to get a change of club if my game was going to advance. I had learned all I could at Tynecastle. I need to get adjusted to the new demands (at Celtic Park). I've also to reach the standard of fitness of a Celtic player. There's a lot more concentration at Parkhead on speed and sharpness than I've been used to."

My performance at my first Barrowfield training session must have been enough to impress Jock Stein, and I was immediately called up for Celtic's league match against Partick Thistle three days after I signed, and it was looming as a very special match. Much of the pre-match press coverage focussed on the fact that Celtic were going into the home encounter against the Jags chasing their 6000th league strike.

Kenny Dalglish was the bookies' favourite to score the historic goal at 9-4, and no wonder. Shortly after we discussed his future in a Glasgow snooker hall a couple of years previously, Kenny had really established himself in Celtic's first-team. The 1971/72 season had seen him scoring 23 goals and he had kept up his prolific record in the season that I joined the club. Football is full of situations like this - so-called 'Sliding Doors' moments. What if Kenny had lost patience like so many other Parkhead youngsters, and had flown the nest? The consequences of that scenario are simply unthinkable. Player's careers are truly on a knife edge and the margins between monumental success and absolute obscurity are often incredibly thin.

In the seven matches leading up to the Thistle encounter, Kenny had scored eight goals as he forged an impressive striking partnership with Dixie Deans. Had Kenny scored an 88th minute penalty against Kilmarnock in a 4-0 league win on the night that I signed, then the turf accountants would have already paid out.

Glasgow bookmaker (and close associate of Jock Stein), Tony Queen, produced a list of odds that also had Dixie Deans at 11-4; Harry Hood and Jimmy Johnstone at 6-1; I came in at 12-1; Bobby Murdoch was 20-1; Billy McNeill was a decent outside bet at 33-1; and goalkeeper Alistair Hunter was quoted at 50-1, which (according to the bookies) made him as likely as Danny McGrain to score the golden goal!

I sat in the home changing-room of Celtic Park at about 2.45 p.m. on Saturday 10th February 1973 and watched Jimmy Johnstone's pre-match routine. This was like being allowed to observe a magician behind the curtain. Wee Jinky had been named in his usual number seven shorts and I just managed to creep into the first twelve with a place on the bench. Jimmy had a pre-match shower, dried off, and then got himself completely kitted out other than that iconic green-and-white long-sleeved jersey. He then walked over to a full-length mirror that was mounted on the changing-room wall, and he pulled the hoops over his head before tucking them into his shorts, fixing the collar to his satisfaction and checking those ginger corkscrew locks of hair.

"Do you still get the same thrill pulling on that top, Jimmy?" I heard myself asking.

Jimmy, later to be hailed as 'Celtic's Greatest-Ever Player' turned and looked at me. "Andy, I swear to you," he asserted. "When I pull this jersey on, I still get the hairs on the back of my neck standing on end."

Wee Jimmy was one of five Lisbon Lions who lined up on my debut, with 36-year-old Stevie Chalmers starting for Thistle:

CELTIC: *Hunter; McGrain, Quinn; Murdoch, McNeill, Connelly; Johnstone, Dalglish, Deans, Callaghan, Lennox (Lynch).*

PARTICK THISTLE: *Rough; Hansen, Gray; Glavin, Campbell, Strachan; Chalmers, Craig, Coulston (McQuade), Rae, Lawrie.*

James Sanderson of the *Scottish Daily Express* with typical hyperbole had reckoned that, "Andy Lynch's debut was another reason for the Celtic fans to pack Parkhead," and a crowd of 32,000 were there to see Bobby Lawrie opening the scoring for the visitors after 36 minutes.

Celtic had not played particularly well, and Jock Stein turned to me in the Celtic dug-out and told me to warm up with about half-an-hour left to play. As I replaced Bobby Lennox five minutes later, I finally achieved everything I had been working towards my whole life. I didn't have time to stand around and be nostalgic about the occasion, however, as we were a goal down and simply could not afford to lose any more ground on league leaders Rangers in our quest for eight-in-a-row. On 71 minutes I had a shot at Alan Rough's goal, but the ball was deflected to the lethal boot of Dalglish. Rough was equal to his future Scotland team-mate's strike, but he could parry it only as far as Bobby Murdoch, who toe-poked the ball home for the equaliser.

Bobby was worthy of the honour as he took his place alongside the millennia legends club, alongside Alex McNair (1000th league goal-scorer), Adam McLean (2000th), Jimmy McGrory (3000th), Jimmy Delaney (4000th), and

Frank Brogan (5000th). After the 1-1 draw, Bobby was presented with the autographed match ball, plus a 21-piece tea set. This regal gift was not provided by the Celtic board, but from popular Parkhead Masseur, Jimmy Steele.

I didn't labour the fact that I had nearly scored such a historic goal for Celtic on my debut, and I was sure there would be many more opportunities to get my name on the score-sheet as we moved into the business end of the 1972/73 campaign still chasing a league and Scottish Cup double.

Jock Stein seemed relatively pleased with my first showing, as he told the *Celtic View*, "Andy needs a few games behind him, but it was good he played a part in the move that brought the goal."

"In a sense," I added when speaking to the club newspaper. "I was lucky that the side still had something to do when I went on against Partick. There was a responsibility thrown on to me. I had to give plenty of effort because something still had to be achieved."

I wasn't initially concerned when Jock then decided to leave me out of the first-team squad after my debut, as I recalled his comments that I had to get myself "Celtic fit," and in any case my groin injury was still bothering me. However, if someone had told me that I would start just two more first-team games in the next season-and-a-half, I wouldn't have been able to comprehend such a depressing predicament.

I managed to score my first goal in a Celtic jersey as we destroyed Motherwell Reserves 5-0 on 21st February 1973. The second-string were a real mixed bag of experience and youthful prospects. Denis Connaghan, Davie Hay, Pat McCluskey and Jim Brogan joined myself among a group of more senior players working on regaining fitness. In the younger camp were two of Scotland's Professional Youth squad (whom I had faced in my only international appearance three months previously). These boys really stood out in the shape of right-winger Brian McLaughlin and 16-year-old striker Andy Ritchie. Both of these youngsters joined me on the score-sheet that night, and it was Andy's Celtic debut following his move from my former junior club, Kirkintilloch Rob Roy.

By the time that I had been at Celtic Park for a month, I still hadn't added to my solitary substitute's appearance for the first team. When the *Celtic View* asked me if I saw myself establishing a place on the left-wing for Jock Stein, I replied diplomatically:

"That's a manager's decision. I'll be happy to follow instructions. On the wing, I like to carry the ball rather than run on to it. I wouldn't say I was the conventional winger dashing for the corner-flag and getting the ball across the goal, I'm more inclined to veer inside and try a shot. I also like to lay the ball off and this probably helped me when I was switched to the middle of the park.

"I'm naturally left-footed, so it follows that I'll use it more often. But I've scored goals with my right as well. I think players who do most of their work with the left catch the eye more. There are plenty in the game who hardly ever strike a ball except with their right but nobody makes an issue of it."

With Celtic having missed two penalties in their previous two matches, the View reporter went on to ask if I saw myself as a serious contender for the job of penalty taker, to which I replied, "When I was in the first team at Tynecastle, I was the fellow most likely to score ten out of ten at training. I got the job and then I missed one against Ayr United. The next came up a few weeks later when I was making my comeback in the reserves after injury, It was against Motherwell and Peter McCloy was in goal. I glanced at him as I prepared to take the kick. He seemed so big standing there that I thought he was filling the whole goal. This must have unnerved me for I changed my mind about where I was going to direct my shot and I finished up making a hash of it. I never wanted to take penalty kicks after that."

My reluctance to take penalties in competitive matches was to remain for another four years. When I finally felt ready to take another one, it was in the most pressure-filled of circumstances. Such a glorious occasion and achievement as I was to enjoy in the Scottish Cup final of 1977 could not have felt further from reality at that moment in time, as I struggled to make a name for myself at Celtic Park.

I had still seen less that 30 minutes of first-team action some six weeks after signing, and Jock Stein all but wrote off the rest of my season. He commented to the Sunday Post that any top-flight football he would get from me in the remainder of the campaign would be a bonus: "I've always believed in buying a good player when he was available. This was what happened in Andy's case. He was signed with the long term in mind. Also he had been troubled with a groin injury at Tynecastle. This re-asserted itself with the intensive training he's been put through since coming to Parkhead. So I'm not looking for anything spectacular from the lad for the time being. Anyway, it's up to the men who have been playing all season to carry us through this sticky spell. Not a new player who has still to get into the swing of things and over a niggling injury."

During this difficult settling in period, I was able to console myself as my wife and I celebrated the arrival of our first-born, Nicola, on 23rd May 1973. The beginning of 1973 had been an exciting and busy time for our family, and we experienced some cherished life-changing moments around about this time.

Our daughter's arrival came just after the eighth league title in-a-row was ground out by a solitary point over Rangers, I still wasn't in the first-team picture, and the longer I was missing, the more focus the press put on my absence. Three months after signing, I told the Sunday Post about my injury woes:

"That has been the worst thing of all - Trying to get fit by doing nothing. As soon as I signed for Celtic, I started hammering it at training. Unfortunately, this only aggravated the strain. So I was told the less work I did the better. Seemingly it is the sort of injury that will heal in its own good time. I would prefer to put in some voluntary training in the close season. But I realise I'd only hurt my chances. So, for the time being, I've to settle for the odd round of golf and a daily walk in the way of exercise. My target is to get a game or two in the Drybrough Cup. That would make all the waiting worthwhile."

Only two signings had cost more than me in Celtic's history at that point, as Harry Hood and Ally Hunter had each been bought for £40,000. The *Sunday Mirror* very kindly reminded its readers that I had cost more than £1000-per-minute of first-team action, and I was keen to play this type of talk down on the eve of a pre-season match against Cork Hibs in July 1973: "I'm glad my injury worries are all over. The only cure was rest. For a time I could not train or even kick a ball, and just sitting around like that was the worst part. Now I only want the chance to justify my transfer."

Jock Stein also seemed keen to wipe the slate clean for the 1973/74 season as he stated, "They are all playing for their places. I only want on-form players in the side at the start of the season. That applies to everyone. I don't care if they were Lisbon Lions or Jackie McNamara, who's on his first tour with us."

We travelled to Eire on a two-match pre-season trip to prepare for our assault on our ninth league title in-a-row. Obviously, I hadn't played as big a part in the previous title win as I would have liked, and I was so eager to start the new season in the first-team squad.

New signing Stevie Murray and I made our first starts against Cork Hibs at Flower Lodge on 22nd July 1973. We ran out 5-2 winners with braces from Harry Hood and Bobby Lennox and an ultra-rare strike by Danny McGrain. Martin O'Neill of Nottingham Forest was one of five guest players to line up for our hosts that evening. Back in '73, he was just a young curly-haired midfielder finding his feet in the game; our paths would cross again much later in life, when Martin was Celtic's Manager and my youngest son played for the club.

Following our victory, big Jock summed up my first start to the *Daily Express*: "I thought Murray and Lynch both played well. I had decided before the game to play Lynch only in the first half, as he has been recovering from a groin strain since last season. They did well enough, all things considered. Don't forget Lynch has only played half a first-team game in the five months he has been with us."

My groin injury finally seemed to have settled down and I felt that I could push myself during our training sessions in Ireland. On one occasion in particular I didn't really have a choice. Jock was unhappy with our performance during the first match and so hard running was the order of the day and a circuit was mapped out. With stop-watch and whistle at the ready, Jock carefully paired players up and I drew the short straw as I was to run with the powerhouse that was Davie Hay. A few of the other players looked at me sympathetically because, although I had always prided myself on fitness, Davie was a machine.

When our turn came around, big Jock warned Davie to go flat out, and he looked at me meaningfully when he gave that instruction. With a blow of the whistle, Davie and I were off and really going for it around the circuit. Big Jock was shouting at Davie not to hold back and I was running as fast as my legs would carry me. Davie knew I was struggling to keep up with him and uttered from the side of his mouth, "You alright, Andy?" I tried to tell him to slow it down just a little but I'm not sure I was able to breath long enough to get the words out. We finished the circuit and were surrounded by bent-over and wheezing bodies as we waiting for our next lap. I looked at Davie as I managed to catch my breath and he was standing there, having failed to break sweat, looking as though he was waiting on a bus. It was no wonder he was known as 'The Quiet Assassin'.

Two days later, and with the Milltown pitch in semi-darkness, I was sent off in the closing minutes of our 1-0 defeat of Shamrock Rovers. I had replaced Jimmy Johnstone at half-time and was more than happy with my contribution as Bobby Lennox scored the only goal of this tough encounter.

After over half-an-hour of my direct dribbling and shooting on sight, Rovers' defender Frank McEwan had a dig at my ribs (and not for the first time) as we waited on a set-piece to be played. I made sure the ref wasn't looking, and I gave him one back, as I threw my head backwards into McEwan's face. The ref turned around and saw my opponent lying on the deck as if he had been executed, and I was called over by the man in black. The referee was a Dublin butcher called John Carpenter, and the colour of his card matched that of my bloodied lip as an otherwise good performance ended in disappointment for me. This type of start to my Celtic career certainly wasn't in the script when I had signed in February and I hoped that my luck would eventually change in our first competitive match of the season, a Drybrough Cup game against Dunfermline.

Big Jock was apoplectic with rage in the changing room after the game, and was tearing strips off some of the players for our lacklustre performance. Then he turned to me and asked, "And what happened to you? What was the red card for?" I offered my most convincing look of innocence and claimed that there had been an accidental clash of heads. Thankfully there were no television cameras at the so-called friendly match and, as the closing stages were played in semi-darkness due to the lack of floodlights, I think I just about got away with my cover story.

"Yes, it was a hard game," confessed big Jock when speaking to journalist Hugh Taylor after the match. "But that was just what I was looking for. We have now reached the match-fitness that we need. It's still a mystery to us why Andy Lynch was sent off though. He is the one with a split lip."

It appeared that my performance leading up to my sending-off may have been a turning point however, as the reports which followed were all particularly positive. Malcolm Munro of the *Evening Times* emphatically asked: "Johnstone on way out to Lynch?" Before adding, "Jimmy Johnstone, Celtic's 28-year-old right-winger is at the crossroads of his career and much depends on how the little redhead attacks the situation. Jock Stein rated him as the best right-winger in Europe and valued him at £250,000 but stated that the days of playing two wingers are over. Andy Lynch (who is big, fast and aggressive) stuck out a mile in the match against Shamrock Rovers, and looks to be a very good buy indeed for Celtic. Johnstone, meanwhile, has made it known that he prefers a midfield role but he is less effective there."

Jock Stein went on to tell the *Daily Record* that he was highly impressed with my display: "Andy did very well when he came on, and the way he got quickly behind the defender and cut the ball back is just what we are looking for.

"He played with great confidence and has a very bright future with us. It was a treat to see him cross the ball on the run with his left foot, the way that Willie Ormond, Gordon Smith and Willie Waddell used to do. He can open up a defence and he is strong."

Thankfully, I held on to my jersey for the three Drybrough Cup games against Dunfermline (6-1), Dundee (4-0), and the 1-0 final defeat by Hibs after extra time. That was Celtic's third consecutive final defeat in the short-lived competition but I was confident that the wing play of myself on the left and the young, elegant Brian McLaughlin on the right was proving a success for Jock Stein. I scored my first competitive goal in the hoops against Dundee on Tommy Gemmell's return to Celtic Park, and I felt comfortable playing with Jim Brogan and Tommy Callaghan as support up the left-hand side of the field.

The one man I had to keep happy - Jock Stein - seemed satisfied with my start to the season, as he explained to the *Observer*: "For a long time we have not had a left-footed player for the left wing. We had John Hughes out there but he was not really a left-footed player. Lynch is one and now we have players for the wings, we will use them. Lynch can get round the back of the defences and get the ball over smartly and accurately. Once the others come to expect this they will score goals from him. In the early matches we have had young Brian McLaughlin on the right wing and we have been able to stretch defences and give the middle men a bit of space."

The performances of the two new wingers - Brian McLaughlin and myself - were again lauded by the press in our opening League Cup fixture against Arbroath on 11th August 1973, as I scored a headed winner in a 2-1 victory. I was looking towards the next fixture against Falkirk on the Wednesday night as my momentum seemed to be gathering pace, and then...

A darkness suddenly befell my entire career.

The pool of first-team players would be typed up on an A4 sheet of paper, and this was pinned up on the home dressing-room wall the day before a game. After a hard training session at Barrowfield, the squad made their way back to Celtic Park to get showered and changed and I felt a genuine excitement at seeing my name on that team-sheet. On Tuesday 14th August 1973, I filed into the changing-room with the rest of the boys, and my heart sank to the pit of my stomach as I read down the pool of players and my name was missing. I had been dropped.

I had never taken anything for granted but I had played in our four competitive games up to that point, scored a couple of goals and performed well. I would admit that I lacked my usual high levels of energy in the Drybrough Cup final against Hibs and had been taken off after an hour, but this was followed up with my match-winning performance against Arbroath in the League Cup. Why had Jock left me out?

For a few moments, I stood there staring at the team sheet in disbelief as the rest of the crowd dispersed. It was Bobby Murdoch who picked up on my puzzled gaze and took me aside before explaining, "This is the way big Jock works. For no apparent reason he will just drop someone, even if he is playing well. It has happened to most of us at one point or another Andy, so don't take it personally. You've been playing really well lately, so keep your head up."

Whenever anyone mentions the late, great Bobby Murdoch, I always think back to that moment of comfort he offered me. He was one of the greatest players I ever shared a pitch with (of that there is no doubt) but it is the humility of the man that I will never forget.

That type of attitude was typical of many of the senior players at Celtic Park. There were others who were undoubtedly more self-centred and only out for themselves, and that was the way in every workplace. It could be a dog-eat-dog environment, but Bobby realised how devastated I was and took some time out to put an arm around me. What a gem of a human being.

Within a month of that conversation with Bobby, he had been shipped off to Middlesbrough. Out to grass? You've got to be kidding. Bobby Murdoch had plenty of years in the tank and became an absolute legend down on Teesside. I don't think Bobby wanted to leave, and there was a fair bit of shock within the squad when he was allowed to. Jock was far too premature in selling him. Remember what I told you about Jimmy Johnstone's pre-match preparation? Well, Bobby Murdoch also had his. For home games he would always be the first to arrive, well ahead of anybody else. He would take a shower, then change into the strip for the game and, like wee Jimmy, he would study his appearance in the full-length mirror. Even after several hundred games for Celtic, Bobby Murdoch took an immense pride in seeing himself in that famous jersey.

"...And Andy Lynch, who had shaped up so well early in the season, isn't in the squad of 15. Stein believes in blooding in new players but not in rushing them. Lynch may well have reached his peak too soon..."

I was written off by the *Evening Times* as the 1973/74 league campaign was about to kick off, and so began the darkest, most frustrating period of my entire life. There are many people who will argue that there are far worse things than being left out of a football team. Within a few weeks, for example, teenager Brian McLaughlin suffered a serious injury in our 5-0 defeat of Clyde and he was physically hampered for the remainder of his once promising career. That was truly tragic. But, in my case, I had invested everything into my football, and my big move to Celtic Park meant the world to me. To be dropped and cast aside without as much as an explanation hurt like hell and I had real difficulty in dealing with such a disappointment.

The walk down London Road from Barrowfield after training to check the team sheet became agonising. My confidence was corroded with each omission from the squad and, like a bad penny, my pelvic injury began to flare up again. This was due to me over-exerting myself in training. I felt that I had to do something extra; something special to catch big Jock's eye. Other than three more substitute appearances and one further start, I was marooned in the reserves for the rest of the season.

"I just can't string it together the way I want to in the reserves," I explained to *The Sunday Post*. "The atmosphere gets me down. I know I could make everyone sit up if I got half a dozen or so games in the league side. But the way things are at present, I appreciate the boss can't do me any favours by changing a winning team with Europe coming up. So I'm working like fury on the mental side of my game, trying to change my way of thinking. My case hasn't been helped any by Bobby Lennox. He's playing so well it's making it very difficult for anyone to get his place in the team."

"When I signed Andy Lynch from Hearts," continued Jock Stein. "Bobby Seith told me he reckoned Andy would go on to win a Scotland cap. Bobby could still be proved right.

"I can understand only too well how fed-up Andy is with reserve football. His ability has never been in doubt. But he's got to be patient. He's got to produce top form in the reserves so that when a vacancy crops up in the team he's ready to take over. I'm confident he can do it, and justify every penny we paid for him."

The Sunday Post weren't as convinced as my gaffer regarding my prospects of a first-team re-emergence, as they summarised: "At £35,000, Andy Lynch is one of the most expensive signings Celtic have ever made. In February, Andy celebrates his first anniversary at Celtic Park, and in that year he has made a mere handful of appearances in the first team. Many people think the young winger simply doesn't have what it takes. Others are bold enough to say Stein has made a very expensive mistake."

I certainly didn't want to be remembered for being big Jock's first expensive flop but I had entered a period of near obscurity which lasted from February 1973 until April 1975, when a series of fleeting appearances in Celtic's first-team proved to be false dawns.

John Clark looked after the reserves at the time and I recall that my lowest ebb came at a cold Celtic Park against Hibs reserves during the winter months of 1973. Big Jock was watching from the stand and he got a message to the reserves' Coach to substitute me before half-time. About five minutes before the break and the number 11 board went up. To suffer the embarrassment of being substituted in the first half of any match was not one I had ever endured and it hurt me to the core. I was disillusioned and distraught as I trundled off the pitch and up the tunnel. About the only saving grace was that I'd have the piping hot bath to myself.

The heat of the bath matched my mood as I sat there on my own pondering my Celtic future. I had just been taken off for Newman, who was as renowned around Scottish football circles as 'Trialist.' Basically 'Newman' was a pseudonym for 'new man' as in new player. Any youngster coming into the reserves would be referred to as such in the following day's match reports, and here I was playing second fiddle to the player without a name.

As I soaked myself clean from 40 minutes' toil, I heard my team-mates entering the changing-room for the interval. Big Jock came into the washing area to use the toilet and, as he turned to offer me a glance, he had a pop at me for my first-half performance and asked me what I thought I was doing out there.

Months of pent-up anger and frustration finally exploded to the surface, and I replied with a volley of verbals towards my highly-esteemed Manager, as he gazed over me nonplussed from the side of the bath. The cutting words flowed out of me like the sweat from my contorted forehead and I remember my closing gambit being, "AND YOU CAN STICK YOUR FOOTBALL CLUB UP YOUR ARSE!"

Surprisingly, the Manager, a man feared throughout football for a legendary temper, just gazed at me thoughtfully: "I hope that makes you feel better, Andy," was his measured response, as he made his way through the door to the dressing room. What happened next is all a bit hazy. I can't even recall getting dried off and dressed, but as I drove home that night I finally came to my senses and realised that my Celtic career was surely over. No-one speaks to the great Jock Stein like that and lives to tell the tale. Now, my neck really was on the chopping block.

As I often did when faced with such dilemmas, I phoned my father later that evening and explained exactly what had happened. He asked me how I was feeling and, upon reflection, I told him that I actually felt alright and that it was good to get my frustrations off my chest. I added that I felt justified in most of what I had said to big Jock. My chat with my dad settled me down a little bit but I still expected to be pulled into the gaffer's office first thing the following morning.

What would Jock have in store for me? If he could ship out Lisbon Lions before their time was up then would I face a similar fate? Would I be sent off to a club down south without notice? Or even loaned out and banished to some Scottish backwater?

Nothing. Not a word. Everything just went along apparently as normal. What was Jock Stein thinking?

A week or so later, the gaffer told me that he had been discussing my injury with Dr Fitzsimons and that I was to take two weeks off. Not only that, but I was to go on holiday and get complete rest for a fortnight.

The rest of the squad gave me some stick for that decision, but I wasn't bothered as I booked up to go to Majorca to escape the grim Scottish climate. I travelled with my wee pal Stevie Gaw, and my older brother Matt, who had just been named Editor of the Paisley Daily Express and so deserved a well-earned break.

The two weeks away certainly gave me plenty of time to think about my career and how I could get it back on track. I was under no illusions that the wheels had come off it in dramatic style. I also knew deep down that Jock truly wanted me to overcome my pelvic injuries and succeed at Celtic Football Club. His signing record had been pretty flawless when you consider the players he had brought in to Celtic Park before me: Joe McBride from Motherwell for £22,500; Willie Wallace from Hearts for £30,000; Tommy Callaghan from Dunfermline for £35,000; Harry Hood from Clyde for £40,000; Dixie Deans from Motherwell for £17,500; and Ally Hunter from Kilmarnock for £40,000.

A stubborn man, he would not welcome having his judgement of a player questioned, and so seemed determined to persevere with me. Also, I knew he still rated me as a player because, with his vast array of contacts in the game, he could have moved me on without too much fuss. A few clubs had enquired about me during my absence and he had knocked them back. I certainly didn't want to remembered as being a failure at Celtic either.

With the boss, you never knew what to expect next. I had been flying at the beginning of the season and he decided to drop me. I then tore strips off him in the dressing room and he granted me a two-week holiday. He was a complex character and I'm still trying to work him out all these years later.

Around about the time of my early troubles at Celtic Park, John Lennon descended into his infamous 18-month-long 'Lost Weekend'. This was the period where he suffered a break up with Yoko Ono and all-too-often sought solace in the bottom of a liquor bottle. My temporary relationship break-down was with Jock Stein and first-team football and, although I didn't turn to alcohol with the same degree of rapacious zest as the Beatles' rock-and-roller, it did play an unexpected part as I languished in my own chasm of despair.

CHAPTER EIGHT
THE LOST WEEKEND

Football can be a labyrinth of dead ends and wrong turns. There are common vices in the game that lead players astray, and a litany of talents have lost their way in the game as a result. I have played with numerous young men who flew too close to the sun like Icarus, and were burned out before reaching their peak. These problems still exist in the modern game, and many onlookers wonder what drives footballers to continually dabble in such seemingly damaging practices?

I must stress right away that there is a footballer's code similar to that of the Sicilian omertà (or vow of silence) concerning such matters, and so I am not willing to be hypocritical by naming and shaming anyone within these pages. What I do think is necessary, however, is being able to provide an insight into the game at the top level and the various stresses and potential pitfalls that go hand-in-hand within such a high-pressure environment.

I will focus on my experience with the one aspect of the game that has ruined more footballers than anything else in Scotland. As I've already mentioned in an earlier chapter, there was a drinking culture at Tynecastle when I was a young player there. I didn't get involved in that, but at the same time I didn't look down on the players who enjoyed going for a few beers with their team-mates after training.

Throughout my career, footballers were 100% focussed all week on their 90 minutes of action on a Saturday. The pressure could be overwhelming at times and not only was your livelihood at stake, but the expectations of the directors and investors, other club employees and whole communities of supporters could weigh heavy on players' shoulders. It should come as no surprise then that these young men would let off a bit of steam by going out for a few drinks together.

Some people believe that footballers shouldn't drink at all, but there can be huge advantages to building team morale around a few pints. This has to be managed though, and the chronic inability of some players to do this in moderation was where a lot of the problems lay. There was a mistaken belief that you could run off a heavy night on the tiles the following day on the training pitch, but this was clearly no way to treat the body of a supposedly finely-tuned athlete.

When I joined Celtic, the Lisbon era still permeated throughout the club. Many of the players involved in that incredible achievement were still there and we were in the process of winning nine league titles in-a-row as part of a sequence that the Lions had started. Everywhere you looked, there was a remnant of Lisbon and that achievement was the standard that every player and manager has had to live up to ever since (and rightly so).

The expectation of emulating the heroes of 1967 was tangible and I noticed an increase in intensity in everything we did compared to my time at Hearts. The training was tougher, expectations on and off the pitch increased, and players were under the media microscope to a far greater degree. In turn, everything we did was approached with the maximum of intensity and this also extended to off-the-pitch activities.

The Celtic team I joined enjoyed going out for a few drinks and letting their hair down. I was part of that sometimes and I saw no harm in it. Being accepted as part of the team came hand-in-hand with going for a few sociable drinks and so it was almost part of my initiation, which I thankfully passed with flying colours. Some of the antics may have been frowned upon but we weren't doing anything illegal and, for the most part, it was all good clean fun. We had it under control and kept our off-the-field endeavours under wraps.

At Celtic, everyone trained like beasts; some of the boys would do double sessions. Sometimes, in the afternoon, the players would go for a few drinks. It was very much the way things were in Scottish football back then. The following day, the players would get back in the saddle at training with the black bin liners under their training gear to sweat out the alcohol, and turn it on again when it came to match day on a Saturday.

Not all of the players drank. I played in a team with Kenny Dalglish and Danny McGrain remember, and these guys were consummate professionals who never went out drinking. Come to think of it though, I can't recall many others who were in that category! When you consider what Kenny and Danny achieved in the game though, then perhaps their approach was the correct way to go about it.

The biggest teetotaller of them all of course was the gaffer, big Jock, and he knew what was going on. He expected us to behave properly and didn't mind us having a pint at the right time. We would go down to Seamill before a big game and it was great because the whole group were together. On occasions such as these Jock wouldn't mind if we all went for a couple of drinks on the first night that we were there. After that and it was back to getting prepared for the game.

At most other times, it must have been a full-time job checking in with all the spies he had across the city. These were trusted aides, who would report back to Jock if players were overdoing it out on the town. I did see him sampling a half shandy once but he famously deplored alcohol. He was far happier once a player was married and settled down because he knew the value of a wife in keeping her husband (and his player) at home of an evening.

I had my own strict rule that I would never drink after a Wednesday if we had a game on the Saturday, even if it was a reserve game. After a match and on a Sunday I would let loose a little and have a few drinks without feeling too guilty about it.

Going for a few drinks was definitely a way of relieving the pressure, and in the dark days when I was out of the team and things weren't going so well I felt even more pressure. I started going out more often, and I can admit now that I was probably drinking a bit too much.

There was a period of a season-and-a-half to two seasons at Celtic Park where I didn't know if I was coming or going; it threw my whole focus and outlook off kilter and my career was in a state of flux. I had waited all my life to play for Celtic and had managed to prove to the great Jock Stein that I was good enough to join his side. I had finally made it to Celtic Park after a big money transfer, and then for a few reasons things weren't working out for me. It was such a difficult thing for me to accept and come to terms with because I didn't see a way back at that point.

I may not have realised it at the time but I had fallen into a deep depression as a result of my stagnation. I wondered if I could have done anything differently, and whether I would ever be a success at Celtic Park. These niggling doubts cast a shadow over every waking moment and affected my very being. I could only take so much of the disappointment and stress, I let rip a few times and I went out more often than I should have done. I could so easily have been caught up in the 'drinking culture' that Jock Stein so despised. It could have gotten a grip of me like it has done to so many others over the years. If I succumbed to these pressures and failed to get back into Jock's first-team, then I faced the prospect of being branded an expensive failure in the annuls of Celtic's history.

Then all of a sudden there was a sea change in my fortunes, and everything started going right for me again. The pendulum began to swing in my favour and my career got back on track in the most unlikeliest of fashions.

Yet, ironically, this only came after one last drinking session with the boys. One more for the road...

Nine-in-a-row was won, as was the Scottish Cup after a 3-0 defeat of Dundee United; earlier, Dundee had caused us a shock in the League Cup final by beating us 1-0, and our European adventure ended at the hands of the brutal Atletico Madrid at the semi-final stage. 1973/74 had been quite a season and the club were never to scale such lofty heights in Europe ever again (Seville apart). But for me it was an utterly forgettable campaign.

I didn't feel part of the team and couldn't possibly enjoy it as a fan.

When you are left out of the first-team as I was during virtually the entire campaign, you feel isolated and detached from all the success and achievement. I felt none of the elation of the highs, and only the despair of my personal lows. As my contemporaries Kenny Dalglish, Danny McGrain and Davie Hay travelled with the Scotland national side to the World Cup Finals in West Germany (along with Jimmy Johnstone), I felt as though I was a permanent resident of football limbo.

I consoled myself with rare bit-part appearances in friendlies and Testimonials. For example, we faced East Stirling in Alex Ferguson's first ever managerial match and beat them 4-3. No-one could have envisaged what the fellow Govan native would go on to achieve in football management.

I also notched a consolation goal, on 2nd August 1974, in a 2-1 pre-season friendly defeat against Preston North End, who were by then managed by one of the few British players to ever win the World Cup - Bobby Charlton. I had travelled down to Anfield three months previously to play alongside the England legend, when he guested and scored for Celtic against Liverpool in Ron Yeats' Testimonial. Charlton was superb that night as he orchestrated the game from the middle of the park. Effortlessly, he stroked 60-yard passes to the feet of Bobby Lennox, who tore through the Liverpool defence time and time again. Charlton scored a trademark screamer from outside the box in our 4-1 win, and was so comfortable with the ball on either foot. I remember he mentioned after the match that, even at 36-years-of-age, he could still play for Celtic because our players made his job so easy.

Playing in bounce games was all well and good but nothing could beat the real thing, and I was missing from the first-team for virtually the entire 1974/75 season following these two exhibition appearances. In my absence, Celtic won their first-ever Drybrough Cup in August by defeating Rangers on penalties after a 2-2 draw. The League Cup was added to the trophy haul after an incredible 6-3 defeat of Hibs in October. I was naturally delighted for the boys and for my team, but I was nowhere near being part of these victories and it was as if I was on the outside of the party looking in. As 1974 drew to a close, I could not have imagined what the future would hold, and the glories it would bring. But there were still a few twists and turns to contend with before I had the opportunity to sample that sweet taste of success.

Before long I was unceremoniously placed on the transfer list by Jock Stein alongside Jimmy Quinn and Jimmy Bone. I was bitterly unhappy with the prospect of leaving Celtic, but respected the gaffer's decision. All I could do then was to keep myself fit and perform as well as I possibly could for the second string. At that stage of my career, there was no doubt in my mind that I needed to play first-team football, either for Celtic or (unthinkably) for someone else.

I wasn't sure where my future lay on the night that I scored a couple of goals against Hearts' reserves on 20th November 1974 in front of Bertie Auld, who was checking out my suitability for his Partick Thistle side. With the greatest of respect to Bertie and Thistle, if I was going to leave Celtic, it wasn't going to be for another Scottish club.

That double against my former side came from a central striker's position, which was slightly new ground for me. John Clark knew that I had been frustrated with playing reserve football and he asked me if I fancied a challenge by playing in a different position. I was open to trying out something new in the hope that it might revitalise my performances. John played me through the middle for a few games and I thoroughly enjoyed my new role. Meanwhile, a young Tommy Burns was playing wide left for the reserves and getting fine praise for his performances from Jock Stein, who stated, "Tommy is the old-fashioned type of winger with a thought behind every move."

At the advanced age of 23, I already had one of Celtic's youngsters wrestling me for the number 11 shorts in the first-team. By that point my theory was that, by playing centre-forward and getting in among the goals, I could grab the attention of Jock Stein (or a potential new club) by slightly different means than my typical rampaging runs down the left wing.

A week later, my goal-scoring touch was not lost as I grabbed another in a 7-0 rout of Morton reserves. With the traditional New Year fixture against Rangers' second string on the horizon, I knew that I was hitting decent form at the perfect time.

An early night was had by the Lynch household, as the clocks chimed us into 1975. The New Year is traditionally a time of contemplation (as well as celebration) and I had a lot to muse over as the slate was wiped clean amidst the breaking of this new dawn.

At nearly 24, I was at a crossroads in my football career as I languished on Celtic's transfer list with Jimmy Bone. Our previous companion (Jimmy Quinn) on that undesirable roll-call had already exited through the Celtic Park revolving door, and I wondered if I would be next. I knew for definite that I didn't want to go into a relegation battle at the foot of England's Second Division (like Jimmy Quinn at Sheffield Wednesday) or to the provincial Arbroath (as Jimmy Bone soon would);

I still wanted to live my dream with Celtic. But I had to be realistic and, with just two starts and four substitute appearances in two years under my belt, I knew that 1975 was make-or-break for me.

Our reserve fixture against Rangers was scheduled for the 3rd January 1975. It was a Friday night game and as good a time as any to get my career back on track. These encounters, although 'just' second-string matches, were still a big deal. There was plenty of media attention on the derby, a healthy crowd usually turned out, and there was always the possibility that potential suitors would be in attendance. This was undoubtedly the most important football match of my season.

A New Year shindig had been arranged for all the first-team players by club captain, Billy McNeill, for the Thursday night, but I couldn't go because I always stuck to my rule of not drinking three days before a match. I had only ever broken this on one occasion in my entire football career, and it was by accident when I inadvertently made my debut for Queen's Park reserves after a night on 'the sauce'. I wanted to give myself the optimum chance of being at the very top of my game, and especially at this crucial stage when I felt that I had a lot to prove. I was a lot older and wiser by the turn of 1975, and there was no way I was going to put my career in further jeopardy for the sake of a few jars of the golden stuff...

"Come out with the boys Andy... Everyone will be there... You'll have the whole day on Friday to recover... Ach, what's the harm in a few drinks? What does it matter? It's just a reserve game..."

Were these the words of my team-mates or the devil on my shoulder? Either way, I succumbed to temptation and made the short journey to the designated pub in Glasgow to begin the players' night out, and I remember thinking that things could not get any worse for me in my football career. I felt a little apprehensive that I wouldn't be at my sharpest the following evening against Rangers. The first-team players didn't have a game on the following day, and I knew that I should have been at home with my feet up in front of the telly.

As the first pint went down, my nerves began to settle and the guilt quickly diminished. As I enjoyed the second, I began to revel in the company of my Celtic comrades, and managed to put the Rangers game to the back of my mind. A few more drinks and a good night out was had by all. The reserve match didn't enter my mind again... Until the following morning.

I awoke feeling rather ropey, and I realised that I better shake off that unmistakeable, alcohol-induced grogginess before I was due to report to Celtic Park. As the game was kicking off in the evening, I didn't have to go in until an hour before the match and it was just as well because I was feeling distinctly rough around the edges.

My mind raced back to my previous indiscretion at my parents' house, but the pounding sensation inside my head this time was not the same sound created by my father's footsteps as he made his way to my bedroom after hearing of my teenage drunkenness. But I was a grown man this time round and no-one had to tell me that I had done wrong, as I fought to banish this dreadful, lingering hangover. After a fitful afternoon nap had failed to ease my weary head, I made my way up to Celtic Park with my heavy head hanging low, and the fearful guilt still set deep within my conscience...

"Four superb goals by Andy Lynch gave Celtic a narrow win over league-leading Rangers in a thrilling reserve clash at Parkhead last night. The value of the transfer-listed winger must have shot up considerably after this devastating display.

"Lynch opened the scoring on 14 minutes, taking a pass from Andy Ritchie before neatly dribbling round 'keeper Peter McCloy before sliding the ball in the net. Just on the half-hour mark, Lynch made it 2-0 when he dived bravely to head a Vic Davidson cross in at the post.

"Rangers pulled it back to 2-2 before Lynch scored the goal of the match. He made a tremendous run down the left wing before beating McCloy to edge Celtic back into the lead. The Rangers' goalie then punched a fierce drive from Ritchie into the air and Lynch pounced to round off his scoring feat on 71 minutes.

"Although Rangers pulled another goal back with ten minutes left to play, an Andy Lynch-inspired Celtic held on to win 4-3."

(The Daily Record, 4th January 1975).

Although we beat Rangers 4-3, and I scored all four goals, I wasn't ignorant enough to believe that my preparations were acceptable. I should never have gone out before this (or any) match, but I got away with it and things began to turn in my favour again. I dread to think what would have happened had Jock Stein found out about my drinking antics but, to the contrary, that performance helped me a lot in the eyes of the gaffer. I had really nailed my flag to the mast and Jock could not ignore such an individual performance.

Looking back on this period of my life now, I realise that my mood was very low. My chronic pelvic problem made it near-impossible to do my job effectively, and I was making decisions that I would never have normally considered. These could have been particularly destructive to my career but I was lucky that I got through it.

How can I justify all of this? Well, being a professional footballer is no ordinary job, and Celtic are no ordinary football club. The opportunity I had with Celtic was a once-in-a-lifetime gig. However, I had no real warning about the roller-coaster ride I was getting on when I joined the club. I had monumental ups and disastrous lows, went around the loop-the-loop a few times, and my carriage stalled on more than one occasion. There were times when I felt physically sick throughout this journey but by the time I got off the ride, I was glad that I had experienced it.

Ultimately, no matter how much management or guidance you receive (or not, as the case may be) a footballer's career is in their own hands unless he suffers a serious injury. I was my own man and I made my own decisions. Some were perhaps regrettable (such as drinking before an important match) but I stand by everything I did and I take responsibility for every part of it.

I can see how so many footballers' careers go off the rails, I really can. The pressure and profile gets to such a high level that you react in a way that you never thought possible. I got through the darkest days of my journey, but sadly many other didn't. There was light at the end of my tunnel and my biggest achievements in the game were all ahead of me.

The first-team were well beaten 3-0 by Jock Wallace's Rangers the day after my four-goal exploits, and Celtic were awful that afternoon. It wasn't long after these Old Firm matches that I started making my way into the first team, as Jock Stein tried everything in his power to stop a slide that would ultimately cost Celtic their tenth championship in-a-row.

Five days after my scoring spree against Rangers, I scored another hat-trick as we defeated Saint Mirren (now managed by the up-and-coming Alex Ferguson) 5-1 in a challenge match. Jock Stein had still not spoken to me all season but, after my seven goals in two games, he told the Daily Mail, "We've taken Andy off the wing. Now he's playing through the middle alongside our main striker and finding some success. I think he is a bit fitter now and there is less tension in him. For a while he was too anxious. If he keeps things going I wouldn't rule him out for promotion soon. You can't turn your back on a fellow who is scoring goals."

"Within the next fortnight," I explained to *The Weekly News*. "I reckon that's how long I have to show Mr Stein that I can be of value to him or to prove to other clubs that I'm worth buying. If I could get back into the Celtic side by then, I'd work like never before to re-establish myself. I've been 'open to offers' for a couple of months now but I'm sure I could still knock it off with Celts. It's so frustrating. I reckon I'm playing as well as ever so it's now or never at Parkhead. After all, if I can't be considered for a place when the team are going through a sticky patch, there'll be no chance when they're back on the crest. It's not that I'm desperate to leave Celtic. There's no other club I'd rather play for. But I must have first-team football. It's all I've known since I was a teenager at Hearts and after almost two years of continuous reserve football with Celtic, I'm missing the big time."

Jock Stein chopped and changed his side as they struggled to find any kind of convincing form in 1975, and my name finally appeared on the team sheet as a substitute prior to the league match against Arbroath on 8th February 1975. It had been 10 months since my last appearance in a competitive match, but the Celtic side I returned to appeared to be in freefall. I came off the bench for Paul Wilson during our 2-2 Gayfield draw, and then was an unused sub in our next three league matches against Dumbarton at home (2-2), Hibernian away (1-2), and Partick Thistle at Celtic Park (3-2).

During this spell, big Jock realised that we lacked cohesion, and his team selection seemed to change with every passing week as he strived to find the correct blend that would spark us back into life for the title run-in. A hastily arranged friendly away to East Fife was designed to iron out some of the side's problems, and I managed to net a brace in a 5-2 victory.

It was the same score-line when we met Morton reserves in a match watched by Cardiff City's Scottish Manager Jimmy Andrews, who travelled up to Glasgow to cast his eyes over myself and Vic Davidson. We both managed to get on the score-sheet that evening, but events of the next few weeks meant that I wouldn't be joining my old Glasgow United team-mate, Freddie Pethard, down in Wales.

Three matches in a week followed, but I wasn't complaining. I scored another two against Clydebank in a challenge match that ended 6-5, and then partnered Kenny Dalglish upfront in our Scottish Cup fifth round tie away to Dumbarton. We won 2-1 to progress to the semi-final but had slipped to second place in the Scottish First Division by the time we prepared to play fifth-placed Aberdeen up at Pittodrie.

It was a real thrill to be back in the first-team picture and I repaid big Jock by scoring a double against Aberdeen on 12th March 1975. My second goal was somewhat unorthodox as I scored with my stomach. Any part of my anatomy would do as I stuck to the premise that my goals would keep me in big Jock's eye-line. My couple of goals weren't enough to stop Aberdeen, as they beat us by the odd goal in five.

I was taking nothing for granted and was by no means a staple part of the first-team at that point of the season. Jock was still tinkering with his side on a match-to-match basis, but it was far from what we now consider squad rotation. He simply couldn't find his best starting eleven and so I stepped back into the reserves for a couple of matches as Celtic secured their place in the Scottish Cup final virtue of a 1-0 victory over Dundee.

While I played in the reserves, John Clark completely understood my situation and was very sympathetic towards me. He was a calm, sometimes quiet, unassuming guy, and he had helped me immensely by allowing me to move around the pitch to discover a new lease of life for myself. Playing upfront had been a massive success, but then the Lisbon Lion threw me a curve-ball by asking me to play at left-back one night against Dundee United reserves. Left-back? I had never played there in my life. However, John had shown some considerable faith in me and I was more than happy to repay him the favour.

I never learned if this move was part of Jock Stein's master plan, or if it was solely down to John Clark, but I was happy to help John out and I instantly felt comfortable at left-back. I noticed a huge difference having the entire game in front of me, as opposed to collecting the ball high up the pitch and turning into defenders. I also knew the psychology of a winger, as I had played in that position my whole life. I knew what made them feel uncomfortable and I took full advantage of these insecurities. I was the archetypal poacher turned gamekeeper.

In the following reserve game, big Jock came into the dressing room at half-time and on this occasion I didn't end the conversation by telling him to stick his club up his back-side! He was focused as he gave me instructions on a one-to-one basis for the second half. I think it was the first time we had exchanged more than a few words since our infamous argument in the wash room, but perhaps both of our views had changed since back then. Jock's side had lost their seemingly vice-like grip on the league championship for the first time under his watch, and he had the matter of a Scottish Cup final against Airdrie to win. I, in turn, was doing everything in my power to claw myself back into his favour, even if it meant playing in the most unlikely of positions. There was a mutual understanding between us.

Few people of a Celtic persuasion will take much pleasure from the final three league matches of the 1974-75 season. We had already thrown the championship away, and given up our coveted crown for the first time in a decade after imploding at the offset of the year. Those trio of matches however, were among the most important of my career.

I walked down London Road with purpose on Friday 11th April 1975. The well-trodden path from Barrowfield to Celtic Park had often been a grim one for me over the previous two years. I had moved further and further from appearing on that team-sheet; pinned up, as it always was, on the first-team changing-room wall.

"Andy, you're in," came the shout from the throes of bodies ahead of me. To this day I'm not sure who broke the news to me that I would be on the first-team coach to Fife the following day but I felt a real sense of vindication. Every player wanted to appear in the last three league matches of the season: against Dunfermline at East End Park on 12th April 1975; Dundee at Celtic Park on 19th April 1975; and up at Perth against Saint Johnstone on 26th April 1975. These three games could get you a golden ticket to appear at Hampden Park on 3rd May 1975 for the showpiece event of the Scottish football calendar.

The team was announced once we arrived at Dunfermline and I was confirmed as being in at left-back. "Your defensive duties come first Andy," asserted big Jock in the Pars' dressing-room. "When we have possession, then you can get up the line and join in with the attack. Billy will keep you right." That was the extent of my instructions. That is all that big Jock had to offer me as I readied myself for my debut in a new position.

Over the years I have been asked so many times about my change of position. People seem to think that the transition took some time but, in reality, I had only played my first game at left-back in the reserves at the beginning of that month. I felt comfortable during our 3-1 win against a Dunfermline side who would fall foul of league reconstruction in the summer despite doing enough to keep themselves in the top flight under normal circumstances. I felt within myself that I played quite well against the Pars and an appearance in the Scottish Cup final was a distinct possibility with just three weeks to go. From the obscurity of reserve team football, I could play three consecutive first-team games at left-back, and be just one step away from a Scottish Cup winners' medal.

"It's a big change for me, but it's one I am enjoying," I explained to the *Daily Record* on 29th April 1975. "I would love to emulate players like Terry Cooper and Frankie Gray in successfully switching my position to left-back. As a striker I was being kicked all over the place. Now I can see what the defender has to counteract. The transition can be tricky, but I think I have enough football ability to make it. It's an easier position. If I'm in the team and we beat Airdrie and then Rangers in the Glasgow Cup final seven days later, I would be very thrilled."

"Forgotten man Lynch set for a final return. From the cold of reserve team football into the heat of a Scottish Cup final… that could be the tremendous turn-about for Andy Lynch. Only three months ago, he was transfer-listed along with Jimmy Bone and Jimmy Quinn, who have since moved on…"

(The Daily Express, 29th April 1975).

"Things looked pretty black, then I started a good scoring run with the reserves," I explained to the *Daily Express*. "I felt this would probably make one or two clubs move for me. Instead, it got me my place in the Parkhead first team. And that made me happier still. I don't mind where I play as long as I'm in the team. Being involved again is the great thing and I realise my future at Parkhead will depend on the next couple of games. I'm not even thinking about the Scottish Cup final. Obviously I'm keeping my fingers crossed that I will be in the pool but I'll just have to wait and see."

After everything I had been through since my dream move to Celtic Park, I was taking nothing for granted as we approached our third (and my first) Hampden cup final of the season. I still felt that there was the possibility that the boss would go with someone who had more experience in the left-back position. Deep down though, I felt that I had done enough to hold on to the position.

Seamill Hydro was big Jock's favoured destination prior to a big match. This normally meant that a trip to the Ayrshire coast was part of our preparations for Old Firm encounters, cup finals and home European legs. He would take us away for a number of reasons I suppose. One of the main ones would be so that he could keep an eye on his squad leading up to the important games. But it also meant that we were well rested because we were away from the glare of the media, the numerous requests for complimentary tickets that would normally precede the bigger games, and away from the wife and kids! We also got the chance to enjoy the sea air, which normally came virtue of a legendary Neilly Mochan walk. Smiler's treks were something of a tradition and it was good to get settled and focussed for the challenge ahead. The boys would always have a good laugh together and the morale within the camp always benefited from our stays at Seamill.

On the morning of the Airdrie cup final, we left Seamill to head up to Glasgow on the coach and the Celtic songs began...

"Sure it's a grand old team to play for, and it's a grand old team to seeeee..."

My heart would begin to pump and the hairs would be standing up on the back of my neck, and I could see the other players were affected too; the whole team, to a man, joined in with our pre-match battle cry.

It certainly was a grand old team to play for and it meant everything to me. I had almost lost my opportunity to represent this magnificent football club. I even went as far as telling big Jock to stick it up his arse. But I didn't mean that and Jock Stein and I both recognised it was said out of frustration, anger and upset. Celtic meant the world to me; in fact, they still do, and I would get emotional as the squad chanted every word to every Celtic song we could muster on our way up to Celtic Park. These were scenes that you would expect from a supporters' bus (minus the cigarettes and alcohol). Thinking back, the players' coach was a supporters' bus back in my day. It was a phenomenal time to wear the green-and-white hoops of Celtic, as we made our way to the national stadium to face Airdrie in the Scottish Cup final...

CHAPTER NINE
POACHER TURNED GAMEKEEPER

"I doubt if I would have made the first team for the cup final if I'd still been playing upfront," I admitted to the Daily Record on the morning of the Airdrie encounter. "I've enjoyed my games in defence. Certainly they have made sure of my opportunity to play at Hampden. But I don't look on being picked as the important thing. What I really want is to help the team win the cup. That is the big thing, that's what counts more than anything else."

Ten eventful years had passed since I danced behind the Hampden goal to celebrate Billy McNeill's headed winner against Dunfermline Athletic in the Scottish Cup final. Now I was at the national stadium to share the same stage with big Billy as a player. Bobby Lennox had also graced the field in the 1965 final, as had our substitute Tommy Callaghan, although 'Tid' had starred for the Fifers that day.

I would have played anywhere on the field to get my Celtic career kick-started and I was sufficiently satisfied with my three appearances at left-back leading up to the cup final to ensure that I went into the match brimming with confidence. Celtic's line-up had been announced the night before the match and I was delighted to hold on to the number three shorts:

CELTIC: *Latchford; McGrain, Lynch; Murray, McNeill, McCluskey; Hood, Glavin, Dalglish, Lennox, Wilson. Subs: Callaghan and MacDonald.*

AIRDRIE: *McWilliams; Jonquin, Cowan; Menzies, Black, Whiteford; McCann, Walker, McCulloch (March), Lapsley (Reynolds), Wilson.*

Paul Wilson had been very much a fringe player at Celtic Park for a good number of years since breaking through with his fellow Quality Street alumni, but 1974/75 was undoubtedly his vintage year. He finished the season as top scorer with 22 goals and earned himself a Scotland cap against Spain. Remarkably, Paul was to score in four domestic cup finals during the season and this was even more admirable when you consider the personal trauma he suffered just before the Scottish Cup final.

Paul's mother had sadly passed away in the days leading up to the Airdrie game and many of the players went to her funeral the day before our Hampden appearance. Big Jock gave Paul the option of sitting out the cup final but he played the match and dedicated his two goals to his mother's memory. I always considered Paul's bravery in the highest esteem and he thoroughly deserved his moment in the glorious Hampden sunshine that day.

Airdrie, although always considered unfashionable, were a solid team and equalised Paul's opener, but we were deserving of our 3-1 win, as Pat McCluskey wrapped up the scoring from the penalty spot on 53 minutes.

"Andy Lynch, the left-winger turned left-back, did well, giving Celtic a lot of movement down the left flank," reported the *Sunday Mail*. "While Lennox still has enough pace and courage to cause trouble as a front runner. Stein must have been happy with Lynch, who has taken some time to make it at Parkhead after joining them from Hearts as a winger. He played as an orthodox left-back against Airdrie and did it as if he had never played anywhere else. Surely he must have claimed the right to a regular place at left-back with this performance."

This was exactly the type of occasion that I had been yearning for since joining Celtic, and it was as fulfilling as I had imagined. The 1975 Scottish Cup winner's medal was my first honour in the senior game and I savoured every moment of our celebrations. My involvement in such an achievement seemed like a distant pipedream just a few weeks before the final, but I had turned things around and I was in the starting line-up on merit. I had suffered a lot of disappointment since joining the club and I viewed this final as the turning point of my Celtic career.

After the match, the squad and back-room team headed to a nearby hotel to celebrate our victory. The BBC cameras were there and were due to go live at 10 p.m. That doyen of Scottish football reporting, Archie MacPherson, requested interviews with myself, Billy McNeill, Harry Hood and Stevie Murray. I began to feel a bit nervous about appearing in front of the camera because I had never given an on-screen interview before. In those days nobody official was on hand to prepare you for dealing with the media, but Harry Hood was there to keep me calm throughout, and told me exactly what to say: "I was delighted to get back in the side. I didn't mind where I was playing, whether it was in attack or defence, as long as I was in the team." Hardly original, but safe and free of controversy. I quickly rehearsed Harry's lines and then repeated them word-for-word to Archie. The following day, a few people told me how well I had come across on the TV. I just nodded and lied, "It was nothing!"

As my career was finally turning around and I was breaking back into the Celtic side, others were on their way out in the ever-changing world of professional football...

Billy McNeill announced his retirement after winning his seventh Scottish Cup medal in his 24th major cup final. It was an honour to play alongside this great man in his 832nd and final game for the only team he ever played for. I will always remember how welcome big Billy made me feel upon signing for the club. His aerial ability was incomparable and, for me, he will always be Celtic's greatest ever captain.

Jimmy Johnstone wasn't considered for the final because he hadn't trained in the week leading up to the match. He had taken a knock against Saint Johnstone, which ruled him out, and he would soon leave the club for San Jose Earthquakes after being handed a free transfer. Jinky had left the NASL by the time that I joined the league, otherwise I would have relished the challenge of facing the wee man as my direct opponent.

I now considered that the left-back position was mine to lose, but one of the potential challengers (Jim Brogan) would be taken out of the equation as he was also given a free transfer, and left for Coventry City.

A footnote in the pages of the press on the morning of the final was the release of six other Celtic players, including Vic Davidson. I had always got on well with Vic, and he was regarded as a great prospect at Glasgow United alongside Kenny Dalglish in our younger days. At one time, every top club in Britain wanted to sign him and he seemed destined to be a revelation. When I think back to our games of snooker as teenagers, and the fact that he and Kenny were both struggling to fight their way into the Celtic side at that time (and remembering they were considered to be equally talented), it is yet another example of the thin line between success and failure that exists at the top level of professional football.

Having played in front of over 75,000 at Hampden Park in the Scottish Cup final, we returned to the national stadium a week later for the Glasgow Cup final. This was what being a Celtic footballer was all about - back-to-back cup finals and Old Firm clashes. I had watched these world-famous derbies at Ibrox and Celtic Park as a boy, played against Rangers for Hearts, and played against Rangers reserves for Celtic, but nothing could prepare me for my first appearance in Glasgow's battle royale.

CELTIC: *Latchford; McGrain, Lynch; McCluskey, MacDonald, Brogan (Callaghan) (Johnstone); Hood, Murray, Dalglish, Lennox, Wilson.*

RANGERS: *Kennedy; Jardine, Greig; McKean, Jackson, Forsyth; McLean, Stein, Parlane, MacDonald, Johnstone. Subs: Miller and Young.*

Over 80,000 tickets were sold for my second cup final in a week and, as the rain lashed down relentlessly, the atmosphere was unlike anything I had ever experienced. The volume from the stands was being swept all around the old stadium and it was breathtaking to be in the middle of such a whirlwind of noise. The entire match was played at an incredibly high intensity, and I am not surprised that many footballers are unable to acclimatise to such a frenetic powder-keg of an environment.

We went ahead twice in the first half through that man Paul Wilson, but Rangers equalised through Colin Stein and Tommy McLean. Wilson ran wild that day (as he often did against Rangers) and his second goal came after a sublime example of dribbling prowess, where he left three Rangers' defenders in his wake.

The game ended 2-2 and the replay was played a year later (when Rangers won 3-1). Little love was shared between the teams on the pitch however, as the tackles were flying in hard and sometimes wildly. It is true that the unique Old Firm atmosphere can get players carried away like debris in a strong tide. I find it difficult to explain but it is unlike anything I have ever experienced. Perhaps I got carried away by the occasion myself that day, because I did something to a fellow footballer that I have regretted for over 40 years since.

As I said, the tackles were hard and fierce from the moment Ian Foote blew his referee's whistle. I found myself coming infield to man-mark the expensive former Hibs striker, Colin Stein. Colin and I exchanged a few heavy tackles on one another and it was clear that we weren't holding back and were both up for the scrap. This continued until Rangers scored their second equaliser, and Stein made a beeline for me. With his teeth clenched and both fists held up to my face in defiance, he came right up to me to celebrate. In a moment of madness, I spat at him. Stein's celebrations instantly ended, he edged backwards and stood on the sodden Hampden turf looking absolutely horrified. We were both speechless and I instantly regretted what I had done but no-one else had witnessed it. Before I knew it, the game restarted and raged on to its conclusion with the spoils shared.

When the final whistle blew, I shook a few of the other Rangers' players' hands, before making my way over to my 90-minute adversary, Colin Stein, to apologise to him. I very tentatively put my hand out and uttered that solitary word that can seem so impotent, even when you really mean it, "Sorry." I would have fully understood if he told me where to go but, to his eternal credit, Colin accepted my hand-shake and apology before replying, "It's alright, Andy; these things can happen in the heat of the moment."

The Old Firm game was a match like no other and I had been carried away by the atmosphere of it. I didn't hate Colin Stein (or any of his team-mates), and I certainly didn't want to treat anyone in such an unacceptable and deplorable way. But I had done and I deeply regretted it. I was disgusted with my actions that day and feel that any footballer who spits on a fellow professional is a disgrace to their craft. I was utterly ashamed of my actions, but knew I would never allow it to happen again. I also realised that I could never again be caught up in the derby day drama like I had been on my Old Firm debut.

I had been at the depths of despair at Celtic Park by being transfer-listed whilst rooted in the reserve team. My reoccurring injuries added to my woes, and I had even uncharacteristically gone drinking the night before a game. But I battled through all of this personal trauma and had gone full circle to play in front of 150,000 fans in two cup finals at Hampden Park. It was the perfect end to the season for me, and I felt that the disappointments of the previous two campaigns were firmly behind me.

At some point during the final five matches of the season, big Jock was giving instructions in the dressing-room when he referred to me as 'Kipper'. If it was good enough for Jock, then it was good enough for the rest of the boys and from that moment I had been re-named. 'Kipper' became my nickname for the rest of my career and I still get called it to the present day. Kipper Lynch? I'd heard Jock calling players a lot worse!

It was no secret that the gaffer and Neilly Mochan both loved a punt on the horses and knew the racing game inside out. John Lynch was a successful jockey who was referred to as 'Kipper' due to his distinctive walking style. It was said that he 'walked like a fish' (I didn't think fish could walk). In any case, Jock called me 'Kipper' because I shared a surname with this jockey, and it stuck. I consoled myself with the thought that the giving of a nickname was often a term of endearment and I wasn't going to argue with that from big Jock.

I was able to look forward to the new season for the first time in a while and, as I looked towards 1975/76, I was determined to prise the league title back from Ibrox and my old Hearts' Coach, Jock Wallace. Everything was going well for me again and I was fully focussed on the season ahead when further disaster struck...

At 3 a.m. on the morning of 5th July 1975, Jock Stein was involved in a near-fatal road accident on the A74 near Lockerbie. He had been travelling home from his summer holiday with the bookie Tony Queen, as well as Bob Shankly and their three wives when his Mercedes was involved in a head-on collision with another vehicle, which was being driven the wrong way up the motorway!

I remember hearing this dreadful news the following morning and I was in absolute shock. The news-flash stated that he was in a critical condition, but I instantly believed that Jock Stein had the mental and physical strength to pull through such a gargantuan setback.

The whole of Celtic Park was thrown into uncertainty. Jock had been a giant figure at the club for a decade and it felt as though we might be a rudderless ship without him. The sombre mood of the squad as we arrived for pre-season training was palpable and we were informed that Sean Fallon would take over the running of the team for the entire season while Jock recuperated. We knew that Jock Stein was irreplaceable, but with Sean at the helm we realised that the place would run smoothly until the gaffer recovered. Sean's instructions were simple and clear: "We've got to win the title for the boss."

I had the utmost respect for Sean Fallon and I approached my training for the new season with the same dedication as I always would have done. Perhaps initially one or two of the players failed to give the new Acting Manager the respect that he deserved but Sean wasn't slow in putting them right; he was no pushover. As a squad we owed it to Jock in his absence to do everything we could to achieve as much success as possible. But we also owed this to Sean, who was a fantastic servant to our club. We didn't want to let him down either.

It was always going to be a season of upheaval with big Jock missing but there were a few other obstacles for Sean to contend with: Brian McLaughlin had never fully recovered from his dreadful injury and was missing from pre-season training while he spent time with family over in Ireland; Troubled George Connelly had walked out of the club on several occasions and would do so for the last time before Jock returned as boss; and Stevie Murray (who had been a very important player since signing in 1973) would also be lost to the game altogether, due to injury. To lose three players of such a high calibre would have tested the greatest of managers, and so there was no doubt that Sean had a massive challenge on his hands.

The groundwork for the near-impossible task of winning the league back from our greatest rivals without Jock Stein took place during a 10-day three-game tour of Ireland. Sean did well to galvanise the squad, and I will never forget our journey to his hometown to play Sligo Rovers. As we travelled to Sligo the night before the game, Sean stood up in the middle of the coach and got everyone's attention. He explained that he wanted to take a slight detour to Rosses Point, because it was an area of fondness from his childhood and he used to go there with his family to play on the rocks as a young boy. He asked most respectfully if we didn't all mind taking a drive there as it was a place close to his heart.

Of course, no one was going to go against that endearing Irish charm and we all agreed. By the time that we reached Rosses Point however, it was dark and most of the boys were tired and hungry. Sean rose from his seat as the coach parked up, and asked if we would all share the view with him. To a man, everyone got off the bus and followed Sean up to these sea-swept rocks.

Sean led the way and then stopped at the edge of the rocks. Every player and director stood behind him, as he silently marvelled at the darkness of the Atlantic. He was clearly reminiscing about his youth and the magical times he had spent there with his family, and you could have heard a pin drop.

After a few minutes, Sean turned around and said to us all in his unmistakeable Irish brogue, "Thank you for sharing this moment with me boys." We all climbed back onboard our coach for the final leg of our journey to Sligo. It was dark and bitterly cold that night, and we were all tired and hungry, but no one complained about our unexpected detour, such was our respect for Sean Fallon.

Our League Cup campaign got off to a promising start, and we topped a group containing Aberdeen, Hearts and Dumbarton. I scored our second against Hearts with a strike from distance beyond my old team-mate Jim Cruikshank, as we overcame them 3-1 at Tynecastle.

We destroyed Dumbarton 8-0 a week before kicking off our first ever Premier Division campaign against Rangers, and the *Daily Express* were full of praise for Sean Fallon's side, who were now captained by Kenny Dalglish: "In the 8-0 drubbing of Dumbarton, Danny McGrain and Andy Lynch were magnificent attacking full-backs and what a profitable player Lynch has turned out to be in the number three shorts."

Even though I had been missing from the first-team for so long, I was now regarded as one of the senior players in the squad. Sean started to bleed youngsters like Jackie McNamara, Jim Casey, Roy Aitken, Tommy Burns, George McCluskey and Andy Ritchie into the side more regularly, and it certainly felt like a time of transition. As we moved into our league campaign, I was more than confident that I was the first-choice left back. My ambitions for that season were to win back the league championship and to play as many games as I could to make up for the disappointment of the previous two seasons I had all but lost.

"My career at Parkhead was at a crossroads," I told the *Daily Record*. "I hadn't hit it off after moving from Hearts and I was put up for sale after asking for a move. Then I got a chance to play at left-back. I was delighted to play first-team football again. I believe the switch has worked out because I know the service a winger needs and likes. And, as a winger, I certainly know what he doesn't like. There is not the same pressure playing in defence. You get more time to read situations and you can move into attack as well. A lot of players have figured in similar positional switches to their advantage. I'm certainly enjoying the experience. But then I'd play anywhere as long as it was in the first team."

We lost our opening league game of the season for the first time since 1961. What made things worse was that our defeat came against Rangers, a side we failed to overcome in five attempts during Sean Fallon's tenure. Our form for the remainder of 1975 was largely encouraging and we topped the league by the end of the year, as my performances continued to attract praise from the press.

The *Times* called me, "One of the Lynch-pins of Celtic's defence," and went on to state, "Andy Lynch is the outside-left who stepped back to become one of Scotland's top left-backs. Lynch is currently having his best-ever season with the Parkhead club since he was signed from Hearts as a left-winger, and then groomed by Celtic to become a highly successful full back."

The Evening Times asserted that our defensive frailties of the previous season had been eradicated under the watchful eye of Sean Fallon: "A defence which towards the end of last season was suspect to say the least has been tightened by the addition of the skilful Icelander Johannes Edvaldsson and the uncompromising displays of young Roddie MacDonald. Andy Lynch's willingness and ability to take on and beat players and turn defence quickly into attack has brought an added fluidity to the side."

Everything seemed to be going well in Jock Stein's absence initially, and Sean Fallon was marshalling the squad admirably. I made my first European appearance as we defeated the part-time amateurs, Valur of Iceland, 9-0 over two legs in the European Cup Winners' Cup first round. European football was something I had to get used to because it was a prerequisite of playing for a club of Celtic's stature. We then went on to reach our 12th successive League Cup final after disposing of Stenhousemuir and Partick Thistle.

Four days before the away leg against Valur, Mag and I had our second child, Martin. The life of a professional footballer can be demanding for your family at times, and I had to leave my wife with our growing brood as I travelled with the squad to Iceland.

By October, the *Sunday Post* went as far to tip us to win the Premier League and Cup-Winners' Cup double, and the *Sunday Mirror* had us as certs for the inaugural Premier Division title. Meanwhile, *The Celtic View* emphatically claimed, "Full-backs, Danny McGrain and Andy Lynch are rapidly becoming the best partnership in Britain."

This was all high praise indeed but our season was to come to a shuddering and disappointing halt.

We shared a hotel, the Casa de Contracao in Espinho, with our Portuguese opponents Boavista prior to the Cup Winners' Cup second round first leg tie. It was clear that this outfit were a far more difficult proposition than the Icelanders of Valur, and Sean Fallon rated them extremely highly, having travelled out a few days before the rest of the squad on a scouting mission. "This team may not be as quick as Benfica were in the days of Eusebio, Simoes and Jose Augusto," explained Sean to the Daily Record. "But they have the same skills and they are magnificently organised at the back... Their number one player is their midfield man, Alves. He is just about as good a player as I have seen."

Sean was also raving to us about Joao Alves and he reckoned that the attacking midfielder was one of the finest Portuguese talents around at the time. Alves was the main topic of conversation when we had the most unorthodox team talk you could ever imagine the day before the match...

Neilly Mochan played an important role behind-the-scenes at Celtic Park, and I am sure he would have had more input in the absence of Jock Stein. Neilly, Sean and Jock had been team-mates back in the fifties and were a tight-nit group in the boot-room. There was no doubt that Sean Fallon was in charge for the season, but I have no doubt that he was intelligent enough to lean on a man of Neilly's experience and football intelligence when it was necessary.

Neilly and his side-kick Jimmy Steele had a remarkable tendency to relax the players in the lead-up to matches. If we were staying at Seamill or in a hotel abroad, one of Neilly's predictable routines involved taking us all for a walk the day before a game. He loved going for a wander when we arrived in some far-flung city or village, but he was also keen to get his bearings so that he knew where the nearest chapel was. The only problem was that he was notorious for getting the players lost (as he had done the night before the European Cup final in Lisbon).

True to form, Neilly decided to take the boys for a walk to relax us the day before the game with Boavista. In his efforts to find a nearby beach, Neilly had got us all completely lost and we were scaling walls and fences, and walking through the locals' back gardens in search of the ocean. We were completely lost when we finally reached the seashore, and Sean was keen to get us together so that we could talk about the following day's match.

I'm sure the Acting Manager would have preferred to use a tactics board but we were in the middle of nowhere and so he improvised and found a bit of driftwood on the beach so that he could mark his instructions in the sand. He patiently drew the pitch, and all the players were marked out in their positions on the field. As soon as Sean turned around to explain his instructions for the following day, the tide came in and washed his hand-drawn tactics into the sea.

We had to laugh but it wasn't because we were being disrespectful to Sean. It couldn't have happened to a more genuine human being. Once he composed himself, Sean began rhapsodising about Alves again. He explained that he was the penalty taker and that, if Boavista won a spot-kick, then it would be hit to big Peter Latchford's right-hand side.

"Remember Peter, he'll strike it to your right. Make no mistake," asserted Sean.

"How will we know who this Alves is Sean?" Asked Peter. "What number does he wear?"

There was a moment's silence.

"I don't know Peter, I can't remember what number he wears," answered Sean impatiently before he went back to waxing lyrical about this so-called Portuguese genius.

"They call him 'Luvas Pretas' over here," continued Sean. "Because he always wears black gloves during the match…"

That solved the problem of identifying Alves, but the roar of laughter at Sean's expense only lasted a few moments, as the sight of a military tank appeared over the sand dunes and into our line of sight. Someone had obviously called the authorities about a group of pale-looking men wandering around suspiciously in their back garden and they had sent the militia, guns and all! Sean and Neilly were forced to smooth things over and we were advised in no uncertain terms to stop bothering the locals, and get back to our hotel immediately.

Our performance the following night in front of a capacity crowd in the Bessa Stadium had Alan Davidson of the *Evening Times* gushing that, "Celtic can make it all the way. They displayed a maturity far beyond the relative European experience of their current side as they earned a valuable goalless draw. I have a growing conviction that the present Celtic, moulded pre-season more in hope than expectancy, can win this competition."

Boavista were a fine side and were sitting unbeaten at the top of the Portuguese League when we came up against them. For various reasons, we had lost a host of international players since the Scottish Cup final including Billy McNeill, George Connelly, Jimmy Johnstone, Steve Murray and Jim Brogan. We were also without Kenny Dalglish and Dixie Deans in the away tie yet we were still able to get an excellent result over there, but only after a late scare.

With five minutes remaining, our hosts won a penalty kick and the man in the black gloves stepped up to take it. We all remembered Sean's team-talk from the day before. How could we forget? Alves struck the penalty well…

Latchford dived to his right, and the Portuguese internationalist was foiled by a fine save.

Unorthodox his methods may have been, but Sean Fallon got his tactics spot on that night.

As we flew back into Glasgow, we were sitting top of the Premier League, were through to the final of the League Cup, and had one eye on the last eight of the European Cup Winners' Cup. It looked as though Sean was steering this great ship out of stormy, dangerous waters.

Sean Fallon took it upon himself to compare me to England internationalist, Terry Cooper, as I continued to enjoy a new lease of life at left-back. "Andy is still learning the position," explained our stand-in boss. "It's true he didn't hit it off with us as a winger. And it was the same story when we gave him a go as a striker, then in midfield. But when Jock Stein suggested Andy should have a run in the reserves at left-back, everything worked out a treat. He has a lot of determination and this, together with his skill and composure on the ball, is standing him in good stead in this position. Through playing in defence, Lynch has considerably more time to assess situations and can use the ball better. It is impossible to minimise the part he has played in our success. Personally, I'm not in the least surprised. The same thing happened to me when I was moved from centre-forward to full-back."

The two Boavista legs sandwiched back-to-back Old Firm games (the League Cup final and a league match) and Sean's most famous game as a left-back undoubtedly came against the Ibrox club back on 19th October 1957. He had enjoyed many memorable victories over Rangers including the 7-1 game, but his failure to overcome them during his solitary season in charge was to ultimately be his undoing at Celtic Park.

We lost the League Cup final to a second-half Alex MacDonald strike and my loser's medal meant nothing to me, despite my own performance generating a fair amount of praise in the press the following day. The League Cup was to be the one domestic tournament that alluded me throughout my career, and I don't even know the whereabouts of my three loser's medals. That is not me being disrespectful. I went to Celtic to be a winner and that is the Celtic way. As Jock Stein's great friend, Bill Shankly once said, "If you are second, you are nothing."

We played Rangers twice in seven days and the league game was at Celtic Park. Although we drew 1-1, I was disappointed at the goal we lost. With the match goalless after 75 minutes, I took a free-kick inside my own half and knocked it the short distance to Tommy Callaghan. Just as I released the ball towards the Fifer, he turned away and Tommy McLean nipped in to knock the ball on to Derek Parlane, who rounded Peter Latchford to opening the scoring. I was livid with Tid, because we were a goal down and he made me look bad. Thankfully Paul Wilson equalised just three minutes later but we should have won that game at Celtic Park to extend our lead at the top of the table.

My fourth European appearance came in the impressive 3-1 second leg victory against Boavista. It was the first time that Celtic wore numbers on the back of the hoops in our history and we matched the occasion with a fine display as we marched through to the quarter-final. What a season this was turning out to be!

Personally, it had also been an excellent season for me and *The Universe* were calling for me to win a Scotland cap, "Andy Lynch has been converted into one of the best full-backs in the Scottish game. So consistent have been his displays for the Parkhead team that he is in line for a Scottish international cap. A consistent member of a Celtic team which has been struggling on occasions in its attempts to win the Premier Division in the first year of operation."

A reporter from *Reveille* (Bryan Cooney) also suggested that I was in line for an international call-up from Willie Ormond. But I was keen to focus on my club, as I responded, "If someone had told me last year that I would become Celtic's regular full-back, I would have laughed in their face. Things have gone well for me in the last few months and it's reflected in my play."

"I'm just happy to be in the side," I explained the following week to *The Celtic View*. "I quite enjoy getting in the tackle as well as being tackled

In any case I'm not tied down to a strictly defensive position. When the opportunity offers itself I can carry the ball forward. Last week against

Boavista for instance I played quite a lot of the game in the middle of the park. They weren't playing with an orthodox winger and I had to move forward to pick up the man I was marking. Coming from the back suits me because I like to be involved in the play.

"After a match I can find it hard to unwind. Last Wednesday night I was pretty tired physically but I couldn't get to sleep for long enough. I kept going over the game in my mind. Once that happens it's not easy to pull down the shutters.

"The Celtic support mean a lot to me. When things are going well you expect everybody to be happy. It's when you're struggling that you really appreciate the supporters' goodwill. I was lucky to get it in full measure at the time when I needed it most.

"I've learned to take things as they come. Like everybody else in the game I want to do well for my club and myself but experience has taught me not to indulge in too many daydreams. One day you can be on top of the world. The next and it can all have crumbled about you."

How true those latter words of mine turned out to be!

Despite failing to beat them all season, we were still three points ahead of Rangers in the Premier League table by the end of 1975. We defeated Ayr United 3-1 in our final match of the year and their right-winger, Johnny Doyle, was sent off for retaliating against me.

Ayr were a good side back then and Johnny was their star man. He had made no secret about the fact that he was a massive Celtic fan and a few reports around about that time had linked him with a move to Parkhead.

I had played against Johnny a few times and he was fast with bags of courage. I realised that he had a short fuse, and so I naturally took every opportunity I could to wind him up. I put in a few heavy tackles on him and could see that he was ready to blow a gasket. He played right into my trap as I went through him again and he swung a punch right at my face. Johnny was sent off and we ended up winning the game fairly comfortably after that.

Three months later, Sean Fallon broke the club's transfer record by buying Johnny from Somerset Park for £90,000. It seemed like a shrewd move at the time. The right-winger would undoubtedly inject some of his unbridled zest into our championship run-in.

On the day that he signed, the boys were all in the home dressing-room when Johnny walked in. There had been a rumour circulating around Scottish football that Johnny actually kept a wee black book containing a hit-list of players who had crossed him. If you were in the book, then you'd get your just deserts!

"Hey Johnny, is Andy Lynch in that wee black book of yours?" asked one of my team-mates, obviously on the wind-up.

"He's near the top of the list," answered Johnny in a heart-beat, and with a dead-pan expression.

"So, what happens now that you're team-mates?" asked our trouble-making colleague.

"Now that I'm a Celtic player and he's my team-mate," a grin appeared on Johnny's face and he winked in my direction. "Andy's name will be erased from the wee black book."

The dressing-room were in an uproar, as wee Johnny immediately endeared himself to his new team-mates. It certainly wouldn't be the last time that he had the boys in fits of laughter. He was such a great character to have around the dressing-room, and we all knew that he just loved representing the club of his dreams.

Johnny's arrival came in-between the two legs of our European Cup Winners' Cup quarter-final tie against the East German side, Sachsenring Zwickau. Our defence had been on the wrong end of some criticism from the press for our patchy form, and particularly after throwing away a two-goal lead against Motherwell in the third round of the Scottish Cup as we relinquished our trophy after a 3-2 defeat.

"In all honesty, I believe we are the best team in Scotland," I explained to journalist Glen Gibbons. "And I feel that much of the criticism the defence has had to take has not been justified.

"I know we have lost daft goals this season, like every other team. But we have also lost goals which, if we had scored them, would have been regarded as brilliant. Anyway, our defensive lapses, such as they have been, were a temporary thing. The same bad patch that every team goes through. I believe we are now coming back to our early season form, when we had one of the best defences in the country. I've every confidence that we'll come out on the right side."

Despite my confidence in our defensive ability, it was another error that cost us a win in the first leg against the East Germans. Roy Aitken had really improved under the guidance of Sean Fallon, but the youngster was exposed and beaten for Ludwig Blank's 88th minute equaliser at Celtic Park. Kenny Dalglish had put us 1-0 up in the first half and Bobby Lennox had a penalty saved before the break; so, we were bitterly disappointed to come away without the advantage.

Alan Davidson of the *Evening Times* commented, "Danny McGrain and Andy Lynch had the skill, heart, and fitness to attack the Germans on the wings and chase back quickly. They and Kenny Dalglish were the outstanding Celtic performers. Lynch saw a ferocious net-bound shot poleaxe a defender."

We had dominated the home leg, and should have approached our trip to Zwickau with some confidence because the East Germans were a poor side. When we got over there, I failed a late fitness test, and was frustrated as I had to look on helplessly on what was to be an utterly forgettable European night for Celtic.

Sachsenring Zwickau may have been the underdogs but their stadium was full to capacity and there was a real feeling from the disenfranchised locals that their club was truly representing them. The home fans (and the dubious referee) certainly assisted the East Germans as they knocked us out 2-1 on aggregate.

Losing that tie was undoubtedly one of the most disappointing results of my football career. The standard of this side was highlighted in the semi-final as eventual winners, Anderlecht, destroyed them 5-0 on aggregate. We had the ability and experience to do the same.

Following our European exit, another blow was struck to Sean Fallon's campaign as Johnny Doyle was injured on his debut against Dundee in a 1-0 win. With all the will in the world, Johnny was unable to get a good run of games in the championship run-in and our season collapsed around our ears. One win in our last seven league matches meant that we virtually handed Rangers their second title in-a-row on a plate, and Sean's solitary season in charge ended trophyless.

From a personal perspective, I was delighted with my own performances during 1975/76. Sean had shown real faith in me as he presided over the season in which I finally established myself at Celtic Park. I would like to think that I repaid him with 50 first-team appearance and enough fine displays as to have me touted for an international call-up.

I had a huge level of respect for Sean and we got on very well. He was honest, principled and hard-working. He had a real disdain for anyone who failed to give 100% for Celtic and he constantly reaffirmed the importance of representing the club. He knew how privileged we all were to pull on the hoops that he so cherished.

He had bought well (I am sure Jock Stein would have had the final say in the acquisitions of Shuggie Edvaldsson and Johnny Doyle) but there was an edge missing at pivotal points of the season. This was undoubtedly down to the absence of Jock.

I feel that, as a team, we might have made the board's decision more difficult for them by winning a couple of trophies for Sean, but that wasn't to be. Our failure to beat Rangers in five attempts would ultimately be his undoing.

The game of football is a brutal business and the Celtic dug-out would be without the great Sean Fallon for the 1976/77 season for the first time since 1962.

I felt sorry for Sean and I know that other senior professionals such as Kenny Dalglish, Danny McGrain, Paul Wilson and Bobby Lennox would be similarly disappointed at his departure. Sean had signed all of these boys as teenagers and had played a huge part in their careers.

Similarly, young players like Tommy Burns, Roy Aitken and George McCluskey had all developed well under Sean's tutelage and they would be forever in his debt.

Ultimately, we had been nearly-men under Sean Fallon and Rangers had enjoyed a clean sweep domestically. Although the season had promised so much for us, it had only delivered us with the second prize and... "If you are second, you are nothing."

But the board's decision wasn't solely a football one. Jock Stein's success had given him an increased level of power throughout every aspect of Celtic Football Club, and there were murmurs that the board wanted to relinquish some of this influence before he returned to the helm. Perhaps the board felt that Jock Stein would be in a weaker position without his trusted aide by his side, and so they decided to remove him from the picture. Was Sean the fall-guy so that the board could divide and conquer? It certainly felt that way as we lost a great Celtic man the day he left the club.

Meanwhile, a powerhouse of European football was waiting in the wings. It had been cold in his shadow but the return of a revitalised Jock Stein would provide us one final swansong in the career of one of the greatest managers of all time.

CHAPTER TEN
RETURN OF THE RAPTURE

One kick.

My entire life had been leading up to that moment; Everything I had ever experienced in the 26 years before Saturday 7th May 1977 had prepared me for one kick of a football: the culmination of all those hours spent as a child, relentlessly striking shots at my poor neighbour, young Jimmy Hawthorn, on the streets of Govan; the countless matches I had played over the years with Our Lady of Lourdes School, Queen's Park Victoria XI, Mosspark, Eastercraigs, Glasgow United, Renfrew Juniors, Rob Roy Kirkintilloch, Heart of Midlothian and finally my beloved Celtic; the support of my parents and all the coaches who encouraged me throughout my life; the painful hours on the treatment table when I saw no light at the end of the tunnel; those strengthening drills around the muddy trenches of Barrowfield - It all boiled down to one kick at twenty past three that cold and wet afternoon at Hampden Park.

So, what made me do it? What made me want to take that penalty kick? After everything I had done in my life, and all the disappointments I had encountered in my career, I felt that my day had finally arrived. I was ready to take the ball in front of over 50,000 fans at the national stadium and place it on that penalty spot. I knew I was going to score. Not a single doubt entered my mind.

Maybe all the injury problems in my career were meant to happen as a test? Perhaps the mental strength I had gained from coming through those terrible years of anguish had prepared me for that single kick in the 1977 Scottish Cup final against Rangers.

I have often considered the theory that you cannot fully enjoy success until you have tasted failure. There might be something in that. There are sportspeople out there who have been successful throughout their careers and I am sure they thoroughly enjoyed everything they achieved in any case. But throughout my journey, the successes were that bit sweeter due to the mental and physical hurdles I had to jump in order to reach them.

I faced Rangers' Stewart Kennedy without fear. The yellow-jerseyed keeper stood in the centre of his goal motionless, as I took six paces backwards...

Six short steps, one left-footed strike, 54,252 supporters, and only one outcome: I wrote my name into Scottish football's history books...

Jock Stein had taken a long time to recover from his car crash. His accident had really rocked the boat at Celtic Park and sent tremors throughout Scottish football. Although Sean Fallon did everything in his power to steady the ship in Jock's absence, the team had under-achieved during the Sligo man's season-long tenure, and Rangers had won the treble. There was no doubt in my mind that Sean still had a good squad at his disposal, but they didn't have the gun at their heads that was the imposing figure of Jock Stein. While Jock was away, some players may have eased off to a degree and we ended up winning nothing as a result. Everything changed when Jock returned, and the entire club got a huge shot in the arm as we entered the 1976/77 campaign.

The gaffer signalled his return with the truly inspired signing of Pat Stanton. What a coup that turned out to be, as the Hibs legend shored up our leaky defence and became one of the main reasons for our terrific success that season. In the short period of time that I played alongside Pat, I realised that he was one of the finest footballers I ever had the pleasure of sharing a pitch with.

Other huge reasons behind our double-winning glory that year were the performances of Danny McGrain (who was named Scotland's Player of the Year), and Kenny Dalglish (who scored another 26 goals in his final, vintage, campaign with the club). Johnny Doyle finally had the opportunity to make a telling contribution, and the resurgent Ronnie Glavin was like a new signing for us.

I played in all but one of our League Cup sectional matches, as we topped a group containing Dundee United, Dumbarton and Arbroath. We secured a place in our 13th successive final against Aberdeen by knocking out Albion Rovers in the quarter-final (6-0 on aggregate) and Hearts in the semi-final (2-1).

Our early season league form was patchier however, as we won only four of our first nine league games, but we still sat second behind Dundee United as we prepared for the League Cup final against Aberdeen on 6th November 1976.

"Stein, of course, has been rebuilding," explained Alan Davidson in *The Times*. "And the indications are that he's got the mixture to just about the right consistency for success in Scotland. The signing of the vastly experienced, subtle Pat Stanton is proving to be a clever piece of business. Stanton's influence from the sweeper's position has steadied and organised the defence, and Celtic now appear to have firmly bolted a back door which in the past was sometimes left ajar. His experience and calm is helping young centre-half Roddie MacDonald to accelerate to maturity and allowing full-backs Danny McGrain and Andy Lynch to do what they're best at, supporting the attack."

Another loser's medal was added to the collection when we were defeated in the League Cup final 2-1 to Aberdeen after extra time. Kenny Dalglish had given us the lead from the penalty spot and I still feel that we had enough chances to win that final. The season was to develop into a memorable one for us all but we were so close to winning the treble, and making it even more remarkable for the returning Stein. Where did I put my runners-up medal? I have no idea…

Celtic supporters have often been called "the greatest in the world". Such claims are not solely self-proclaimed, and praise has been forthcoming from such global icons of the game as Franz Beckenbauer, Xavi, Paolo Maldini, Clarence Seedorf, Cristiano Ronaldo, Oliver Kahn, Steven Gerrard, Lionel Messi, Andres Iniesta, Zlatan Ibrahimovic, Carles Puyol and Gerard Pique.

But what does that accolade actually mean? That they are the most loyal? Or that they turn out in the greatest numbers? How can anyone really gauge with any certainty, just who has the greatest set of fans in the world? I think by being the 'greatest' supporters, they have to be able to actually influence and determine the outcome of a match through their support; to truly be the side's twelfth man. Here is just one example of what the Celtic fans are capable of. And why for me they are the greatest in the world:

I always enjoyed going back to Tynecastle as a Celtic player but as Willie Gibson completed his hat-trick on 33 minutes to put Hearts 3-1 up against us on 20th November 1976, it felt as though my former club had come back to haunt me. This was the type of situation that would have floored our team during the previous, tumultuous campaign. But it wasn't so much the intervention from the dug-out that reignited our spark on Gorgie Road that afternoon, it was the massive travelling support. As we prepared to kick the match back off, the Celtic fans stood shoulder-to-shoulder on the concrete slopes of the away end. The green-and-white scarves were held aloft and the haunting, uplifting chorus that has become Celtic's rallying cry echoed around the stadium:

"WALK ON, WALK ON, WITH HOPE IN YOUR HEART. AND YOU'LL NEVER WALK ALONE!"

The sea of green-and-white; the hymn of the downtrodden, but never beaten, throes of disciples. The concoction was inspiring, the effects other-worldly.

I literally felt the hairs on the back of my neck standing on end, and three minutes later Bobby Lennox pulled another goal back. The support continued to lift us through song and applause and it really felt as though we were sparked back into life. They had and have that remarkable ability to get an extra ounce of energy out of players and they are undoubtedly capable of lifting their team to another level. In the second half, with that magnificent support behind us, we equalised through Dalglish on the hour mark. With just three minutes left on the clock, Ronnie Glavin sent us back to Glasgow with an unlikely 4-3 victory.

We followed up our win in Edinburgh with a 1-0 victory at Ibrox, with the winner being scored by £60,000 signing from Partick Thistle, Joe Craig. We were a different beast under big Jock, but we would go into the festive season without the experience of the last remaining Lisbon Lion - Bobby Lennox. Bobby had broken his ankle early in the Old Firm encounter after a typically fierce challenge by John Greig.

"Bobby Lennox is a shining example to all the critics who say that after the age of 30 you slow down," I explained to the Scottish Catholic Observer. "One of the major factors of Bobby's keeping fit is his tremendous will-power, which enables him to push himself to the limit in training. Unfortunately, Bobby is suffering from a broken leg, a hazard that every professional footballer hopes will never happen to him. But happily, with his tremendous will-power, I am sure he will overcome this temporary setback as quickly as possible.

"Many end their careers, not because they have lost any skill, simply because their legs cannot do the running. Examples of this may be seen in the cases of men like Neilly Mochan at Celtic Park. You can't help but notice in our five-a-side games that he must have been a very good players in his day."

Despite the loss of the livewire Bobby Lennox, we entered the New Year full of optimism and went top of the league after another 1-0 Old Firm victory, this time at Celtic Park. "As it was, the winner was an own-goal," reported the *Evening Times*. "A short corner was played to Andy Lynch and his cross was headed in by the towering Roddie MacDonald. Colin Jackson, off-balance, got his head to it... and diverted the ball away from his own keeper."

Under Jock Stein, the edge had returned to our play and the treble-winning Rangers were firmly on the back foot as we also looked to progress in the Scottish Cup replay against Airdrie on 2nd February 1977. This would be my 90th appearance for Celtic, almost four years to the day since I joined the club.

"Andy had a hard time when he came here," Jock Stein told the Sunday Mail. "Because he was troubled with a groin injury and was trying too hard to prove he was worth the money we had paid. He got a chance in a new position and he took it."

We destroyed Airdrie 5-0, Hibs 4-2, and Hearts 5-1 on the bounce at the beginning of February as we really hit top form at the best possible time. The confidence and momentum was flowing through the side and Alan Davidson was clearly impressed, as he proclaimed in the *Sports Times*, "Celtic have that Lisbon look again! 14 goals in three matches is positive proof that Celtic are Scotland's form side and the one every team with a championship or Scottish Cup ambition will have to beat." Davidson wasn't wrong.

I scored my tenth goal for the club in a man-of-the-match performance against Ayr United, as we came back from behind to win 4-2. I then made my 100th appearance for the club against Partick Thistle in another 4-2 win.

Then I picked up a leg strain against Aberdeen, as we lost only our third league game of the season but still managed to remain top of the league. Ex-Rangers' midfielder Alfie Conn had been a surprise £65,000 purchase from Tottenham Hotspur and made his debut up at Pittodrie as we went down 2-0. I thereafter missed six games in-a-row with a bad bout of flu, and my number three shorts were ably filled by Scotland's under-21 international Tommy Burns. As much as I loved young Tommy, I wanted them back as soon a I felt better!

The final match I missed was a 1-1 draw at Easter Road on Wednesday 30th March 1977. The events surrounding this fixture proved to me that Jock Stein was back to his uncompromising best in more ways than one.

The Scotland under-21 side were due to play Switzerland on the same evening, and this led to a war of words between our esteemed leader and the Scottish League because Celtic players were missing from our first-team squad due to being included in the Scottish pool. Celtic requested that the league fixture be rescheduled but were denied by the powers-that-be.

"To us it seemed - and still does - a quite inexplicable instruction," exclaimed Jock Stein. "On that night, according to the ballot, we should have been playing at Hampden against Dundee in the semi-final of the Scottish Cup. But because two of our young players were required for Scotland duty, the tie was deferred for a week. Yet, in the full knowledge of this and the absence of our two youngsters (and hampered further by illness and injury to key players), we were being forced to play in another, and no less vital, domestic competition. Eventually we were allowed to withdraw one of our youngsters, Tommy Burns, from the Scotland squad and, as everyone knows, we fulfilled our instruction to play Hibs, but only under protest.

"We got a valuable point and were quite happy. Hibs, who were so insistent that the game should go on and even advertised the fixture before consulting us, got a gate of under 12,000. I can't remember when a meeting of our two clubs at Easter Road attracted fewer spectators. We, at Celtic Park, have always insisted that football is a spectator sport and that it is the man who puts his money down at the turnstiles who counts first and last. It seems as if the Scottish League are more concerned about a minor fixture backlog than the people who keep them and us in business.

"Our last word on this unhappy affair, it's not unknown in football for folk to talk about Celtic 'having a chip on their shoulder.' We would rephrase it this way - where Celtic are concerned, natural justice does not always seem to apply. This incident merely adds to the evidence that has accumulated over the years to support this contention."

The Big Man was back!

I was also back, in the side and back to winning ways in April 1977 against Hearts away (3-0), First Division Dundee in the Scottish Cup semi-final (2-0) and Kilmarnock at home (1-0) before one of the most bizarre nights of my football career took place at Fir Park.

We travelled to Motherwell knowing that a point would secure the championship. The squad were on a great run of form and the mood was positive in the camp. We weren't over confident having been knocked out of the Scottish Cup by Willie McLean's side the previous season but we were now firing on all cylinders with big Jock back at the helm, and had more than enough in the tank to clinch the title.

"By the look on Andy Lynch's face as he left the Fir Park pitch last night, you would have thought he had just sold six volumes of national defence secrets to the Russians," claimed Chick Young of the *Evening Times*. "Two own-goal blunders in the last three minutes of a match in which your side needs only one goal to clinch their very first Premier League title made Andy the villain in green and white, but that Celtic didn't greet this morning as champions is hardly his fault.

"Suggesting that Motherwell are a better team than the Celts by three goals is akin to inferring that Frank Sinatra is a poor man's Sydney Devine."

It's true; I now have the unwanted distinction of scoring two own-goals against Celtic in one game. Trailing by a first-half goal to nil, and going all out to attack, two shots were ricocheted off me and ended up in Roy Baines' goal.

The *Daily Record* claimed that it had been "The most horrific five minutes of his Parkhead career," but little did they know that it didn't come close. Obviously I was disappointed at losing to Motherwell 3-0 but I had to put it down to being one of those freak results.

"The first one just simply cannoned off my leg into the net," I explained to the *Record*. "I didn't know a lot about it. The second was a misunderstanding between 'keeper Roy Baines and myself."

Is scoring two own-goals against Celtic in one match my worst record? Maybe, but if you heard the Scottish Cup final record we cut in a Glasgow recording studio later that week, you wouldn't be so sure!

The bubbly was only kept on ice temporarily as, three days after my Fir Park fiasco, we wrapped the title up at Easter Road after a 1-0 win. I felt it was fitting that Pat Stanton won his only title at his spiritual home. What an outstanding season he had enjoyed with us and it was a privilege to call him my team-mate.

"The door to European football's greatest prize has opened again to Celtic," enthused Alan Davidson of the *Evening Times*. "Almost exactly 10 years after their night of triumph in the Portuguese city of Lisbon. Manager Jock Stein's rebuilt side, an amalgamation of shrewd signings and Parkhead-produced players, won a 30th league championship for the club at Easter Road on Saturday.

"Hibs were determined that Celtic weren't going to open the champagne at their expense. They came close on a few occasions in the first half to spoiling the party, particularly when an Arthur Duncan shot beat Peter Latchford, only for Andy Lynch to clear off the line. Lynch, in fact, put the painful memory of those two own goals in the midweek match with Motherwell firmly behind him. Apart from stopping what seemed a certain goal, he was strong defensively and dangerous going forward."

The prospect of a tilt at the European Cup was one I looked forward to, especially after the disappointments of our previous two campaigns. Following on from our quarter-final exit at the hands of the East Germans under Sean Fallon, we had been unceremoniously dispatched out of the club's first-ever UEFA Cup campaign in the first round by the Poles of Wisla Krakow. It was clear that in order to reclaim some of the fading European prestige gained, Jock Stein would need to strengthen his championship-winning side.

Before concerning ourselves with continental trips, we had the familiar journey to the Ayrshire coast and Seamill to prepare for the 92nd Scottish Cup final. Ronnie Glavin had enjoyed a vintage campaign in which he was top goal-scorer with 26 goals, and my former Glasgow RC Schools' team-mate was thoroughly deserving of his international call up ten days before the final. Ronnie had picked up a knock though, and didn't make the cut for Jock Stein's side.

This posed another problem for the manager. Six of Ronnie's goals had come from penalties during the season, and seven of Kenny Dalglish's total had also been attributed to spot-kicks. The natural penalty taker in Ronnie's absence would have been his fellow top goal-scorer but Kenny had missed a few during the season, and Jock Stein arranged a competition the day before the final.

I had only taken two penalties in my senior career (for Hearts), and I had missed them both. I had no designs on becoming a regular penalty taker but my performance in the spot-kick competition suggested otherwise as I failed to miss a single shot and converted more than any other player in the squad.

As Kenny and I walked up to the hotel to get changed, we were discussing who should take the kick the following day should we get one. Unbeknownst to us, Jock had been listening in to us and, as he held the door open for us approaching, he remarked, "There's you pair arguing about who should take the penalty... If I got the opportunity to take a spot-kick in the final against Rangers I'd bite your hand off for it."

Jock was right. What a privilege it would be. "I'll take the penalty tomorrow if we get one Kenny," I insisted. Kenny didn't argue.

That was me in 'the zone' from that moment on. I was composed and ready for the cup final. My frame of mind was strong and positive and I felt great as we wound down for the evening.

When I look back throughout my career, there were certain games where I could do nothing wrong. I had prepared the same way as I'd always done, and undoubtedly possessed the same ability as I had done during other, less successful, performances. Yet, on these specific occasions (where I was able to tap into the correct frame of mind), I could play a blinder. During these games, I came to realise that I was tuned in mentally. Nothing could encroach my positivity or affect my confidence. Nothing could knock me. I believe that the finest players, those who are able to maintain an incredible level of performance consistently throughout their careers, have mastered this process.

I was at Hampden Park to be one of the winners. That was what I had visualised. I didn't allow any thought of defeat to enter my mind. On the flip-side, I had played in many games where I may have felt mentally or physically tired before a game. On these occasions, I'd maybe not feel right until I was on the pitch and then the whistle would blow and I'd be switched on. Sometimes, it hinged on my first touch. If I made an error and the doubt crept in then it could affect my entire game.

I was 'in the zone' the day before the cup final. Winning the penalty kick competition and nominating myself for any spot kicks definitely helped me immensely in my preparation. I woke up on the morning of 7th May 1977 feeling that I would perform well and that Celtic would win the Scottish Cup.

CELTIC: *Latchford; McGrain, Lynch; Stanton, MacDonald, Aitken; Dalglish, Edvaldsson, Craig, Wilson, Conn. Subs: Burns and Doyle.*

RANGERS: *Kennedy; Jardine, Greig; Forsyth, Jackson, Watson (Robertson); McLean, Hamilton, Parlane, MacDonald, Johnstone. Sub: Miller.*

The ball-boys are waiting in the Hampden Park dug-outs with their 'QPFC' rain-jackets on. 12 years earlier, I had been one of them.

Jock Stein and Jock Wallace lead out their respective sides. The two great Jocks that I have known (the only two Jocks that I have known!). There is no time for sentimentality on my part, I want to ruin Jock Wallace's day.

Jock Stein had believed in me. I had come to realise that. No matter what I had been going through, he had stuck by me. We had come to verbal blows but he didn't get rid of me, and now here I was, ready to repay him even further.

Kenny Dalglish leads the players, followed by Peter Latchford, Danny McGrain and then myself. I don't look back to see who is behind me. I'm focused on moving forward, on getting on to the Hampden turf, and on winning this match.

"ALMOST SIBERIAN CONDITIONS AT HAMPDEN PARK THIS AFTERNOON..."

The pre-match white tracksuit tops were a one-off. Neilly Mochan had arranged to have 'League Champions 1977' emblazoned across the backs of them in green. Every Rangers player behind John Greig is reminded as they run out the tunnel, just who the top dogs are in Scottish football. Jock Stein is back.

"AN INTERESTING RIG-OUT FOR CELTIC WITH THESE NEW TRACKSUIT TOPS..."

Bob Valentine from Dundee is the referee. He's 36 but looks older. It is his first cup final. We line up for the national anthem, but only half the crowd joins in.

"GOD SAVE OUR GRACIOUS QUEEN, LONG LIVE OUR NOBLE QUEEN, GOD SAVE THE QUEEN..."

We do the obligatory handshakes with the SFA's President, Rankin Grimshaw, and make it as quick as possible so that we can get kicked off.

"ONE OF THE BIG DISAPPOINTMENTS IS THE CROWD OF ONLY 54,252. THIS IS THE SMALLEST CROWD IN OVER 20 YEARS FOR THE SHOWPEICE OF THE SCOTTISH FOOTBALL SEASON. THIS ATTENDANCE CASTS DOUBT ON THE SFA'S DECISION TO TELEVISE THE MATCH LIVE..."

I'm snuffing out the blue jersey I'm up against and am able to get up into attacking positions. The ball breaks to the edge of the box after 17 minutes, and I spot Stewart Kennedy off his line. I loop a header from outside the box and he scrambles back. It looks like a certain goal but he manages to palm it past for a corner kick.

"THIS IS A GREAT HEADER BY ANDY LYNCH. HE READ THIS SITUATION VERY WELL, SAW THE GOALIE WAS STRANDED, AND KNOCKED IT STRAIGHT OVER THE GOALKEEPER'S HEAD. KENNEDY DID EXCEPTIONALLY WELL TO GET JUST A LITTLE TOUCH TO IT AND PUT IT AROUND THE POST..."

For a couple of minutes it looks ominous for Rangers while their 'keeper is being treated for an arm injury. But he recovers to face the corner taken by Alfie Conn.

"OH ALFIE ALFIE. ALFIE, ALFIE, ALFIE, ALFIE, ALFIE CONN!"

Alfie flights the dead-ball in from the same corner of Hampden Park that Charlie Gallagher had back in 1965. Another header towards goal, but it's big Roddie MacDonald this time and not big Billy. The ball is stopped on the goal-line but Derek Johnstone has used his hands.

"THAT IS MOST CERTAINLY A PENALTY KICK. MOST CERTAINLY..."

10 Rangers jersey surround Bob Valentine but he's turned his back on them and is ushering them away. I make my way to the penalty spot and every Celtic player knows that I'm taking this kick. The Rangers players slowly disperse and Stewart Kennedy still has the ball. He throws it to me as he reaches his goal, and I place it on the spot. 12 years ago I was behind that goal...

"THERE'S THE ICE-COOL ANDY LYNCH..."

I've waited my whole life for this. Behind me, Tommy McLean frantically points down to Stewart Kennedy's left in an effort to help out his 'keeper. He tells him exactly where I'm going to put this penalty. It doesn't matter if he knows.

"AND ANDY LYNCH IS TO TAKE THIS. WHAT A NERVE-WRACKING MOMENT..."

I take six steps backs. Run six steps forwards. Sweetly strike it with my left foot, low to Kennedy's left, tight to the post...

*"AND THERE IT IS. ANDY LYNCH MAKES IT ONE-NOTHING TO
CELTIC..."*

*"...CELTIC'S LYNCH-PIN! ANDY MADE NO MISTAKE FROM THE
SPOT!"*

Joe Craig, then Kenny Dalglish, and then Roy Aitken grab me in
congratulation. The embraces are fleeting as we still have 70 minutes to
play, but I have given us the lead.

*"WHEN THE CELTS GO MARCHING IN! OH, WHEN THE CELTS
GO MARCHING IN..."*

I make one mistake during the whole match. After about 25 minutes, I
try to flight the ball across the field. It get caught mid-flight in the wind
and intercepted. Rangers break and the move could have killed me. But it
doesn't, as we have the great Pat Stanton shoring up the defence.

*"THE WHISTLE HAS GONE. CELTIC HAVE WON THE SCOTTISH
CUP FOR THE 25th TIME..."*

*"IT MUST BE NERVE-WRACKING TO TAKE A PENALTY KICK IN
ANY CUP FINAL, NOT LEAST A RANGERS V CELTIC FINAL LIKE
THIS ONE. THERE WAS A TENSE ATMOSPHERE IN WHAT WAS
SOMETIMES A TOWSY, BRUISING GAME..."*

Big Jock runs on to the field and congratulates his captain, Kenny Dalglish.
It's Kenny's first and last cup win as Celtic captain. He will cross the border
in the summer (and a year later he'll win the European Cup with Liverpool).

But before he does that, he leads us up the Hampden steps to shake hands
again with Rankin Grimshaw and to collect our winners' medals.

*"DANNY MCGRAIN, PLAYER OF THE YEAR AND THE MOST
COMPLETE FOOTBALLER ON THE FIELD, WAS OUTSTANDING
FOR CELTIC. BUT CLOSE BEHIND WERE ANDY LYNCH AND
RODDIE MACDONALD, WHO WAS ALWAYS MAGNIFICENT IN
THE AIR. AND ALFIE CONN, WHO BECOMES THE FIRST PLAYER
EVER TO WIN THE SCOTTISH CUP WITH BOTH CELTIC AND
RANGERS..."*

The glittering prize is passed from Kenny, to Peter, to Danny, and then to me. As I hold aloft the Scottish Cup, the sounds of Celtic fans singing in my ears plays like a symphony. I never want it to end.

"WALK ON, WALK ON. WITH HOPE IN YOUR HEART. AND YOU'LL NEVER WALK ALONE..."

We do a lap of honour and Kenny loses his gong. "I've never been so pleased to see a policeman in my life," he stresses after the match. "He had found my medal."

"WALK ON, WALK ON. WITH HOPE IN YOUR HEART. AND YOU'LL NEVER WALK ALONE..."

Big Jock had grasped the nettle and seen something in me. Why else had he kept me so long? He was very patient and had a lot of faith in me. His belief in me shone through and I had now paid him back.

"NATURALLY I FELT A BIT EXCITED ABOUT TAKING THE PENALTY ARCHIE. PREVIOUS TO THAT I HAD MISSED TWO WITH MY FORMER CLUB, HEARTS. WE WERE DISCUSSING IT LAST NIGHT WITH MR. STEIN AND IN THE ABSENCE OF RONNIE GLAVIN WE HAD DECIDED THAT IT WOULD BE BETWEEN EITHER KENNY OR MYSELF. WHEN THE PENALTY WAS AWARDED, I FELT LIKE HAVING A GO..."

It had been hammered into me since the day I joined Celtic Football Club - This club is for winners. It is ingrained in you; We must win at all costs.

I love Celtic and sometimes I found it hard when things weren't working out for me. Maybe I had been too hard on myself. Maybe I had trained too hard. Sometimes I looked around the training pitch and I had to pinch myself. I was playing with my heroes.

But not now. Now no-one could argue that I had established myself in my own right as Andy Lynch of Celtic F.C. I had played over 100 games and won three trophies. And now, I had scored the winning goal in the Scottish Cup final.

My life would change forever. People would ask me about that penalty kick for the next 40 years. I'm sure they will be asking me about it for the rest of my life. It was all down to one kick of a football.

One kick.

CHAPTER ELEVEN
THE EMPEROR'S LAST STAND

In my first four years at Celtic Park, I played under three captains: Billy McNeill, Kenny Dalglish, and Danny McGrain.

Billy McNeill retired in 1975, and took his rightful place among the pantheon of Scottish footballing greats. Such were his natural leadership qualities, I wasn't surprised when he took his first tentative steps into management with Clyde, before sparking a resurgence at Aberdeen in 1977/78.

The captain's armband was then handed on to a new type of hero in Kenny Dalglish. Kenny was an icon of the terraces and led us with style throughout the spectacular 1976/77 double-winning campaign. But he broke the hearts of a generation of Hoops' supporters when he signed for Liverpool in a record-breaking transfer before we were able to build on our success the following season.

The entire squad felt the loss of Kenny just as badly as the fans did. We realised only too well that he was not the type of player that Celtic could replace. He had signed for the club ten years previously and developed under the unparalleled leadership of Jock Stein's boot-room. By the time that he left Celtic Park, there was no doubt that he had been the sweetest fruit from the Quality Street vine. We sold Liverpool the finished article, and Celtic did not operate within the type of market that housed players of his quality. Even the £440,000 that the club received could never have bought another Kenny Dalglish (not that the parsimonious board would ever have dreamt of spending such a vast sum of cash on one player).

Jock decided to make Danny McGrain club captain as we entered the new season, and I don't think there would have been many objections to that decision. We did have another ready-made leader in the shape of

Pat Stanton, but I felt it was right that Danny should take over such an honourable position after his flawless service to the club. The international right-back's leadership lasted just 11 matches however, as Celtic's season unexpectedly de-railed in disastrous fashion.

The influential Pat Stanton and mercurial Alfie Conn were both injured on the opening day of the new campaign in a scoreless draw against a Dundee United side who would soon be challenging for the league title. Pat would never recover from a seemingly routine cartilage operation and was eventually forced to retire from the game, which was such a loss to Celtic and Scottish football. Alfie was also out with knee trouble, which required surgery, and he was missing from action until the November of that year.

Both of these losses added to the impact of Kenny's departure, but there was even worse news in store for Jock Stein, as Danny McGrain succumbed to a reoccurring ankle injury in a league game against Hibs on 1st October 1977.

Our 3-1 victory against Eddie Turnbull's side was just our second win in seven league outings, and we were also to lose the next two against Partick Thistle and Saint Mirren. There was no doubt that these were desperate times and the side who had performed so well during the memorable double-winning season were beginning to look like a shadow of our former selves.

I nearly joined the list of experienced absentees, as my own chronic pelvic problem had resurfaced during pre-season, and I was forced to miss the entire far-eastern and Australian tour, although I did travel with the squad. We had gone on to win a lucrative tournament, which featured Red Star Belgrade, Arsenal, a Singapore XI, and the Australian national side. I have a much-cherished photograph of me standing by the pool-side with Tommy Burns in Australia. Tommy would have only been 20 years-of-age during that tour but he was really coming into his own as a terrifically gifted left-sided midfielder. I thought the world of him as a player and as a human being (although he was always up to high jinx). That photograph always brings a smile to my face - and not just because Tam is wearing denim cut-off shorts and a Snoopy sweater! We are standing with our arms around one-another looking suitably satisfied that we were together on the other side of the world representing the club we both loved.

My own smile was hiding the disappointment that my complex injury problem was rearing its ugly head again, and players of my era were unfortunate in that our club's did not have the expertise to treat such complaints. Celtic used an independent specialist called Doctor Abrami, who had administered countless cortisone injections into my groin to allow me to play since I had returned to first-team duty. If it hadn't been for these pain-killing injections, I would have required absolute rest. That was clearly not an option for me or the club after I had already missed almost two years of competitive football due to this intermittent injury.

"Do you have any qualifications outside of football?" enquired Doctor Abrami one afternoon as he prepared his syringe and flicked it for good measure.

"Well, I completed part of my apprenticeship as a printing compositor Doctor..." I tailed off. "Why are you asking me this?" I pressed, as the morbid point of his question began to sink in.

"Andy, I can't continue to give you these injections, as they will inevitably lead to complications for you. You can't go on like this."

It had never crossed my mind that this injury, which had plagued me throughout my senior career, could force me to retire prematurely. My heart sank. I was just 26-years-old. Clearly, I had to find some alternative.

My saviour was a Dutch acupuncturist from Troon called Jan De Vries.

Mr De Vries had been treating Danny McGrain and, as a last throw of the dice, Jock Stein suggested that I should go and see this world-renowned clinical naturopath. By that stage, I was prepared to try almost anything to save my career.

The late, great Jimmy Steele picked Danny and I up in Glasgow in his big Mercedes and drove us down to Troon to see Mr De Vries. Celtic's two full-backs sat in the back-seat of Steelie's motor as he kept us both amused throughout the journey. The masseur would tell us jokes non-stop and, when Danny and I fell into fits of laughter, Steelie would turn around to join in the fun. We would be screaming at him to turn around and face the oncoming traffic as our laughter turned to panic; Steelie's car journeys were as memorable as the man himself.

I was introduced to Mr De Vries, who was a soft-spoken Dutchman, and I explained to him as much as I could about the pelvic problems I had been suffering. I realised that I hadn't brought along any x-rays and apologised to him for this omission, to which he replied, "X-rays are of no interest to me Andy." I got the feeling that this genius knew what was wrong with my body just by looking at me. Maybe he had x-ray vision!

Mr De Vries asked me to take off my shoes, as he pulled together two sets of stand-on scales. He then asked me to stand with one foot on each scale, and requested that Danny and Jimmy come over to read the scales. To all of our amazement I was 14 pounds heavier on one of the scales.

Mr De Vries explained that, over the years, my body had been over-compensating for my pelvic problems and my spine and pelvis had readjusted through time. He went on to explain that he could get them back to normal using acupuncture.

He got me to lie on his treatment table and asked me to pull my knees up one-at-a-time. I pulled them up as far as I could but there was a lot of resistance and not much flexibility. I could barely pull them up beyond my waist. Then the Dutch master proceeded to give me a deep stretch, and the cracking sounds of my back and pelvis echoed around the room to Danny's grimaces and Steelie's amusement.

A 30-minute acupuncture session followed, and I was asked to pull my knees up again one-at-a-time. The freedom and flexibility I had on both sides was remarkable. I thought Mr De Vries had fixed me in little under an hour.

This incredibly insightful and intelligent man then described how I would need realigned during the winter, when the heavy Scottish pitches would give my body a pounding. To my relief, he told me that my condition was manageable if I visited him every six weeks for acupuncture. I kept my appointments with him religiously and we developed a solid friendship. He even went as far as introducing me to his family. Mr De Vries treated me until I left Scotland in 1980, and then he recommended me a list of reputable acupuncturists in North America, who would be able to carry on his fantastic work.

There is absolutely no doubt that Jan De Vries saved my football career.

Danny McGrain's recovery was not as forthcoming, but I was to benefit from my colleague's misfortune. Jock Stein had made me temporary captain in Danny's absence and, after a couple of months, he called me into his office. Jock explained to me that there were serious doubts about Danny's future and that he may never play again. I was astonished at that news because Danny seemed like one of those invincible characters who could bounce back from almost anything. He had already recovered from a fractured skull and I thought if anyone could overcome this ankle injury then Danny could.

"I'm going to announce to the press that you're officially the club captain Andy," explained the gaffer. "I know things aren't great around here at the moment, and I need an experienced head in the changing-room to keep the players focussed. You know what this football club demands and it's important that the new boys know what's expected of them."

I felt privileged to be handed the honour of captaining this magnificent football club. This was the team that I had always supported and the sense of pride I felt in being asked to wear the captain's armband is amongst the most satisfying moments of my life. That pride wasn't simply reserved for myself but for my entire family, who had supported me throughout my career. As far as I was concerned, I had achieved everything I possibly could for Celtic. I had already won the League and scored in a Scottish Cup final against Rangers, and now I was being asked to captain Jock Stein's team.

I was part of a sequence that read: McNeill, Dalglish, McGrain and Lynch (albeit, I was never in the same class as those other players). The magnitude of that responsibility was not lost on me, and I realised that I would be carrying on a blood-line of bona fide club legends to have worn the captain's armband. I am eternally proud and humbled to be quoted among their ranks. Having overcome my own personal injury woes, my career had gone full circle, and I felt that this was the most satisfying reward anyone could ever have bestowed upon me.

But, with my new responsibility, I was truly entering the lion's den. Our side had been decimated since the Summer and Jock Stein, normally the shrewdest of operators in the transfer market, had failed to adequately replace those on the injured list. Dalglish couldn't be replaced, not even by a manager of Jock's stature.

A procession of players were brought in but they had failed to reach the heights of the almost flawless list of previous Stein signings: My ex-team-mate, Roy Kay, was a full-back signed on a free transfer from Hearts; Centre-half Ian McWilliam arrived from my other former club, Queen's Park; Forward Tom McAdam was a £60,000 capture from Dundee United; John Dowie was a midfielder, who came in from Fulham for £25,000; Right-back, Joe Filippi of Ayr United was swapped for Brian McLaughlin plus £15,000; and a further £20,000 was shelled out to bring centre-half Frank Munro in from Wolves.

The Celtic fans must have wondered whether Jock had lost his Midas touch. I'm not about to slate my fellow professionals but only one of those half-dozen players (the solid and adaptable Tom McAdam) enjoyed a Celtic career that continued beyond the end of 1979. Most of the others were given free transfers before then.

Perhaps these guys had performed well at their previous clubs (Roy Kay had certainly been a promising youth at Tynecastle), but Celtic were never going to win another league (never mind a European Cup) by signing that calibre of player.

By the time we approached our final league outing of 1977, we had already succumbed to the Austrians of SWW Innsbruck in the second round of the European Cup. The Luxemburg amateurs Jeunesse Esch had been dispatched with ease 11-1 on aggregate but Innsbruck (the first Austrian side Celtic had ever played) were a different class of side altogether.

We won the first leg 2-1 at home, with Tommy Burns scoring the winner on 78 minutes after my shot had been blocked, but the second leg was an unmitigated disaster. I approached the game with confidence that we could salvage a draw over there but we were 3-0 down after half-an-hour in neutral Salzburg. The frustrations of a disappointing season got the better of me, and I was sent off for punching Austrian internationalist Gunther Rinker with ten minutes left to play to round off a truly desperate evening.

THE EMPORER'S LAST STAND

Innsbruck were knocked out in the next round by Borussia Monchengladbach, who in turn were beaten by eventual winners Liverpool in the semi-final. As we accepted the fact that we were undoubtedly European also-rans, our departed Kenny Dalglish went on to score the winning goal in the European Cup final, as Bob Paisley's side overcame Brugge 1-0 at Wembley Stadium.

Ayr United beat us 2-1 at Somerset Park on Hogmanay and Brian McLaughlin scored the winning goal to rub salt in our wounds. My former team-mate would go on to become a cult legend and fans' favourite for the Honest Men and, had it not been for that career-threatening injury he sustained early in his career, there was no doubt that he could have crafted out a similar role for himself at Celtic Park.

That result at Ayr was the first of five league defeats in-a-row, as we slipped to a lowly eighth of a ten-team table going into March 1978. That level of performance was quite simply unthinkable and unacceptable to a club like Celtic, but it was difficult to stop the rot once we had succumbed to such depths.

During that five-match sequence I was struck down by appendicitis and was forced to miss seven league and cup games. This was nothing like as serious as my fellow full-back's untimely illness however, as Danny McGrain was also diagnosed with diabetes. Jock Stein must have thought he was cursed as he lost four captains in one season!

In my absence, Jock played Frank Munro, John Dowie and Tommy Burns at left-back as he attempted valiantly to salvage at least a cup from an otherwise disastrous season.

We drew 1-1 with First Division Kilmarnock in the fourth round of the Scottish Cup and Killie's right-winger, Davie Provan, was the best player on the park. I had discussed this matter with the gaffer before the game because I had been highly impressed with the young wing-man when I faced him the previous season. First Division player or not, I realised that Davie Provan was capable of causing any of our inexperienced left-backs serious problems.

I had one eye on the League Cup final against Jock Wallace's Rangers on 18th

March 1978 as being the match in which I could make my comeback, and I was determined to lead my side to an honour at the national stadium. I also wanted to complete my domestic trophy-haul having lost two League Cup finals in-a-row. The day after I was discharged from hospital, I went into Celtic Park to get the once over from Dr Fitzsimons. As the Doc was checking me out, Jock Stein entered the treatment room and asked for a prognosis. Dr Fitzsimons suggested that I'd be out for another two weeks, which meant that I'd miss the final, so I piped up that the hospital told me I could start training in a week. Jock knew exactly what I was up to but I was desperate to play at Hampden and do something to turn around what had been a hugely disappointing year.

Frustratingly, I had to sit out the Scottish Cup replay against Killie at Rugby Park, and I again feared for whomever was handed the number three shorts. Jock Stein gave them to John Dowie, who had hitherto been a midfielder for English Second Division side Fulham.

Part of my role as captain of the club was to support the less experienced players, and this is something I'd have done in any case because I saw the value in it when I was a youngster.

I pulled John aside in the Rugby Park dressing-room, and explained that Kilmarnock's right-winger was one to be watched. I added that I had come up against him the previous season and did everything in my power to subdue him. John was told to mark him tightly and shut him down as soon as the ball went anywhere near him because he could hurt us.

No matter how much mentoring or one-to-one coaching I could provide, the fact was that the unfortunate John Dowie was out of position and out of his depth. The inevitable consequences ensued - Davie Provan ran riot and Kilmarnock won 1-0.

Davie joined us the following season and I'm sure those two Scottish Cup performances went a long way to sealing that deal. I recall discussing these matches with him when he joined me at Celtic Park. He explained that he was sitting in the Kilmarnock dressing-room before the replay, and when the Celtic line-up was read out without Andy Lynch he clapped his hands together, and knew from that moment that he would wreak havoc down the right wing. I took that as a compliment but it was painful to watch as I sat in the Rugby Park stand knowing that I could do nothing to stop him.

Having been unceremoniously dumped out as holders of the Scottish Cup to First Division opposition, I knew that the only chance we had left for silverware was in the League Cup final against Rangers 12 days later.

Our passage had been secured by beating two Premier League sides (Motherwell 4-2 on aggregate in the second round, and Saint Mirren 5-1 on aggregate in the quarter-final) and two First Division sides (Stirling Albion 3-2 on aggregate in the third round and the recently relegated Hearts 2-0 in the semi-final). After the Killie game I assured big Jock that I'd be back for the final, but I'm sure he would alrcady have had his team pencilled in.

No matter how poorly the two sides were playing, there were no guarantees in any Old Firm encounter. The players all knew that, the fans knew it, and the bookies certainly did as we went into the League Cup final at 5-2 to win, which were surprising short odds given our woeful form.

As well as our three long-term absentees, Joe Craig, Johnny Doyle and I were injury doubts for the final. Meanwhile, our new signings, Tom McAdam and Joe Filippi, were cup-tied. Johnny Doyle and I passed late fitness tests down at Seamill on the day before the game but Johnny could only make the bench. Thankfully I was handed a starting place, although I definitely wasn't 100% fit. These are the risks that professional footballers take. There was no way that I was going to let a cup final against Rangers pass me by and I was desperate to appear and help save our season.

I had stood in that Hampden tunnel as a ball-boy and ran out behind my team-mates for cup finals before, but this was my first (and only) occasion where I was privileged enough to do it as captain of Celtic Football Club. As I led my troops out alongside my Rangers counterpart John Greig, the magnitude of my responsibility did not phase me. Like the Scottish Cup final the previous year, where I was ready to take the decisive penalty kick, I felt confident within myself that I could lead Jock Stein's team into battle.

Again, Neilly Mochan decked us out in one-off pre-match cup final Umbro tops, and the 'League Champions' stunt of ten months previously seemed like a distant memory now, such had been the depth of our demise. The 1978 pre cup final tops were not of the typical tracksuit variety, but were unusual bottle-green cardigan-cum suit jackets that had two button-down pockets on the breasts. I led our side out hoping that I could finally put a League Cup winners' medal in one of those pockets once the battle was over.

Incredibly, this was Celtic's 14th successive League Cup final appearance and my third in-a-row. More remarkable still was the fact that we had won less than half of them.

We went into the game wearing our traditional green-and-white hoops but with the addition of the club crest on the left breast. This was the first time Celtic had ever appeared in a cup final wearing the crest on the club's famous jersey. The fans were unhappy about this 'commercialisation' of their sacred tops and many thought that the badge desecrated their hallowed hoops. Fast forward almost 40 years and we now have two sponsors, players' names, and even numbers on the hoops! Who'd have thought?

The Celtic side that lined up for the final included just five of the previous season's Scottish Cup-winning side:

CELTIC: *Latchford; Sneddon, Lynch (Wilson), Munro, MacDonald; Glavin (Doyle), Dowie, Aitken; G. McCluskey, Edvaldsson, Burns.*

RANGERS: *Kennedy; Jardine, Jackson, Forsyth, Greig; Hamilton (Miller), MacDonald, Smith; McLean, Johnstone, Cooper (Parlane).*

We played well in the first half but an error from Ronnie Glavin allowed Rangers a chance, and the late Davie Cooper made no mistake with a fierce strike in 38 minutes to put Jock Wallace's side 1-0 up at the break. Johannes Edvaldsson (who was playing upfront that afternoon) equalised late on to send the match into extra time but my lack of match fitness meant that I couldn't last the duration and was replaced by Paul Wilson, with Tommy Burns covering for me at left-back. The manner in which Rangers scored their winning goal left a decidedly bitter taste in our mouths, as we felt that Peter Latchford had been impeded before Gordon Smith slotted home on 118 minutes, but the record books state that Rangers won the cup. No-one remembers such dramas once the dust settles.

My 1977 cup final jersey is framed and given pride of place at chez Lynch. It is a symbol of success and is emblematic of a lifetime's effort. In comparison, the 1978 crest-endowed (or should that be crestfallen) jersey is a footnote in the history of Celtic Football Club and offers me no sense of satisfaction whatsoever. It is a second prize, just like the medal which accompanied the occasion. I promised myself that my next medal would be another winner's one as I looked towards putting the season from hell behind me.

I still look back to that cup final match and consider how closely we ran a Rangers side who went on to win the domestic treble that season, their second in three years no less. This was an excellent Rangers team, make no mistake, but we could match them on a one-off basis and we proved it over 90 minutes in the cup final. Seven days later, we went one better in our league encounter at Celtic Park.

In what would be Jock Stein's last-ever Old Firm match, we salvaged some pride by beating the best team in Scotland 2-0 through first-half goals from Ronnie Glavin and Roddie MacDonald. Alas, it was too little too late and our season will forever be regarded as an unmitigated disaster. Perversely, as bad as the season was for the club as a whole, I became club captain and Jan De Vries saved my career so on a personal level I had two major life-changing positives to console myself with.

Our final match of the season was at Love Street against a well-organised Saint Mirren, who could boast Tony Fitzpatrick, Billy Stark and Frank McGarvey in their ranks. The Saints were deserving of their 3-1 victory in what would be the final match in charge of their respective clubs for the two managers that day - Alex Ferguson and Jock Stein.

If ever there was a changing of the guards; a passing of the baton from Europe's finest manager to his young pretender, then this was it. By the beginning of the following season, Jock Stein had lost his job and was replaced by Aberdeen's Billy McNeill. Alex Ferguson took big Billy's place up at Pittodrie and started a revolution.

This must have been so frustrating for Jock Stein. He had previously been able to maximise players' performance and supplement his team in the transfer market with almost perfect accuracy. He had won the European Cup once and I felt that the double-winning side of the previous year could have put together a decent run in the competition. The team were solid and growing in confidence, especially at the back, but the loss of

Dalglish, McGrain, Stanton and Conn was too much of a fight even for our celebrated doyen of European football.

That fight would not only be on the park and on the training pitch but also in the boardroom. He had sold Kenny Dalglish and brought in six new players for around a quarter of the transfer fee received from Anfield. When reinforcements were required, they simply never arrived.

It was no secret that Desmond White was tight-fisted and I am sure that he would have made things far more difficult for Jock than they should have been. The enduring vision that I have of the club's Chairman was of him walking out the Celtic Park tunnel before matches. We would all be warming up on the pitch and he would come walking out to survey the terraces. You could almost hear him adding up the attendance as he rubbed his hands together.

There is no doubt in my mind that the board failed to back Jock sufficiently in the transfer market that season and then, when we failed to get the results, he was hung out to dry. The Jock Stein of ten years previously may have been able to turn things around but the sands of time were running low on his Celtic career and his empire was crumbling. It was a sad ending to a gloriously success-laden journey.

There was only one man who could rebuild the reputation of a club who once dined at Europe's top table, but who now struggled to secure a fifth-placed finish in the Scottish Premier League.

I had called him my hero, my team-mate, and my captain. Now it was time to call Billy McNeill "Boss."

CHAPTER TWELVE
WHEN TEN MEN WON THE LEAGUE

The winds of change swept through the East End of Glasgow like a whirlwind during the Summer of 1978. For the first time in 13 years, that galactic figure of Jock Stein would not be imposing his methods and theories upon a chosen eleven from his Celtic Park throne. His pedestal was not a comfortable, heated seat within the hub of the stadium's modern main stand, but took the form of an oft-times cold wooden bench amid the shadows of Celtic's concrete home dug-out.

It was from this pitch-side perch that he was able to instruct a golden generation of players, see them sweat, and sense their combative spirit, or indeed their fear. Very little had escaped Jock during his historical tenure, and he could switch his side's entire game with a volley of invective or an arm around their shoulders. But his final twelve months had seen his star fading, and what at one time had been unthinkable became almost inevitable - Jock was gone.

Although we had endured what could only be described as a nightmare season the previous year, it still came as a shock when Jock Stein was relieved of his duties. At one time I thought he would go on forever. There was no doubt that the gaffer had been hampered by a number of poor signings - players who should never have been in a Celtic jersey - but I always wondered why there wasn't more money made available to him by the board.

It wouldn't have helped his cause that Sean Fallon wasn't there to assist him when things began to go awry. The boss had just recovered from a horrendous, life-threatening situation, and I am certain that the support of his long-term comrade would have been welcome to him upon his return. Jock and Sean had proved that they were the greatest managerial partnership we had ever had, so why break it up?

The players were never particularly well-informed on the goings-on at the end of 1977/78. We knew that the atmosphere around the club wasn't right, but we only heard of the changes through the press. There was no announcement to us as a group of players.

Jock Stein's Lisbon-era boot-room had now been almost completely depleted following the hastily-arranged departure of Sean Fallon. Bob Rooney was also soon to retire, but we still had a bloodline to that glorious unit with the presence of Neilly 'Smiler' Mochan and his trusted side-kick Jimmy Steele.

Jock Stein and Billy McNeill had worked together as Manager and Captain of the club for a decade. They had also been together while Billy was a youngster and Jock coached the reserves. I am sure that the new man in charge had learned enough from his mentor over the years, but he would have wanted to be a success on his own terms and in his own right.

Farewell Jock; Hail Cesar!

When we returned for pre-season training, Billy McNeill called me into his office, and we had a frank discussion about the situation that Celtic were in. He realised that I knew the club inside out, and wanted me to lead by example in order to quickly galvanise the changing room.

Billy explained that it took a lot of persuasion for him to leave Pittodrie. He was enjoying life up in Aberdeen and his family were settled there. He also had a very good pool of players, whom he had led to the runners-up position in the league the previous season. Although Billy had welcomed the opportunity to take a step out of the goldfish bowl of the Old Firm upon his retirement as a player, I could see that he was just bursting with excitement and enthusiasm to get started in his new role. The lure of his first love had been too much and he was determined to get Celtic back on top.

I told him I was delighted to have him back and that the lads all felt the same way. Billy and I had always got on well as team-mates and, although there was around a ten-year age gap, we did have a solid friendship. On one or two occasions on our days off as players, I had a few rounds of golf with him and Tommy Callaghan and we'd go for a couple of pints afterwards. But I knew our relationship would inevitably be different now because he was my boss, and I was prepared for that.

Danny McGrain was still out injured and we didn't discuss the captaincy directly, but it was clear that this was a Manager to Captain conversation. Big Billy demanded that we got off to a good start following such a poor campaign and I assured him that all the boys were right behind him.

A few times over the years it has been levied to me that I was given the Celtic captaincy by default due to the departure of Kenny Dalglish and the injury to Danny. But the way I view it is that virtually every captain gets the armband by default. Kenny was given the title when big Billy retired, and then Danny was the ideal recipient when Kenny left. I only got it because Danny was injured but I fulfilled the role with pride, and it certainly doesn't make it any less of an achievement to me. All I wanted to do now was lead our side to a trophy.

We didn't plunge straight into the transfer market, even though I felt that the team of 1977/78 were six players short of a title-winning side. Billy did make some shrewd changes behind the scenes though.

First up was John Clark, who became Assistant Manager. I had great admiration for John, because he had been something of a confidante during my time in the reserves and I never forgot that. It was also 'Luggy' who convinced me to take a huge backwards step into the left-back position, and so I can honestly say I am due him my eternal gratitude. He was the quiet man, who was always at Billy's side. He had fulfilled that role on the pitch and they were a great team off it too. John was a calming influence and they complimented one another perfectly. He had a very understanding personality, and that is particularly rare in top-flight football.

Jimmy Lumsden was brought in to assist with coaching the reserves. He had been a useful midfielder for Clydebank, but his arrival had not been with the intention of utilising him as a player. We were so threadbare at one point however, that even Jimmy appeared in the first team!

As I entered my sixth full season at Celtic Park, my contract was for a basic weekly wage of £120, plus permitted bonuses. Despite being at the club since 1973, I had only three full seasons behind me where I was playing regularly. Under a new manager, my ambitions for the forthcoming term were to stay in the team as captain and to win a trophy. Winning the league title was going to be a huge task, especially with the resurgent Aberdeen and Dundee United joining the treble-winning Rangers as our main threats.

In terms of preparation for the new season and for matches, there were no great changes made by Billy. There were some similarities between him and Jock in terms of his managerial approach but the new man in charge was more demonstrative and outwardly enthusiastic. I think it was these attributes that helped the players to get over the disappointment of losing Jock Stein, and it propelled us to a positive start to the new campaign.

We won our opening nine league and cup games before our first Old Firm encounter - the litmus test for all new managers at Celtic or Rangers.

"Our start to the season will have surprised quite a few people," I explained to the Daily Express on the eve of our first league meeting with our greatest rivals. "It's only a start, of course, there's a long way to go. But we'll certainly be going into Saturday's game against Rangers with more confidence than we did for any Old Firm match last season.

"One reason for the good start is that the lads were very anxious to show everybody that they aren't as bad as some of last season's results suggested. Everybody's working hard in training and, just as importantly, working for each other out on the park. The spirit is terrific."

9th September 1978

Scottish Premier League

Celtic   3 *(McAdam 2 & 76, McCluskey 14)*

Rangers   1 *(Parlane 49)*

CELTIC: *Latchford; Filippi, Edvaldsson, Aitken, Lynch; Glavin, Conroy, Burns (Casey), Doyle, McAdam, McCluskey (Craig).*

RANGERS: *McCloy; Jardine, Jackson, T. Forsyth, A. Forsyth; Russell, A. MacDonald (Miller), Johnstone; McLean (Cooper), Parlane, Smith.*

I played in over 20 Old Firm games during my career, and it took me a few matches before I managed to get my strategy right. I quickly established that the key was to win my own personal battle. Everyone on the pitch had one, and there was no room for passengers. I had my own philosophy and I couldn't allow my mindset to change. I played in successful Celtic sides (1976/77 and 1978/79) and unsuccessful ones (1975/76 and 1977/78) but I could not allow myself to worry too much about weak links in our side. I had to concentrate on doing my own job and winning my own battle.

Overcoming Rangers in our first derby of the season carried on the momentum we had enjoyed since the arrival of Billy McNeill. Our new gaffer made his first move into the transfer market after the Rangers game when he brought Bobby Lennox back to the club from Houston Hurricane of the NASL.

This signing raised a few eyebrows but Bobby was a very inspirational figure to have around the place and he could still trouble opponents. His experience was immense and it was great to have another Lisbon Lion back at Celtic Park.

Our first defeat of the season followed at home to Hibs, when a first-half goal from ex-Celt Willie Temperley was enough to give Eddie Turnbull's men the points. Directly after this defeat, Celtic moved into the transfer market again, this time in dramatic fashion.

Billy McNeill had seen enough to know that a few changes were required. He had been patient and analysed his squad for a few months before breaking the Scottish record transfer fee when he purchased Davie Provan from Kilmarnock for £120,000. I had been a long-time admirer of Davie's and was delighted that he'd be on my side from now on.

The reshaping continued with Paul Wilson leaving for Motherwell and Joe Craig joining Blackburn Rovers. Football can seem shallow at times but players come and go. I had known Paul and Joe for a few years but you cannot ponder anyone's departure because there is always another important match just around the corner.

We scraped a couple of league victories at the end of September and I scored penalties in each match (3-2 away to Partick Thistle and 2-1 at home to Saint Mirren), but we then went on a dismal run of form between 4 October 1978 right up to the end of the year. During this sequence we won just one league game in 11, and slipped down to a depressing sixth place in the table.

In the run-up to the second Old Firm match of the season, another important signing was secured when £100,000 was paid to Dumbarton for midfielder Murdo MacLeod. It seemed unlikely at the time that the promising young player could do anything to save our season, as our league challenge had derailed in quite drastic fashion.

Before we were due to face Rangers again, we had a League Cup quarter final first leg to play against unfancied Division One side Montrose. The Gable Endies went a goal up on 23 minutes through ex-Aberdeen striker Ian Hair and it looked as though there was a shock on the cards. The importance of the 10 penalties I scored throughout this season cannot be under-estimated, and I managed to score another one to save our blushes with a 1-1 draw at Links Park.

"Andy, you must have some bottle," offered Davie Provan in the changing room after the game. "If we had lost that match, people would have remembered it along with shock results like Berwick Rangers beating Rangers in 1967. Did you consider the importance of that when you took the penalty?"

"I tried not to Davie!," came my reply.

But the new arrival was absolutely right. It wasn't every player who wanted to take the added responsibility of a penalty over and above the normal pressures of the game. I remember that no-one ever offered to take them when we were a goal down or level with the opposition, but sometimes they'd be keen to ask when we were coasting. "I can't remember seeing you volunteering when we were a goal down against Montrose," became my party line.

11th November 1978

Scottish Premier League

Rangers 1 *(A. Forsyth 55)*

Celtic   1 *(Lynch 52)*

RANGERS: *McCloy; Miller, Jardine, T. Forsyth, A. Forsyth; McLean, Russell, A. MacDonald; Watson, Johnstone, Smith. Subs: Parlane & Cooper.*

CELTIC: *Baines; Filippi, MacDonald, Edvaldsson, Lynch; Aitken, MacLeod, Burns; Provan, McAdam, Doyle. Subs: Lennox & Casey.*

The Old Firm match wasn't every player's cup of tea. I witnessed quite a few skilful players, who didn't fancy the more physical aspect of the clash, being swallowed up by the occasion. I was a Glasgow boy born in the shadows of Ibrox, and so I knew all about the history of the encounter. I was one of the wee guys outside the stadium looking after the fans' motors and then running up the steps of Ibrox to watch the last 20 minutes of the action. I was doing all of that as a kid having been brought up in a Celtic family. I loved playing in Old Firm games, and I thrived on their intensity.

The best advice I could give players who were playing in their first Old Firm matches (and Baines, MacLeod and Provan were all debutants in this particular fixture) was, "Who dares wins." It was that simple. If a player went into this match with any level of apprehension then they would lose their own personal battle, which made them a liability.

We never went into an Old Firm game looking for a draw, but on this occasion that is exactly what we got. Rangers were playing their home games at Hampden Park due to reconstruction work at Ibrox, and I remember pushing on because we were pinning them right back. I exchanged a perfect one-two with Murdo MacLeod and struck it beyond McCloy to put us a goal ahead. It was my second and final Old Firm strike and they both came from the left-back position.

Rangers scored an equaliser almost immediately from the penalty spot and there was very little between the sides. John Greig's men were strong (having won two trebles in the previous three seasons with Jock Wallace at the helm) and, despite our marked improvement under Billy McNeill, it was clear to us that they were going to be difficult to beat over the duration of a long and unremitting Scottish football season.

The serious challenge would not only come from Ibrox, as the emergence of Alex Ferguson's Aberdeen and Jim McLean's Dundee United was tangible and could not be ignored. Our record shows that, in our eight league meetings against Scotland's so-called 'New Firm', we managed just two wins.

Four days after the Old Firm draw, we managed to overcome Kenny Cameron's plucky Montrose in the second leg of the League Cup quarter-final 3-1, and I scored yet another goal from the spot.

Danny McGrain made a rare appearance at right-back, but he was clearly not ready for a fully-fledged recall just yet. I had a great understanding with my fellow full-back and it was just great to see him back on the field of play. He had been out for a season-and-a-half and it took a lot longer before he could play regularly again. Regardless of his performance, it was great to have him back, however fleetingly.

Our victory against lower-league opposition set up an Old Firm semi-final, but we failed to reach the final for the first time in a remarkable 15 years.

13th December 1978

League Cup semi-final

Rangers 3 *(Jardine 26 pen, Jackson 80, Casey og 113)*

Celtic 2 *(Doyle 10, McAdam 65)*

RANGERS: *McCloy; Miller, Dawson; Jardine, Jackson, MacDonald; McLean, Russell, Johnstone, Watson, Cooper (Smith). Sub: Parlane.*

CELTIC: *Baines; Filippi, Lynch; Aitken, MacDonald, Edvaldsson; Provan, Conroy (Casey), McAdam, Burns, Doyle. Sub: Conn.*

No matter how you were feeling, or how the team were performing, you had to lift yourself for the Rangers game. The idea of going out there and taking a trouncing was absolutely unthinkable. Any defeat would take weeks to get over, and the Old Firm match could finish careers. If a player had a shocking performance against Rangers then there was the possibility that he would never recover. That was the magnitude of this incredible encounter.

Young Jim Casey fell victim to these almost impossible demands and he was dreadfully unlucky when a Baines save ricocheted off his leg and into the net to give Rangers the win in extra time. The poor guy never recovered from that. He was simply standing in the wrong place at the wrong time. As I said before, the Old Firm game can destroy players.

Following the disappointment of our League Cup exit, we drew 1-1 with Dundee United at home, where I netted yet another penalty to open the scoring before David Narey drew United level on 74 minutes.

The 1-0 defeat at Cappielow the following week in our final league encounter of 1978 did not bode well as we edged closer to the New Year languishing four points behind leaders Dundee United. The 89th minute winner had come from the penalty spot courtesy of Morton's cult hero, Andy Ritchie.

I had played in Andy's reserve team debut at Celtic when he was just 16 and I could see even then that he had bags of potential. There was no doubt that Jock Stein had thought a lot of him but he was eventually allowed to leave in a swap deal involving Roy Baines. The individuality of the mercurial Ritchie was something the Celtic fans would have undoubtedly warmed to, but his lack of application didn't suit our ex-gaffer and, like so many other talented players before and since, Andy had to carve out a career for himself elsewhere.

The desolation of Scottish football due to a freak period of cold and frost, meant that Celtic had a league hiatus which lasted from 23rd December 1978 until 3rd March 1979.

Other than a couple of Scottish Cup games, again at Montrose (where we won 4-2) and at home to Berwick Rangers (3-0), we went without competitive football for over two months.

Keen to re-energise the squad after our end-of-year blip, Billy McNeill had the inspired notion to take us for a break to Estoril in Portugal, where Celtic's European Cup winners had been camped during their unforgettable trip of 1967. The trip worked a treat, and it was great to get the boys together for a few days in the sun. Billy's plan to revitalise was a success because, when we returned to Scotland, our season began to turn around.

We played Aberdeen three times in 11 days and, although they beat us 2-1 in the Scottish Cup quarter-final replay, we were able to record an important 1-0 victory against them in the league. The winning goal was scored by Alfie Conn, who would soon be on his way out of Celtic Park after a clash with the gaffer.

I came up against Gordon Strachan in two of the matches against Alex Ferguson's side and I rated him highly. He was a fiery wee guy, but I guess he had to be considering his size. I generally managed to keep him at bay, but I wasn't surprised that he went on to forge out a lengthy and successful career north and south of the border. Wee Gordon was one of those players who seemed to get better with age.

A massive boost for us was the return of Danny McGrain for the triple-header against the Dons, and I had no hesitation in handing him back the captaincy. It had been an honour and a privilege to hold court at the captain's table, and no-one can ever take that distinction away from me. If I lost the captaincy because Danny's career had been saved then how could I complain?

It was just great to have Danny back. You could detect a slight limp in his run, and wingers were enjoying a more fruitful time against him than they normally ever would. But Billy realised the importance of having such a stalwart back in the side as we threw everything we had at one final challenge for the title.

There was no doubt that Peter Latchford was our first choice number one, but the departure of his understudy, Roy Baines, back to Morton at the beginning of March meant that a new name appeared on the team-sheet against Motherwell - ironically on St Patrick's Day 1979 - Pat Bonner.

Pat had been Jock Stein's final signing before he left the Celtic Park hot seat and what an inspired acquisition he turned out to be. I think big Packie followed in the footsteps of Tommy Burns and Roy Aitken as a new generation of Celts began to shine. But the big Irishman had a ropey start.

I know it seems strange to say it now, when his vast achievements in the game are considered, but Pat was a nervous young man in his early days. He was just a teenager, who had flown the comforting nest of his family, and come over to Glasgow from Ireland. I think he was dreadfully homesick and he had a shaky performance, which left the poor guy in tears in the dressing room. He wanted to go home and give up his career at Celtic but the boys rallied around him and thankfully he changed his mind. Pat showed a real strength of character for such a young boy and he got over his early period of doubt to craft out an incredible career at both club and international level. He became a global icon for legions of Irish fans in the years that followed, and rightly so.

We went on an excellent run of eight wins in 11 league games and then came up against league-leaders Dundee United on 28th April 1979.

It is at this point that I wish to discuss the art of penalty kicks - for it is an art. I had been the club's recognised spot-kick taker since my exploits at Hampden brought the Scottish Cup back to Paradise in 1977. Ronnie Glavin had taken one or two during the period since but I was the recognised taker of the penalties.

During the memorable 1978-79 season, I scored 10 from the spot to take my tally for the campaign to 13 league and cup strikes, which was a personal best for Celtic. I was joint-top league goalscorer with Tom McAdam, which I'll take as another feather in my cap.

I did miss one during the season, but I scored with the rebound so I didn't lose too much sleep over it. I was facing Scottish international goalkeeper, Alan Rough, on 7th April 1979 at a heavy and wet Celtic Park. We were already 1-0 to the good through an early goal from Mick Conroy when Davie Provan won us a penalty on the hour mark.

The last time I had taken one against Roughie, I had scored to his right, so I decided to vary it this time around. I went for power down to his left, but the ball lifted slightly higher than I'd anticipated and Scotland's international goalkeeper parried it out. Thankfully for me I had followed in my strike and was able to slot the ball home from six yards.

We didn't have video analysis like they do nowadays and players would watch Scotsport and Sportscene like everybody else to gauge how their opponents were playing. Keepers knew that I was on Celtic's penalties and would be looking out for my approach, so I tried to vary things slightly.

I think that I benefited from taking them whilst playing at left-back. This meant that I had a distance to walk from my defensive position up to the opponent's goal, and it was during this stroll that I would take a few things into consideration:

What is the weather like?
How heavy is the pitch?
Have I taken one against this goalie before?

I gave myself time as I walked and jogged up to the penalty spot for my moment of reckoning. I always went through this mental check-list but there was one golden rule above anything else - Never change you mind.

The Dundee United encounter came during our magnificent run, and we were high on confidence going into the match with Jim McLean's side. Johnny Doyle equalised a Davie Dodds opener and then we won the penalty kick on 68 minutes.

This was an extremely nervy moment for me. I can't remember feeling any nerves in the Scottish Cup final but this was different. We were chasing United at the top of the table and I could get us the all-important win. I went over my mental tick-list:

What was the weather like?

It was extremely windy that day; the wind was howling. So much so that this was my biggest consideration. I had to keep my body over the ball to get it on target.

How heavy was the pitch?

I was more concerned with the penalty spot itself. The paint on the pitch was sticky, and the groundsman had piled it on the penalty spot to make it visible over the mucky surface. I didn't want the ball to stick to the paint and so placed it just off the spot.

Had I taken one against the goalie before?

Hamish McAlpine had been in goals when I scored a penalty against United four months previously. I knew he was left-handed, not that tall, but very flexible.

I started walking back from the spot and was composed, until George Fleming (who had been my team-mate at Hearts) started throwing muck at the ball. He was picking it from the studs of his boots and throwing it to put me off. His United team-mates followed suit and were also throwing muck at the ball in an effort to break my concentration. They were trying to taunt me but it's all part of the game, and I wasn't about to show any weakness by getting the ref to intervene.

"Bottom right Andy... Keep over the ball..."

As I started to run towards the ball, the wind blew it right off the penalty spot. I heard a collective gasp from the Celtic Park crowd, then there was a hush. I had to go after the ball and stop it myself. Like that penalty at Montrose, no-one was about to help me out.

I got the ball and walked back to the spot. The pressure was all on me as I re-placed it just off that sticky white paint.

"If you miss this Andy, the championship could be gone..."

The dirt was flying... the wind was howling... I ran six yards...

I got over the ball and smashed it hard. It was a bit higher than I had intended. Hamish McAlpine got a glove to it, but the power took the ball beyond him and into the net. The Celtic fans erupted into bedlam. They knew, we knew, and the Dundee United players knew, that the Celtic machine was on full throttle and we would not lose that game now. I had won my battle of the wits against Hamish McAlpine, and our tilt at the league championship was back on.

5th May 1979

Scottish Premier League

Rangers 1 *(A. MacDonald 57)*

Celtic 0

RANGERS: *McCloy; Jardine, Johnstone, Jackson, Dawson; A. MacDonald, Russell, Smith; McLean, Parlane, Cooper. Subs: Denny & Urquhart.*

CELTIC: *Latchford; McGrain, Aitken, Edvaldsson, MacLeod, Davidson (McAdam), Conroy, Burns (Lynch); Provan, McCluskey, Doyle.*

We followed up our 2-1 win over Dundee United with a 3-1 victory over Hibs, before going to Hampden Park for the penultimate Old Firm match of the season. By that time I was 28-years-old and I had began to pick up niggling injuries here and there. These types of physical complaints meant that I missed the odd game like our victory over Hibs, and I only made the bench against Rangers.

Although we were beaten 1-0, and were left trailing league-leaders Rangers by a point, we knew that we could overtake them and win the championship if we won our final four league matches.

Due to the fixture pile-up, our final game of the season was once again against John Greig's men, and we managed to beat Partick Thistle (2-1 away), Saint Mirren (2-0 away), and Hearts (1-0 at home) to set up the battle royale at Celtic Park.

Our season culminated magically and we knew that we required a win, with Rangers just needing a draw virtue of them having a game in hand. The two managers, Billy McNeill and John Greig, had been tremendous opponents on the field and now they were going head-to-head for a league championship in what was one of the most famous Old Firm encounters of all time.

The Glasgow derby was the biggest football match in world football. I have no doubt that. There are huge derbies throughout the globe but I think the Old Firm match had an added intensity that could not be matched anywhere else. The fact that the two sets of fans largely originated from two distinctive religions had a huge amount to do with the level of rivalry, because that created divisions that went beyond football. A win against Rangers always meant everything to us, but the magnitude of a victory in this particular match carried even more weight and importance than ever before.

I had never played against a weak Rangers side, but the power of this Ibrox team cannot be understated. In our two trophyless seasons of 1975/76 and 1977/78, Rangers had won two trebles and they were a rock solid unit. They had a consistent structure and a fantastic blend of brains and brawn. Rangers had a settled side and we were still in transition.

Sandy Jardine was an outstanding, international-class full-back. Their motto was, 'Thou shall not pass,' and they were a very physical side as a consequence of that. They had the experience of Derek Johnstone, who was dangerous in the air, but this was allied with the flair of players like Davie Cooper, who could be exceptional, and Bobby Russell, who was a playmaker. They were a strong side, and there was no doubt that it was going to be one monumental task for this relatively new Celtic side to overcome the Rangers juggernaut. But we were at home, and we had the glorious Celtic support behind us. They became our twelfth man (or on this occasion our eleventh). Yes, that's right, because we needed one.

The stage was set for an enthralling climax to the season...

We're right down to the last game of the season. This was a match that wasn't even on the fixture list. A January victim of an unforgiving Scottish Winter of burst pipes and frozen pitches. We haven't trained in recent weeks, it has been relentless with matches being played back-to-back, but now it all comes down to one game of football. This isn't just any game - it's the Old Firm derby.

We could never have envisaged that we'd be here after the tumultuous Summer we suffered back in 1978. We lost a football great, but it seems that some of this alchemist's magic has been sprinkled on his old captain, Billy McNeill, because we've been dragged to the pinnacle of a league championship in the most unlikely of circumstances.

If we win this match then Billy will be a managerial great. We are ably assisted by the Quiet Man, John Clark. He gave me belief in myself during my darkest days, and I want to pay him back. Billy and John knew what it took to beat Rangers as players; they knew what it entailed to defeat anyone in Europe!

The game is being played on a Monday night and we all stayed at home the night before; no trips down to Seamill, just a short drive to play the game that could cast heroes or villains over a 90 minute set.

We're a fairly new group, with a mixture of experience and youth. Our new buys, Murdo and Davie, have done well and bedded themselves into the unit. Bobby and Vic have added plenty of wisdom and a calming influence that only comes through years in the game.

I say a prayer on the day of the match. I pray for the victory that will give us the league...

Billy McNeill reads out the team, "Left-back: Andy Lynch"…

Celtic Park is already rocking. The atmosphere is unlike anything I have ever witnessed before.

"WE LOVE YOU CELTIC, OH YES WE DO. WE LOVE YOU CELTIC, OH YES WE DO. WE LOVE YOU CELTIC, WE DO. AWH, CELTIC WE LOVE YOU."

The wave of the fan's chorus washes over me, and the hairs on my neck and arms are standing to attention at the instruction of this incredible Celtic crowd. I've never felt anything like this. It feels as though I've just had a shot of adrenaline and I'm ready to go to battle.

The velocity of this match is unbelievable, and there isn't a moment to catch my breath. Tommy McLean switches wings with Davie Cooper and I know that I need to stay tight on Davie, because he can hurt us. He gives chase to the corner flag, and I'm pinning him to that corner of the field when he manages to turn and fire a waist-high cross into our box. We know all about Alex MacDonald's late runs but he's made it on his own and ball is in the net. Nine minutes gone and we've suffered a sucker-punch. The wind is momentarily out of our sails.

We manage to get in at half-time to regroup and know that we need two goals in the second-half. But can we do it against this treble-winning Rangers side? The Celtic choir are still with us, and we can hear them from the changing room:

"WALK ON, THROUGH THE WIND. WALK ON, THROUGH THE RAIN. FOR YOUR DREAMS BE TOSSED, AND BLOWN. WALK ON, WALK ON, WITH HOPE IN YOUR HEART. AND YOU'LL NEVER WALK ALONE…"

We're back out of the traps and then disaster strikes. Doyley is caught up in the emotion and he's kicked Alex MacDonald off-the-ball. There is the flash of a red card and wee Johnny cuts a lone figure as he trudges up the tunnel; our hopes of a league win are in tatters.

"WHEN YOU WALK THROUGH A STORM, HOLD YOUR HEAD UP HIGH…"

I can only hear Celtic fans, and they erupt when Roy Aitken pulls us back into it on 66 minutes. Eight minutes later and George McCluskey puts us 2-1 ahead. I'd seen these boys coming through as teenagers and they were now becoming stalwarts of this Celtic side. It was time for them to become legends.

Rangers go right up the pitch and win a corner. I'm on the left post and Danny's covering the right.

"SHUGGIE, MAKE THIS YOUR BALL. GET THIS AWAY!"

Joahannes wins the ball, as I knew he would, and clears it to the edge of the box. But it's dropped to that clever ball player, Bobby Russell, and he's struck it cleanly...

"ZING!"

It's hit the post. That was the sound of it hitting the metal post. I turn to my right and Danny's still standing there, but the ball is behind him, nestled in the net. I look ahead and there is a pyramid of Rangers players celebrating. They only need a draw. I grab the ball and launch it up to the centre circle. Let's go again.

Wave after wave of attack, and still the Celtic fans are creating a cacophony of noise. I glance over at the dug-out and Neilly raises his five fingers. We're running out of time. George McCluskey crosses in, but Colin Jackson has won the ball in the air. The ball flies past Peter McCloy and Celtic Park erupts - Celtic 3 Rangers 2.

John Greig is waving every blue jersey to attack the ten men of Celtic. They throw everyone forward, and Neilly's holding up one finger...

The ball breaks to Murdo, and I give chase. The Rangers team are left standing in our box and there is only one defender facing three oncoming cavalier Celts.

"HOLD IT MURDO!"

I don't know how my legs are still moving but we're charging ahead as we reach the 25-yard mark. Don't give this ball away Murdo...

"HOLD IT MURDO... HOLD IT!"

MacLeod strikes it towards Peter McCloy's goal...

"MURDO! YA STUPID BAS......"

The ball dips, and it's in the top corner as a green-and-white frenzy explodes all over the terracing of Celtic Park. What a phenomenal strike. We've won the league. I can't believe that we've done it. Ten men have won the league!

21st May 1979

Scottish Premier League

Celtic 4 *(Aitken 66, McCluskey 74, Jackson og 85, MacLeod 90)*

Rangers 2 *(Russell 9, MacDonald 76)*

CELTIC: *Latchford; McGrain, Lynch; Aitken, McAdam, Edvaldsson; Provan, Conroy (Lennox), McCluskey, MacLeod, Doyle. Sub: Davidson.*

RANGERS: *McCloy; Jardine, Dawson; Johnstone, Jackson, A. MacDonald, McLean (Miller), Russell, Parlane, Smith, Cooper. Sub: J. MacDonald.*

The history books will tell us that 'The 7-1 Game' was undoubtedly Celtic's greatest victory of the 1950s, and there is no doubt that the 2-1 European Cup final victory over Inter Milan was the pinnacle of the 1960s. So what about the greatest game of my decade? There is no doubt in my mind that the players I lined-up alongside on the evening of 21st May 1979 became crystallised for the rest of time as being part of the club's most memorable result of the 1970s - 'The 4-2 Game,' (when ten men won the league).

Who were those players?

Peter Latchford had really established himself as a dependable 'keeper over the period of five seasons and I feel that he matured and improved every year. As a defender, I trusted having big Peter behind me. There were a few goalies I played with at Celtic Park who I couldn't say that about but Peter was very reliable. Despite his size and presence, he had such a gentle personality off the field and he was well liked by the entire squad.

Danny McGrain made a really inspirational comeback during the season and it is remarkable that he was able to re-establish himself for club and country after suffering such serious injuries and illness.

Even though he had not regained 100% fitness, he was still a massive presence and a huge influence on the team. His legendary status at Celtic Park is assured and it was a pleasure to play alongside such a classy defender.

Roy Aitken was a player who impressed me from the moment he broke through as a teenager. By the time that we won the league in 1979 he was a fully established (and extremely important) cog in the machine. His performance against Rangers was pivotal to us winning the match and his calm and confident approach to the game marked him out as a possible future Celtic captain. I cannot recall Roy ever getting nervous before any game. He knew exactly what was expected from him and the players around him and he went out there and performed consistently from a very young age. I was not surprised that he went on to have a fabulous career in the game because he could be an inspirational figure even back then.

Tom McAdam was a very underrated figure in that league-winning side. Sometimes a player's adaptability can go against them, as it may be difficult for them to establish a specific role within the side. Tom perhaps suffered slightly from that but I was very impressed with him while I was at the club. His strength was in winning the ball and he was particularly strong in the air. Tom never failed to give his all for the team and his dedication was very important to our success.

Johannes Edvaldsson was cut from the same cloth as Tom McAdam. They could both play centre-half or centre-forward and were equally as effective in both positions. I enjoyed having Shuggie's powerful presence on the field. He was another player who seemed to relish the Old Firm encounters, and he always seemed to be good for a goal against our greatest rivals. Shuggie enjoyed throwing his weight around, and he played with no fear.

Davie Provan came in and played an important part in our success that season. I had been impressed with Davie while he was at Kilmarnock and he was a great signing for us. I know how difficult playing on the wing can be and you can sometimes be out of the action for lengthy spells during the game. Davie didn't allow that to happen because he wasn't a lazy player and he'd come back and help out defensively if things weren't going our way in an attacking sense. He wasn't afraid to put himself about and track back, which is a dream for a full-back.

Mick Conroy was just establishing himself under Billy McNeill, having been brought through in Jock's final season in charge. He had been a promising young player and I think that final game really made him at Celtic. He was fairly small but was strong in the tackle and didn't look out of place during a battle against Rangers. Winning the title must have been amazing for a young player like Mick, who was just coming into the picture.

George McCluskey had been slightly inconsistent in his younger years. If things weren't going our way he could disappear from the action and didn't fancy the defensive duties as much as someone like Davie Provan. I felt that George was finding more consistency under Billy McNeill however, and he was showing his undoubted talents on a more regular basis. When George was on song he could be a match winner and he was so vitally important the night we beat Rangers 4-2.

Murdo MacLeod adapted very quickly to life at Celtic Park. Like Davie Provan, he had been a star player in a small team and it can sometimes be difficult for this type of signing to excel at a club like Celtic. If we had a stronger squad then perhaps Murdo wouldn't have been thrust straight into the first-team but he responded very well to the step up. His contribution was very important and he was a strong, workmanlike, box-to-box player with a ferocious strike. The stunning goal he scored in the 4-2 game will live long in the memory (even though he should have passed it to me).

Johnny Doyle enjoyed the celebrations as a relieved man that night! We were all so glad that it turned out well for him in the end. I was always very fond of Johnny, and I loved the fact that you could rely on him to give us absolute dedication on the pitch for 90 minutes (if he stayed on that long!). He was so in love with Celtic that he sometimes got too emotional during games. Even if he wasn't on form though, wee Johnny would give you an explosive performance, and that could kick-start other players into action on the pitch. Looking back now, had we failed to win the title, his sending-off could well have adversely affected Johnny's career at Celtic Park. But on the other hand, maybe Johnny was the hero. Who knows what might have happened if we hadn't have had a man sent off?

Vic Davidson was a low-key but very inspired signing by Billy McNeill. He had gained so much experience since leaving Celtic Park that he was a calming influence in the run-in to the title. Vic wasn't easily fazed and it was good to see that he was able to come back to Celtic and taste some success having been given a free transfer earlier in his career.

Bobby Lennox was another one who added much-needed experience to our squad. Even at such an advanced stage of his career, he could contribute with a goal, and big Billy was very wise to bring him back in when he did.

His presence instilled confidence in some of the younger players and we all knew that we could rely on Bobby on the pitch and behind the scenes, which was vitally important during our time of transition.

Tommy Burns didn't feature in the final game of the season but he deserves a mention for his contribution throughout the campaign. A Celtic man through-and-through, Tommy would have enjoyed the celebrations as much as the punters in the Jungle that night. I had observed Tommy, Roy Aitken and George McCluskey developing as players at Celtic Park, and I was so happy that these guys were now established members of the side. It was (and still is) so important to have a nucleus of home-grown players around a club like Celtic. These men were steeped in the traditions of the club, and act as role models for the next generation of youngsters coming through. I was confident that Tommy and Roy had matured into the type of figures that could lead Celtic on to further success throughout the 1980s.

What a difference a year makes in football. The previous season had ended in the worst way imaginable, and no-one thought it was possible to turn around the Celtic side in the way that Billy McNeill had somehow managed to.

If my two years in the football wilderness taught me anything, it was that you simply must celebrate the good times, for you never know how long they will last. A stark reminder of that lesson was lying in wait just around the corner for me, as I was to enjoy just one more season with the club I dearly loved.

CHAPTER THIRTEEN
ON THE ROAD AGAIN

"Your registration for Celtic Football Club has been cancelled as from this date."

Ernie Walker, Secretary of the Scottish Football Association, Ltd.

17th April 1980.

Thirteen short words that ended my Celtic career, and indeed my time in Scottish football. The dream was over less than a year after our emphatic league win, but how did it all come to this?

I had captained the side, and assisted Billy during a period of immense change, at a time when he required as much experience as possible. By the end of the season I was the top league goal-scorer and we won the championship against all the odds. Yet the stats will show that I made a miserly two first-team appearances the following season.

I realised early on in this game that you have to grow-up quickly in football, and you need to realise when the tide is turning. Otherwise you will be left out in the cold. Sure, I had some niggling muscle strains in my final season at Celtic Park, but I was still fit enough to play regularly - I was only 28 and reaching my peak in the game.

During the pre-season, I had confidence in the gaffer to make the right moves in the transfer market, and it was obvious to me that we still needed a striker. The younger players such as Roy Aitken, Tommy Burns and George McCluskey now had the added experience of having been part of the quite astonishing league win the previous season. They would now be vital features of the 1979/80 campaign, and they would supplement the newer signings, who were now fully bedded into the side.

So where did that leave me? I initially had great optimism for the season ahead, and I really wanted to be involved in the European Cup matches. But it was clear from the offset that I wasn't going to be an automatic choice.

There was no fall-out, and no discussion with Billy about this. I trained throughout the pre-season in as committed a fashion as I always had done, but when the 1979/80 season got underway, someone else was wearing the number three shorts that had been on my peg for four years. It was Danny McGrain who started the new term at left-back, and Alan Sneddon was now deployed at right-back.

The only match I remember being unfit for was the away game against Dundalk in the European Cup second round. I had a recurrence of my pelvic injury and couldn't run freely, and I had to be honest with Billy. By that stage of my career, I had taken enough painkillers to last me a lifetime, and I was not prepared to take any more. The rest of my absences can be attributed to me being unceremoniously replaced.

As soon as I was left out of the side when I was fully fit I decided that I would be leaving the club. The decision was made pretty early in my own mind because the penny never takes long to drop for me. I also had to carefully consider my future for my family's sake. Mag and I had just had our third child (Andrew) on 15th November 1979, and stability was of paramount importance at that stage of my career.

Around about this time, I was chatting to Doug Baillie, an ex-Rangers player who was a journalist for *The Sunday Post*. We got on well and would meet up now and again for a catch-up.

"What's happening with you, Andy?" Doug asked me, over a coffee.

"My time is up Doug," I confessed. "It happens to us all sadly, but I've accepted it and I'm looking for a move."

"Where do you fancy going?" enquired the experienced newsman.

"I'm going to try my luck over in the States," came my bold reply.

North America had made a lasting impression on me when I travelled there as a teenager with Hearts in the late 1960s, and the lifestyle and climate held a real attraction for me. Many British players had gone over to play in the North American Soccer League (NASL) for one last pay day, and they hadn't really planned on making a go of it long-term. My intentions were quite the opposite, as I wanted to eventually embark on my coaching career in the States.

I had completed my UEFA B Licence with the SFA in 1978. This involved a one-week trip to Largs, where my instructor was the future Scotland coach, Andy Roxburgh. There were players and ex-players from all over the country there, and Andy was delighted that he had representation from Celtic because not many of the boys had gone for their badges. Jim Craig was one of the few other Celts from my era to have also completed the course, and I recall having a conversation with the Lisbon Lion about its value. Jim had gained further experience in South Africa and at Sheffield Wednesday after leaving Celtic Park, but he was of the opinion that players of our background would find it difficult to get coaching jobs in Scotland.

Was bias and religious prejudice really so prevalent in the Scottish game back then? I would find out to my cost some years later that it most certainly was. For now though, I was intent on fulfilling my very own American dream.

"I am in touch with George O'Neill," revealed Doug.

"He is currently the Assistant Manager at Philadelphia Fury, and I know that they're looking for experienced players."

"Tell him I'm interested," I replied. "But let him know that I have a few options over here as well."

My absence from the Celtic first team had alerted Burnley City (who wanted me as a player/coach) and Cardiff City, and both sides were keen to sign me. I was definitely going to pursue any interest from the NASL, but didn't wish to seem too keen in front of the middle man.

Neither of the English-based sides had made a formal offer, and I was not on the transfer list, but clubs had ways and means of letting you know that they were after you (as my transfer from Hearts to Celtic perfectly illustrated some years before). Burnley and Cardiff were decent outfits but my heart was set on a move to America. One thing I knew for sure was that I wasn't staying in Scotland.

George O'Neill was a Scotsman, who was around ten years older than me. He had started off his own career on the books of Celtic in the early sixties, but made a name for himself as a left-winger with Partick Thistle before eventually making the move to the States. He had even been capped for the USA whilst playing for the now-defunct Philadelphia Atoms. There was no doubt that he would be a good link in my transfer chain.

Eddie Firmani was the South African Manager of Philadelphia Fury, and he had plied his trade as a prolific striker in England and Italy (most notably for Inter Milan in the early sixties under Helenio Herrera). The Italian internationalist moved to America at the end of his career and famously won the Soccer Bowl on three occasions (twice with New York Cosmos sides featuring Pele, Franz Beckenbauer, Giorgio Chinaglia and Carlos Alberto).

Shortly after planting a seed with Doug Baillie, he called me back and we arranged another incognito meeting.

"George O'Neill was surprised that you're available," explained Doug. "He has spoken to Eddie Firmani and they are both excited at the prospect of signing you. They want you over there, and are wondering if Celtic will give you a free transfer."

"You know what Celtic are like Doug," I offered. "I'll speak to Billy McNeill and get back to you."

The wheels were now in motion, however, I knew that the thriftiness of the Celtic board may well be a stumbling block to making this a swift move. I went into Billy's office to discuss my release.

"I have an opportunity to move over to the States, and I am very interested in going," I explained. "I'm not going to leave Celtic for another Scottish club and I'm not too keen on moving to England either, Billy. With the greatest of respect, I don't want to stay here and sit on the bench when I could be over in America. I have loved playing for Celtic, but something is telling me that the time is right for me to move on... So, what are the chances of me getting a free transfer?"

"I'm not too sure, Andy," Billy shook his head. "You haven't even asked me if I want to keep you here. You're just out the team and this is the first time we've discussed the situation. I need to think about it. Let me discuss this with Dessie."

'Dessie' was Celtic's notoriously tight-fisted Chairman, Desmond White. My mind was made up and I didn't want him throwing a spanner in the works just so he could make the club a few quid out of my move.

"Celtic will be looking for a transfer fee of £20,000," revealed Billy during our next meeting. "They won't give you a free transfer. That's the way they run the club, Andy, and there isn't much I can do about it."

Until I had gone in to see Billy about my move, we had never discussed my future. There was still the possibility that he wanted to keep my experience in the pool, especially when you consider the injuries that Danny McGrain had suffered in recent years. I had played a few games with the youngsters during my spell out of the first-team, and there were a few talented boys coming through in the reserves like Charlie Nicholas, Jim Duffy, Willie McStay and Danny Crainie. No-one had asked me to assist these up-and-coming guys, but I had offered them as much advice and support as I could while I was playing alongside them. I was still young myself, and wasn't ready to take a step back from playing first-team football just yet though. I had to look after my own career before I worried about anyone else's, and that meant getting a free transfer.

I had been with Celtic for seven years and so didn't qualify for a Testimonial match. The only way of me making a decent amount at that stage of my career was to be granted a free transfer from the club. What normally happened was that the buying team would be able to negotiate a one-off payment with the player because they didn't have to stump up a transfer fee. The amounts were usually between £10,000 to £15,000, and this allowed you to plan your next move once your career ended.

I had seen plenty of guys leaving Celtic on free transfers, and they hadn't contributed nearly as much as I had done to the club. There were plenty of players who were way past their best, who secured a couple of free transfers at the tail end of their careers, and walked away with a cool £30,000 in their back pocket. This had now become a point of principle for me.

Celtic wouldn't budge on the transfer fee and Philadelphia Fury were keen to get me over to face Johan Cruyff's Washington Diplomats on 13th April 1980. The negotiations inevitably dragged on and I kept Doug Baillie updated so that O'Neill and Firmani knew that I was doing everything I could to push the transfer through.

My discussions with Billy had become more and more heated, although there was no long-term bad-blood between us. I appreciated that this really was out of his control, but was assured enough to explain that I had never been a mercenary (Billy knew what my wages had been during my time with Celtic). I just wanted to take advantage of an excellent opportunity, and get the financial reward I felt I was due.

Billy then called me in and informed me that Desmond White was prepared to give me a tax-free amount of £1,000 from the transfer fee. A grand? I knew it was out of Billy's hands. I had always respected him, and didn't want to fall out at this late stage, so I agreed.

I let Philadelphia Fury know that Celtic would require a transfer fee of £20,000 from them to conclude the deal. I also spoke to their General Manager over the telephone to agree on a signing-on fee. Thankfully, the NASL side showed a real enthusiasm for getting me over to join them in Pennsylvania, and they agreed without hesitation.

I had to make a concerted decision not to let this final few weeks of my Celtic career sour my time with the club. The stories of their 'biscuit tin' mentality are well-known, and I witnessed that penny-pinching approach first hand. The pleasure I had in representing this magnificent football club over a number of seasons will always outweigh the dealings I had with a miserable Director or Chairman. I have been a Celtic supporter my whole life and that unfortunate run-in over a relatively small amount of cash will never influence my love of the club.

My registration was cancelled on Thursday 17th April 1980, and I went up to the office at Celtic Park to find out what was to happen next. I was told that Philadelphia Fury had paid Celtic the agreed fee, and that I was to make my own arrangements with my new club in the States.

I seemed to be the only person in the stadium; all the players had finished training and had left for the day. I took a look around and then walked down to the boot-room. The door was open but Neilly Mochan was nowhere to be seen, which was unusual. I wanted to ask him if it was alright for me to take my boots!

The smell of boot polish and liniment filled the air as I took in a deep breath. This was really it - I was leaving my beloved Celtic. I went over to my peg, where 'Lynch 3' was written on a plaster above my two pairs of boots. There wasn't even a bag lying around, so I took my footwear in both hands and walked out of the boot room. My stride didn't break as I then walked out the front door of Celtic Park, and into the car-park.

I was looking around as I made my way to my car, but not a soul was around. Once inside my motor, I placed my boots on the passenger's seat and rolled down my window to take one final glance at Celtic Park.

There was no fanfare... No farewell... Not even a handshake...

Paradise can be such a wonderful place... Ten minutes passed, as I thought back to all the glorious memories I had enjoyed there over the years. My father and I had stood on the terracing and cheered on our heroes so many times before. Then, years later, I had ran out of that tunnel with the hoops on, and was able to give my auld man a wee wave or a wink. I knew that made him proud. I reminisced for a moment about lining up alongside the greatest Celtic men that I had known: Latchford, McGrain, Lynch, Murdoch, McNeill, Stanton, Johnstone, Aitken, Dalglish, Burns and Lennox. What a team that would have been! I had scored goals, heard the fans in the Jungle chanting my name, and captained the glorious Glasgow Celtic to victory. I helped my team to two league wins and two Scottish Cups. Less than a year earlier we had made our fans' dreams come true when we somehow beat Rangers with ten men to win the league. But never again would I enjoy such life-affirming moments. Tears were running down my cheeks. Paradise can be such a lonely place...

Within 24 hours, I was on a flight from Glasgow to Philadelphia. During the near-eight-hour transatlantic journey, I had plenty of time to ponder the unexpected path my career was taking. There was no doubt that my early visit to America with Hearts had planted the initial idea that I might end up there one day. But the NASL was in its infancy back then, and I had been too focussed on my career in the Scottish league to spend too much time pondering such a move. This all changed of course, when I lost my place in the Celtic first-team.

Playing for a club like Celtic is a hugely intense experience. The pressure is relentless, and you never really get enough time to take your foot off the gas and relax; you don't get much of a chance to smell the roses. I finally realised that I needed to escape from that environment. I had to travel, clear my mind, and learn more about the game.

This transition to a new country was undoubtedly going to challenge me in ways I had never imagined, but as I travelled over to meet George O'Neill at the airport, my instinct told me that it was the right move for me and my young family. I knew a few Scottish players who had gone to the play in the NASL, and it was obvious that their moves were financially motivated. I'm not criticizing them for making a few quid, because without a Testimonial match, free transfer, or coaching career to fall back on, retired footballers in my day had to go out and find a job once the floodlights faded.

My motivation for moving to the other side of the world was to develop myself as a coach. I had my badges, and my masterplan was to learn as much as I could in America from the multi-cultural NASL. The league allowed its teams to import a huge amount of overseas players into their ranks, and I looked forward to learning new techniques and methods from all over the globe.

If I thought my financial negotiations were disappointing with Celtic however, then I was in for an even bigger shock when I arrived in Philadelphia. George O'Neill met me at the airport and we got on well, as we were two Scots with a leaning towards the green-and-white half of Glasgow. Once the word got out that I was interested in going to the States, a few other NASL sides showed an interest. Initially, it really wasn't too important as to which club I eventually joined, as long as I made the move over there. However, Philadelphia Fury had shown that they desperately wanted me to be part of their team, and perhaps that was what I really needed at that stage of my career.

George took me to the hotel and got me booked in. He told me to rest, and that he would pick me up the following morning for training before meeting the General Manager, Tom Fleck, who would have my registration papers for signing.

I made my way downstairs at around 8.30 the next morning, and ordered scrambled eggs, toast and tea for breakfast. This was my first lesson about life in America. The plate arrived and was piled high with hash browns, tomatoes, sausages, bacon, fried eggs and beans (but no black pudding). It was the largest breakfast portion you could imagine but I somehow found my scrambled eggs in there, and managed to stick to a much lighter pre-training option.

George picked me up at 9.30 and took me along to the stadium for my first Stateside training session. We were able to train at our stadium because the pitch was laid with artificial Astroturf, which was so-called as Houston's Astrodome had been the first stadium in the world to be fitted with the material back in the 1960s. What can I say about this plastic surface? Well, it was better than training at Barrowfield!

The Veterans Stadium was huge and we shared it with the American Football side, the Philadelphia Eagles. We would split the pitch half-and-half with them to train, and the Eagles' players were absolute giants. I used to watch them crunching into challenges and was glad I had chosen the game the Americans called 'Soccer.' The clubs would exchange complimentary tickets, so our players were able to sample one of this country's true sporting obsessions whenever we were free.

The sun was shining, and I felt the benefit of that straight away. Once I was introduced to the players, Bruce Hayne took us out on the pitch for our warm-up. Bruce was a pleasant and knowledgeable physiotherapist / trainer. It was clear to me that the American game was streets ahead in many aspects in comparison to the Scottish set-up. For example, Billy McNeill had only just secured Brian Scott as Celtic's physiotherapist prior to me leaving Glasgow. Before Brian's arrival, the amateur way that they treated injuries was abysmal. Philadelphia Fury on the other hand had a real expert in Bruce.

Our physio started the session by strapping up the ankles of a lot of our players for added protection, before embarking on a 20-30 minute period of stretching. This may seem really obvious now, but our warm-up at Celtic had been a few laps around the park. Stretching? The attitude back home had been that such preparation was for athletic sports such as gymnastics. What the Scottish game had failed to realise was that footballers were athletes too, and many of them lost weeks and months of the season due to muscle strains, pulls and tears.

I sat on the Astroturf and stretched my legs out as wide as I possibly could, which wasn't very far. Bruce laughed as he came over to see me. "You Brits are all the same, Andy," he explained. "The lack of flexibility you have is unbelievable." And he was right, because when I looked around the pitch, the other players' legs were wide open, and I was struggling for another inch.

Where did that lack of flexibility come from? I think the climate and the training facilities had a lot to do with it in Scotland. We had nowhere to stretch indoors, and certainly at Celtic we couldn't sit on the muddy trenches of Barrowfield for half-an-hour because we would be freezing cold and wringing wet before a ball was kicked. It was no wonder my pelvic problems plagued me throughout my career back home.

Around half of the pitches in the NASL were Astroturf, and I enjoyed playing on it. Many of my team-mates didn't, but I think that was more down to the fact that the ball obviously bounces more and this demands better control. The players who didn't fancy the synthetic surface probably didn't have the necessary skills to adapt to it.

As well as the additional spring to the surface, you had to be very careful with slide tackles. This is something I only discovered after losing most of the skin on one of my thighs and hips. I was in agony for weeks after a last-minute tackle, which was something I was normally used to performing on a regular basis.

The other downside to the artificial pitches was a condition known as 'Astroturf Toe,' and I fell victim to that a few times. This normally happened when your boot would catch the turf before the ball, and your toe would stub badly on the solid surface, whereas on Scottish pitches you would generally kick right through the grass and mud (like a golfer taking a divot).

I met Eddie Firmani for the first time during our training session. My new gaffer had been one of the most successful managers in NASL history, having won three Soccer Bowls with two different sides, and he was delighted to have an ex-Celtic captain in his ranks. He asked me if I was prepared to move around the pitch and perhaps play some games in midfield if I was needed. I was more than happy to oblige, as I soon discovered during our bounce match that the squad we had was far from great.

They had a lot of raw, young American players in their pool, and there was a league ruling that stated two North Americans must be fielded by each side at all times. These boys were fit and strong but lacked any real skill. Peter Osgood, Alan Ball, Johnny Giles and Frank Worthington had previously been star-names for the Fury in recent years, but they had all gone, and we now lacked that 'marquee' attraction that almost all of the teams in the NASL had.

It wasn't for the lack of trying, as Firmani had made efforts to sign Johan Cruyff and Gerd Muller without success, and legend has it that a young Argentinian was offered to the club back in 1978 but they turned him down for being too small. His name? Diego Armando Maradona.

After training, I was taken up to the General Manager's office to sign my registration forms and officially become a member of the Philadelphia Fury. I had conducted all my negotiations myself and, as I picked up the pen to sign on the dotted line, I asked the General Manager (an ex-marine called Tom Fleck) when I would receive my agreed signing-on fee... There was a moment of silence and, as his smile evaporated, Tom uttered, "What signing-on fee Andy?"

I couldn't believe this was happening after all the hassle I had to deal with at Celtic. I was also tired after a long-haul flight and in no mood to come up against a stumbling block at this late stage of the deal. I'm not sure what created this mix-up but Philadelphia Fury believed that Celtic were paying me my lump-sum. I could see that Tom was genuinely surprised so I put it down to poor communications. This was the early eighties after all, and I didn't have the luxury of an email trail that could be produced as proof of our agreement.

I had to stand firm though, so I explained that I'd be on the first plane back to Glasgow unless the money was paid. To his credit, Tom Fleck asked me to give him 24 hours so that he could speak to the owners of the club. I agreed, before heading back to the hotel with George O'Neill.

Sitting at the hotel bar that night, George gave me the low-down on the financial state of the club. He explained that it had a real Rock 'n' Roll background and had been bankrolled by none other than Paul Simon of Simon & Garfunkel fame; Rick Wakeman, of Yes; Peter Frampton, who had a star on the Hollywood Walk of Fame; and Peter Rudge, who was the Rolling Stones' Tour Manager. I hoped this wasn't going to turn into a Rock 'n' Roll circus!

The Philadelphia Fury had risen from the ashes of the Philadelphia Atoms in 1977, but by 1978 the franchise were losing $500,000 a year and Rick Wakeman jumped ship. With a lack of finances, the star names had all been moved on. This, in turn, had the predictable effect on attendances, with the average gates falling from over 8,000 to under just 5,000 in three seasons. All was clearly not well.

The following day, I went back in to see Tom Fleck. Tom described how he had pleaded for hours with the owners to release the extra cash, and had explained to them that the team really needed my experience. A smile appeared on his face, as he offered me his hand and confirmed I was getting my signing-on fee. I shook his hand emphatically, for Philadelphia is the 'City of Brotherly Love' after all.

As I signed my contract, I explained to Tom that I would train the younger lads at the club free of charge. I wanted to use all of my experience to assist them to develop, and at the same time work on my own coaching technique. Philadelphia Fury had already sufficiently shown their desire for me to join their team, and their sense of loyalty really impressed me. I assured him that I was in this for the long haul, and he would not regret signing me.

Now, I was finally ready to go on the road with the Philadelphia Fury.

DANNY BHOY: Danny and I celebrate our league championship win in Billy McNeill's first season in charge.

SAFETY IN NUMBERS: Big Shuggie and I snuff out
a Rangers attack in the 1977 Scottish Cup final.

HEADS UP: Tommy McLean and I give chase
in the 1977 Scottish Cup final.

KIPPER & THE BIG YIN: Billy Connolly had St Philomena's Church Hall in an uproar during this charity event. Away from the stage he is a lovely guy and a massive Celt.

FUN IN THE SUN: We retraced the Lisbon Lions' footsteps in 1979 when we visited Estoril. Here I am with Tom McAdam, Murdo MacLeod and Vic Davidson.

HALCYON DAYS: I will always remember the late Tommy Burns as being full of fun and mischief. He will forever be revered as a one of Celtic's best-loved sons.

SIGN OF THE TIMES: Jimmy Steele takes some of the squad for a relaxing walk at Seamill.

THE LEADERS: John Greig and I captain our sides in the 1978 League Cup final. I was desperate to lead Celtic to victory but it wasn't to be.

THE HAMPDEN ROAR: Another goal against Rangers, as I wheel away in delight with Murdo MacLeod and Tommy Burns on 11th November 1978.

ON YOUR TOES, SON!: I can almost hear the roar of Jock Stein from the dug-out.

THE CELTIC FAMILY: Kids and grandkids join Jock Stein, Pat Stanton, Bobby Lennox, myself, the late Johnny Doyle, and Paul Wilson.

WRONG WAY ROUGHIE!: My penalty kick ritual beats Scotland's number one.

THE STARS: I made the right move to Montreal and had a fantastic few years in the NASL.

PENALTY KING: I never missed a spot-kick for Montreal Manic in the NASL.

IN THE PRESENCE OF GREATNESS: Standing next to two of the greatest wingers in the history of British football: Sir Stanley Matthews and Charlie Cooke.

MANIC STREET PREACHER: As Head Coach of Montreal Manic, I relished the extra responsibility of managing a squad of professionals.

THE ART OF FOOTBALL: In Lake Placid with revolutionary Dutch Coach Wiel Coerver, whose methods have been practiced all over the world.

KEEPING IT IN THE FAMILY: It couldn't have been easy for my son Simon, as he followed in my footsteps at Celtic Park. I'm very proud of what he achieved.

All images are from Andy Lynch's personal photographic archive

CHAPTER FOURTEEN
THE MANIC & THE FURY

A ball of flames entering the earth's atmosphere adorned the Philadelphia Fury club crest. It was meant to signify the arrival of the sport in the city, like a fireball of excitement. The Americans did things differently, that's for sure.

They knew how to make a game of soccer more of a box-office event because they had to. Take the Fury for example, they were just three years old when I joined them, and they had no real history to speak of. They were a franchise who played in the multi-purpose Veterans Stadium. This was a huge arena, where over 60,000 spectators could converge for sporting events or musical shows.

In order to fill as many of those seats as possible (and generate some serious cash in the process) the clubs of the NASL had to approach the marketing and promotion of the game completely differently. They did not have a century of goodwill to rely on. Some of their ideas were inspired, whilst others were verging on the insane!

The colours of Philadelphia Fury's uniforms (that's what they called strips) were a bold yellow and maroon. They were created by fashion designers to also appeal to the female audience, who made up 45% of NASL's spectators.

Squad names and numbers were already old-hat when I arrived in 1980. When the English Premiership introduced them in the early nineties, football executives in England thought they had reinvented the wheel. I was number 12 on the Philadelphia Fury roster for my first season, but I thereafter reverted to the familiar number 3 for the following campaign.

They certainly knew how to brand the teams. Even the names had a touch of the razzmatazz about them: San Jose Earthquakes, Chicago Sting, New

York Cosmos, Houston Hurricane, Toronto Blizzard, Calgary Cougars, Vancouver Whitecaps. Everything was geared towards appealing to a live and TV audience.

The NASL realised long before the British game that television revenue was paramount to the league's success and had secured a major network TV deal with ABC, which adequately lined the pockets of the 24 participating teams.

The league set-up was also completely different. There were six small divisions of four sides. Philadelphia Fury were in the Eastern Division alongside Tampa Bay Rowdies, Fort Lauderdale Strikers and New England Tea Men. Not only would we play the teams within our own division but, throughout the season, we would go on the road to play every club within the other five divisions.

Going on the road was necessary due to the vast geographical distances between many of the sides. This meant we would play three games away from home in quick succession against teams from roughly the same area. Then we would play a few games in-a-row at home. We certainly racked up plenty of air-miles on our travels, which might explain why wee Jinky didn't last long over in San Jose!

We were awarded six points for a win, and one bonus point for each goal up to a maximum of three. There were no draws. Once the league fixtures were completed, the top two sides from each division automatically made it to the play-offs. The two third-placed teams with the highest points total also qualified for the knock-out stages. There is no doubt that the structure of the Champions League of today strongly resembles what the NASL were doing back in the 70s and 80s.

Going back to there being no draws, I thought this was a great idea. The spectator knew they were going to see a winner, and that very much appealed to the North American ethos. In their minds, there are just winners and losers, and they have no interest in ties. If a match was level after 90 minutes then we would have a short water break before playing 30 minutes of extra time. If the sides could still not be separated then we would have a 'shoot-out' to decide on a winner.

This was a 'Beat The Shot-Clock' sudden-death event, and there were two illuminated Countdown-style clocks on each side of the field. Players started 30 yards from goal and had five seconds to beat the goalie. The ref blew the whistle and the klaxon announced when the time was up. This might sound easy for the player, but trust me it is a very difficult and pressure-filled situation to be in. I found it entertaining, and perhaps even better than the conventional penalty kick shoot-out.

When I discussed the NASL with friends back home, some of them would sneer at certain changes that the Americans were making with 'their' game. Many fans felt that the NASL was a Mickey Mouse set-up, but I detected that some of the criticism only came due to an element of envy.

We had the glitz and the glamour, we sang the national anthem before league matches, an organ would play over the loud speakers to rouse the crowd if a team were on the attack, and we had cheerleaders going through their repertoire pre-match and behind the goals. It was all about entertainment.

Certain quarters of the British game turned their noses up at what was going on in the NASL, but I think that a huge part of that was down to an inherent fear of change. The vast crowds of the 50s and 60s were a distant memory in British football, but the national associations stuck to their traditional philosophies despite a huge number of new threats to their 'product' such as the collapse of heavy industries, and the effect of television.

Anything that enhanced the game as a spectator sport was positive as far as I was concerned. I believe that the elements of the NASL's approach that are now prevalent in the English League and Champions League speak volumes in terms of the Americans' forward-thinking attitude. It took European football a generation to catch up to their way of thinking.

The league's organisers wanted soccer to be the number one sport in North America. The scale of that ambition was gargantuan when the popularity of American football, baseball, ice hockey and basketball is considered. However, parents realised that soccer was one of the least dangerous sports compared with the others I've mentioned, and they understood that it was enjoyed throughout the rest of the world, so why not in America?

In my time, there was far less focus on grass-roots development, and more emphasis on getting in big names from all over the world to appeal to the expectant public. Pele had been the biggest name in the world, and he played in the league for three years before I arrived. Some of the superstar players I faced included: Franz Beckenbauer, Giorgio Chinaglia, Johan Neeskins and Carlos Alberto of the New York Cosmos; George Best of the San Jose Earthquakes; Charlie Cooke of the Memphis Rogues; Johan Cruyff of the Washington Diplomats; Teofilo Cubillas and Gerd Muller of the Fort Lauderdale Strikers; and Hugo Sanchez of the San Diego Sockers. It read like a who's who of fantasy world football.

In order to compete with such talented individuals, we had to prepare to the absolute hilt, and this was where I was first educated in the field of sports science and nutrition. Our pre-match meal at Celtic was chicken or steak - people would laugh at you now if you ate a steak before a game of football. It won't have digested in time for your body to feel the benefit of it, but that's what we did back then. Not in America though.

We ate our pre-match meals around five hours before the games, and these were served at a hotel banquet. We were fed mounds of pasta, spaghetti, rice, bread, chicken, beans, potatoes and carrots. Bruce Hayne explained to me that I needed to stock up on energy because 90 minutes in the heat and humidity would really affect my energy and fluid levels. We'd then be sent for a pre-match sleep, and then have some more tea and toast before the game.

We'd be weighed before and after every match and I was losing an average of six to seven pounds every time I played. The sweat would be pouring off me and we changed our sodden shirts at half-time (I can just imagine Neilly Mochan's reaction if a Celtic player was ever to ask for a change of jersey during a match!). The fluids would be replaced after the game of course, and sometimes it was with a well-deserved beer.

With such a dearth of big-name players, Philadelphia Fury had invested their hope in the decorated Eddie Firmani. After winning the Soccer Bowl with the Tampa Bay Rowdies and twice with New York Cosmos, his stock was at an all-time high. Having said that, Eddie had the luxury of having Pele and Franz Beckenbauer at his disposal at the Cosmos, so it would have been pretty difficult not to win it. In fact, he once confessed to me that training in New York normally consisted of playing head tennis.

I once asked him why he left the Cosmos and he told me a quite astonishing story. Warner Brothers owned the club, and they had close links to Giorgio Chinaglia, who was one of Eddie's star strikers. The South African manager had been advised that he was not to substitute Chinaglia unless he was injured. For the most part this wasn't an issue because the Italian internationalist was a top class player and consistent performer. However, the ex-Lazio man hit a sticky patch of poor form and was struggling for a goal, so Eddie decided to hook him off half way through the second period of a match at the Giants Stadium. As Chinaglia slowly walked past the Cosmos bench on his way up the tunnel, he turned to Eddie and threatened, "You'll regret that." The next day, Eddie Firmani was fired.

As unbelievable as the chain of events sounded, I was quickly learning that anything was possible in the NASL. I thought Eddie was fine at first. He was softly-spoken and liked a laugh. He seemed to be everyone's friend, but I was to later discover that I couldn't trust him. Later on, when we both moved to the Montreal Manic, Eddie felt threatened by my growing reputation as a coach and tried to get rid of me. For now though, we were on good terms and he seemed happy to embrace my top-flight experience.

My NASL debut arrived on 19th April 1980 (just two days after my Celtic registration was cancelled), and I lined up against the Memphis Rogues in front of 9,574 fans at the Veterans Stadium. We ran on to the pitch to signature music and cheerleaders doing their thing, and lined up for the 'Star-Spangled Banner.' It was all a world away from my last league appearance for Celtic at a dismal Cappielow Park in Greenock.

The heat and humidity took care of the pace of the game, and I felt that tactically the approach was very similar to what I was used to. One thing that did take a bit of getting used to however, was the blaring organ whenever one of the teams were on the attack. It sounded as though the cavalry were on their way, but it was all about entertaining the crowds.

Alcohol was served in the stadiums, which weren't policed, and there was no crowd trouble that I can recall. The venues were all-seated, and the clubs were able to manage crowd-control solely with stewards. Fans would be able to sit at the game with a cold beer in one hand and a burger in the other and enjoy a game of soccer. It all went without a hitch.

Some of the bigger matches were sold as double-headers, whereby the entertainment after the game came from a well-known band, and fans could buy a ticket for both events. I remember playing the New York Cosmos, and after the match all the players got showered and made their way up to the stand. A team of construction workers hurried on to the pitch to erect a temporary stage, and the announcer started the countdown clock to challenge them with the NASL record, which I think was twenty minutes. In the meantime, the crowd were being served food and drink while we waited on the show.

Eventually these pink Cadillacs appeared and were being driven around the trackside. There were five of them, and each of them had a Beach Boy sitting on the roof waving to the crowd. They then got on stage and The Beach Boys played a full set. It was all quite incredible.

We also seen Billy Joel playing a concert after our match with George Best's San Jose Earthquakes. They played at the Spartan Stadium, which was one of the smaller venues with a grass pitch and a terrific atmosphere. I was playing sweeper that day, and we were 1-0 up with a quarter-of-an-hour left to play. Best had been marked out of the game and didn't really look all that interested.

With 15 minutes to go, the former Manchester United man picked the ball up on the right wing and lost his marker with a drop of his shoulder. As the centre-half approached the Belfast wizard, he drilled the ball into the top corner from all of 20 yards. Five minutes later, Best went on a mazy run and set up the winner. During the 90 minutes, he had the ball twice and he punished us on both occasions to win the game. Was I in the presence of a truly world class performer? Without a shadow of a doubt.

After games, if there wasn't a show arranged, we would get showered and make our way up to the player's room. This lounge was open to everyone, and the players were actively encouraged to attend after matches. This meant that we were able to enjoy a beer with the fans, who were keen to rub shoulders with footballers, get their photos taken and ask us all

THE MANIC & THE FURY

manner of questions about the game. All the time that they were doing this however, they were also buying food and drink at the bar. It was a sure-fire way for the clubs to make even more money.

I met some interesting people from all over the world in those player's rooms. One such fellow was an ex-bus driver from Knightswood in Glasgow called Maurie Greening. What did we have in common? Celtic Football Club of course. Maurie had emigrated with his wife, Jessie, and they settled in Woodbury, New Jersey. We became great friends, and he'd regularly invite me over to his place for a drink or barbecue. Maurie had a den under his house, where he had a bar full of Celtic memorabilia. He introduced me to Country and Western music and we'd go to see bands in fantastic Country and Western bars all over the place. To this day, the one song that reminds me of my time in North America more than anything else is Willie Nelson's 'On The Road Again.' The sentiment of this beautiful composition speaks for itself really, and I could honestly relate to the lyrics describing life on the road.

The Fury's co-owner, Peter Rudge, looked after Mick Jagger and his band when they were on the road, and this once led to a chance meeting with The Rolling Stones' front-man in the tunnel before a game. We were playing the Cosmos when this little bundle of energy came up to speak to us. He shook my hand and was very pleasant, but I must confess I was more of a Beatles fan; so, I wasn't overly excited!

Peter Rudge was a memorable character. He would come into our changing room before the games and speak to us all to try and get us motivated for the upcoming match. The way he dressed made him look completely out of place, but the boys would go along with it and humour him. Then, when we were out warming up, Peter would join us on the pitch wearing his shirt, tie and winkle-pickers, and start shouting for a pass of the ball. Again, the players duly obliged and it was obvious that this guy had never played football in his life. A Director coming on for the warm-up... Can you imagine seeing that at Celtic Park or Ibrox?

My wife and children joined me in the States around four weeks after I arrived, and we rented a lovely family home in Haddonfield, New Jersey, which was about 25 minutes' drive from our stadium in Philadelphia.

Most of the players rented property, such was the nature of the game over there. Many of the Brits were only out there short-term, and some were actually on loan from their parent clubs. My team-mate, Fran O'Brien, did things slightly differently to most of us.

Wee Fran was an Irishman, who had managed to get a few trials for English clubs earlier in his career without anything materialising. He decided to try his luck out in America, and he's still out there. Fran was a big Celtic man, had a great sense of humour, and needless to say we got on like a house on fire.

Talking of houses, Fran rented out the apartment that the club gave him, and he bought a house to renovate. If he ever picked me up, his car was always full of old toilets, bags of cement, and tools. It was filthy. But he stuck to his guns and managed to finish his house. He did the same when he moved to Vancouver, and then to Seattle. A clever wee Irishman, who did well with his business ventures.

Fran was actually one of our better players. He was a box-to-box midfielder, who was two-footed and could get us goals. He was also partial to a wee Bicardi and Coke, a habit I was exposed to when we roomed together whilst we were out on the road.

We were back at our hotel one night after playing Toronto Blizzard away from home, and Fran was getting itchy feet. He suggested that we sneak out for a beer, and it didn't take too much persuasion for me to agree (after all, I had lost half a stone in fluid during the match). There was a club curfew, but we couldn't sleep and what harm would a quiet drink do?

We found an all-night diner and ordered a couple of pints before finding a quiet booth. As we were enjoying our night-caps, something caught Fran's attention at the counter. "Shit, keep your head down," he whispered, as he slouched down as if to hide in the booth, and I followed suit. "A guy's just pulled a gun out at the till," added Fran, as I slowly turned my head to see the stick-up in full progress. The till attendant looked petrified as she emptied the takings into a bag, before the assailant disappeared into the night. We decided not to have another beer, and headed back to the apparent haven of our hotel instead.

Our next fixture was against the mighty New York Cosmos. When we arrived at the hotel, we were given an itinerary, which allowed us some free time to explore the different cities we were visiting. Our goalkeeper, Bob Rigby, and defender, Bobby Smith, were a pair of Americans who would just disappear into their hotel room for days on end. They would camp out in their room for two days, close all the curtains, and crank up the air conditioning system. Then they'd order pizzas, and watch movies non-stop until it was time for us to leave. I went to check on them one day because no-one had seen them since our arrival. I knocked on their door, and waited a few moments before I heard some movement from the den of iniquity. The door eventually creaked open, and Bobby Smith was standing there with his long hair and beard looking rather dishevelled. There was a thick and potent haze of smoke filling the room, where Bob Rigby lay on one of the beds. These two American internationalists had been in there the whole time smoking copious amounts of dope!

By the time that we played the Cosmos in New York, our side had won just six matches to the loss of 20. I had played in all 18 matches since my arrival, and I managed to chip in with four goals. What had become crystal clear to me was that we were a weak side, who were the whipping boys of our division.

What we lacked in flair however, we more than made up with team-work and sheer brawn when necessary. Against the New York Cosmos, Carlos Alberto was on the rampage when he let the ball run too far in front of him and I went in solidly to the tackle. The Brazilian World Cup-winner didn't take too kindly to my tough-tackling approach and he pushed me with two hands to my chest. This caused a bit of a scrap between quite a few of the players, and during the furore our ex-Chelsea centre-half John Dempsey unceremoniously booted Alberto right up the backside. I had never seen such a blatant assault on a football pitch in my entire career, and I couldn't stop myself from laughing. The image of this big no-nonsense Cockney defender booting the silky smooth Brazilian up the arse epitomised our season - we were a team of workers, who lacked the necessary flair and skill to make the play-offs.

The Cosmos narrowly defeated us 2-1, and our goal was scored by Ronnie Glavin's younger brother, Tony. The Celtic connection was never far away even on the other side of the world, but I always welcomed that. I recall during our next match against Houston, I went over to the trackside to take a throw-in when I heard a Scottish voice from the crowd shouting, "Here Andy, you wouldn't get a game for Celtic playing like that." I just smiled up at the crowd, as I had no idea who my heckler was.

After the game (which ended in a 2-0 defeat), I was in the player's room when a tall guy came over to me. He was about 40 years of age, and was with his girlfriend. "How are you doing Andy?" he asked in a Glaswegian accent. "Awh, so you're the one who was giving me stick out there tonight," I smiled. It turned out that this fan came from Govan, and had settled in Houston a few years before.

We got chatting, and George O'Neill joined us. We were just three Celtic fans at a bar on the other side of the world shooting the breeze. It was one of those nights where the atmosphere was infectious, and we felt that we were among friends. Our new best friend invited us back to his home for some supper and a night cap, and we all jumped in a cab. I knew I had a pass as I was with the assistant manager, and we stayed up until the wee small hours drinking and singing. As we left at 8 a.m. the next morning to get back to the team hotel, George and I shook hands with the Govan expatriate having enjoyed a full evening of Houston hospitality. We managed to get back to our hotel for breakfast and had a sleep on the flight home. I never saw or heard from that big guy again. No matter where I've been in this world, I've ended up bumping into fabulously hospitable Celtic supporters.

Being an ex-Celt also helped me in a somewhat unexpected way on the field during an encounter with Chicago Sting. In those days, FIFA referees were permitted to have a working holiday in North America, and were allowed to officiate NASL matches whilst on their travels. Before this particular match, the ref came into our dressing-room to check the players' boots and have a word with us, as is usual practice. The ref was a Dubliner and he started chatting away to Fran O'Brien, whom he clearly knew.

I recognised the referee, but he didn't remember me. Perhaps it was because the stadium that Celtic had played Shamrock Rovers in back in the pre-season of 1973/74 was in semi-darkness by the time the part-time butcher sent me off - it was John Carpenter!

When we went out for the warm-up, I explained the story to Fran (who found it all hilarious), and I asked him to introduce me to his fellow countryman. We were desperately needing a win, and I thought there would be no harm in making friends with authority. I was duly presented to the ref, and I regaled him with the tale of me flattening Frank McEwan seven years previously, resulting in a red card. John Carpenter started laughing, and I joined in before wishing him all the best for the rest of his holiday.

Ten minutes into the match and one of our forwards went down in the penalty box after a challenge from Chicago Sting's goalkeeper. The decision could have gone either way, but the ref pointed straight to the spot. The 'keeper began to remonstrate and was promptly shown a red card for his troubles. As the reserve goalie was being stripped, Fran just winked at me and observed, "I think that was a stone-waller, Andy. The goalie left the ref with no option..." That was one of only ten wins we managed all season, and it was partly down to hoodwinking the referee.

As much as I had enjoyed my debut season in the unique surroundings of the North American Soccer League, we finished bottom of our division, a massive 56 points adrift of the New England Tea Men. I wasn't used to holding the rest of the league up from the foot of the table, and I knew that imminent changes were required.

Our predecessors, the Philadelphia Atoms, had averaged crowds of between 10,000 and 11,000 but our attendances had plummeted to below half of that. It was obvious that the fans swarmed to see the big-name imports, but the Fury were unable to afford that type of player any longer. The cavernous Veterans Stadium didn't inspire any confidence either, as it was a venue devoid of atmosphere when it was less than a tenth full.

As the supporters continued to stay away, the Rock 'n' Roll owners decided to sell the franchise so that it could be relocated elsewhere. The destination? Montreal in Canada.

Molson Breweries were based in Canada and they bought the franchise on 26th November 1980. My wife and I had to consider the move carefully because we had a young family to think about. However, our children had embraced the earlier change or surroundings when we moved to New Jersey and we felt that the experience was beneficial to them at such an early stage of their lives.

My new team wore blue and white and would be called the Montreal Manic. Molson already owned the highly successful National Hockey League side, the Montreal Canadiens, and were confident of introducing a soccer club to the city. In doing so, the locals would have their first professional soccer team since the Montreal Olympique disbanded seven years previously.

The move to Montreal was one of the most important of my football career. It was there that I was finally able to embark on my coaching endeavours, after building up my experience with the Philadelphia kids. Eddie Firmani and eleven of my Fury team-mates joined me on the journey, and I was delighted that one of them was my wee Irish room-mate, Fran O'Brien.

The ball of flames that made up the Philadelphia Fury's designer club crest had crashed and burned to earth with the velocity of a meteor. From the embers of its wreckage, I had another life-changing opportunity ahead of me in Montreal.

My first year in the NASL had been a real learning curve for me, and anything but dull. My North American adventure was just beginning, but, as I looked optimistically towards living in another new country in 1981, I hoped that my new club would be 'Le Manic' in name alone.

CHAPTER FIFTEEN
BIG BANG OF THE COSMOS

My debut season as Montreal Manic's first-choice number three had been hugely successful for me and the club. I played in 31 of the Manic's 38 matches throughout 1981, as we made it to the play-off quarter-final before being knocked out after three games against Chicago Sting.

Our roster of players was largely similar to the Philadelphia Fury's final season, but we averaged an impressive 23,704 through the turnstiles, which was second only to the New York Cosmos. This had been an eventful maiden campaign for the club, and it looked as though Molson Breweries had made some inspired choices in acquiring the franchise for a reported $2 million, and moving it to appeal to its Francophone fan-base.

Eddie Firmani hadn't made wholesale changes to the Fury's squad but added some important elements in Nigerian striker Thomson Usiyan, England internationalists Tony Towers and Gordon Hill, and ex-Middlesbrough striker, Alan Willey.

Even though we were travelling extensively all over America and Canada, sometimes for 10 days at a time, I felt less tired than I had done during a typical Scottish league season. I'm sure this was down to the improvements in preparation and diet that I had embraced since moving to North America.

Visiting this vast array of cities was an education, and I found it all very exciting and refreshing. I felt at ease in the relaxing surroundings of the West Coast, and always enjoyed playing in San Jose, Los Angeles, San Diego and California. The weather was hot, and I remember that hundreds of fans would set up barbecues from the back of their vehicles in the stadium car parks, and there would be a fantastic pre-match atmosphere as we arrived at the venues.

When we were in Florida, I would make a point of catching up with another ex-Celtic left-back - John Gorman - who was one of the Tampa Bay Rowdies' star players at that time. At one point, John was being offered so many commissions for his magnificent artwork over in the States that he was actually considering a career away from football.

In the deep south of Dallas, the men would go about their business wearing sharp suits, white shirts and colourful ties. This ensemble would be topped off with a Stetson hat and cowboy boots, complete with stars. They resembled something that had walked straight off a TV set. Put it this way, if they strolled along Sauchiehall Street in that kind of get-up, the locals would think they were in fancy dress!

Chicago was the hub for airport travel, and we spent more time waiting on flights there than any place else. When the time was right, this gave the team an opportunity to bond during 'happy hour' in the airport lounge. Although we had such a mixed bag of players from a variety of backgrounds, the one common denominator was football. When a few sociable drinks were added to the equation, we were guaranteed lots of laughs, and that became my endearing memory of Chicago.

Games against fellow Canadian sides Toronto Blizzard and Vancouver Whitecaps were regarded as derbies, even though the teams were hundreds of miles away from us. Leeds United icon, Johnny Giles, was coaching the Whitecaps, and I remember one encounter against them in particular at their remarkable Empire Stadium (a venue memorable in itself for having a roof). The pivotal moment of the match came when we were awarded a penalty kick, which was taken by our Yugoslavian striker, Dragan Vojovic. Dragan had us all on the edge of our seats as he nonchalantly executed the spot-kick using the method made famous in 1976 by Antonin Panenka. It is a risky technique, which involves the penalty taker chipping the ball straight down the middle of the goal. This is all very well if the goalkeeper commits himself to a dive, which thankfully he did on that occasion. Dragan could be a real match-winner on his day, and he was later to prove as much during the most important NASL match I was ever involved in.

The events of one particular winter's evening in 1981 very nearly prevented me from ever seeing Dragan's sublime skill ever again...

The Montreal winters were severe, and the temperatures would fall dramatically to between minus 20 and 30 degrees. It was a dry cold, and the locals would prepare for the conditions by changing the tyres on their vehicles to see them through this Baltic spell. In turn, the NASL prepared for such stark climate changes by operating a wintertime indoor league.

I had been invited on to Ted Tevan's late-night cult radio show, and was due to be interviewed at 11 p.m. Ted was a well-loved broadcaster, whose passion for sports in Canada was second-to-none.

These commercial engagements came through my association with my first-ever football agent, Allan Turowitz. Allan was a Montrealer, who had been looking after the affairs of several ice hockey and American football players for several years. He moved into the soccer market when the NASL was on the rise, and represented a few of the Manic's roster. When I eventually took over the role of coach, I encouraged the youngsters to work with Allan, but warned the agent not to take advantage of these inexperienced players.

Allan and I both lived around 25 minutes' drive from the radio station, but we took separate cars to Ted's show. During the live broadcast, I was asked all about my time at Celtic and the mean streets of Glasgow where I was brought up. It seemed that this was the general perception of Glasgow over in North America. I actually thought that it could get a lot more sinister in downtown Montreal, but I wasn't about to shatter the illusion.

Once the interview was finished, Allan and I decided that we would head back to his place for a coffee. It was late, but the experience of being on Ted's live show had stirred up my adrenaline, and I was in no mood to sleep.

Allan was a local and knew the roads well. He warned me that, even though the freeway had been gritted and cleared of snow, I would need to be careful as there were some microclimate areas of the road that could freeze over.

We set off in separate cars, with me following Allan, and I quickly realised that the road was clearly used by Toronto and Montreal haulage firms, as truck after truck hammered past us in the opposite direction. With Allan's warning in my ears, I kept a safe distance behind him as we made our way back to the tranquillity of the suburbs.

All of a sudden, I saw the flash of Allan's break lights in front of me, and so I slowed down with my feet touching the break ever so slightly... My car went into an unexpected and dizzying tail spin. I was completely helpless as I pirouetted down the freeway before colliding with the concrete central reservation, and coming to a stop on the opposite side of the road. I managed to compose myself (as I was now facing the oncoming haulage trucks), and quickly slipped my car into reverse. As I revved away backwards to return to my side of the road and out of danger, a truck careered down the road towards me. With the horns blaring in my ears like the klaxon bell announcing time-up, I turned back into the other lane, and was inches (and milliseconds) away from being involved in unthinkable carnage.

My near-death experience seriously shook me up, as I pulled into a layby to be met by a shocked-looking and distinctly pale Allan Turowitz. He thought I was a goner; I was seconds away from being wiped out on the road. When you've faced death like that, and stared into the white of its eyes, it helps to put other aspects of life into perspective.

Following my narrow escape, I contracted a bout of hepatitis, which kept me out of almost all of the 1982 campaign, and eventually put paid to my playing career altogether at the age of just 31. My professional football journey - which had began at Tynecastle, Edinburgh on 6th October 1969, and ended at the Skelly Stadium, Tulsa, Oklahoma on 1st April 1982 - was over.

The matches that book-ended my career both came against American opposition. My debut was against Dallas Tornado, and my farewell appearance was in a 1-0 defeat to the Tulsa Roughnecks. My entire playing career had been enveloped within 11-and-a-half short years.

Like everyone else in the world of sport, I wanted to play on for as long as I possibly could and had envisioned a career that would last until I was at least 35. However, by hanging my boots up prematurely, I was given the early opportunity to focus on my coaching career.

Molson Breweries representative and Montreal Manic's Vice President and General Manager, Roger Samson, convinced me to stay on at the club. Our vision was to develop a Manic reserve side, and I agreed to set this up from scratch. As well as focussing on the youth, I was also appointed as Assistant Coach to Eddie Firmani.

"This is one of those mixed emotion situations, similar to seeing your mother-in-law driving over a cliff in the new Cadillac."

As opening salvos go, the first three lines of this eccentric letter from Roger Samson, was possibly the most memorable I had ever read. He went on:

"We are sorry your playing career has ended but it ended as it should: with you riding a crest. Conversely, we are delighted at our good fortune of having access to your coaching, teaching and organisational abilities, and I am happy that you have chosen to remain with this organisation. Sorry to see you go (as a player), but a sincere and official welcome to the family on another important level."

A month after my final game of football, Mag and I celebrated the arrival of our fourth child, Simon, who was born in downtown Montreal. We felt that our children were settled and enjoying a great opportunity to embrace a vastly different lifestyle to the one they would have had back home. I was delighted for myself and for my family to commit our future to the Manic. We had purchased a house in Montreal (following advice from an exiled Dundonian Estate Agent called George Wylie), and were in an area that was largely populated by Anglos. I was disappointed to bring the curtain down on my playing career, but life was good and we envisioned that our family's long-term future would be in Montreal.

My playing career ended in the Spring, and I quickly busied myself in setting up Montreal Manic's reserve side, 'le Manic II', who began to play games in June 1982. Young North American amateur hopefuls lined up for a chance to trial for our second string, knowing that it may lead to a professional contract with our first team. Most of these boys ended up being sent back to their amateur sides however, as they simply didn't meet the required standard.

I worked as an all-round goodwill-ambassador for the club - A Manic Street Preacher if you will - and attended regular commercial events to enhance the brand of Montreal Manic among the Quebecois. It was obvious to me that the locals were delighted to have a professional soccer team on their doorstep again, and I was keen to tap into that burgeoning enthusiasm.

I started attended a gymnasium on the West Island, and took part in a game of five-a-sides. The word was soon out that an ex-Manic player was mingling with the locals, and the game eventually turned into a 15-a-side affair. We had players from all walks of life - 19-year-old plumbers to 60-year-old company executives. We'd play for a couple of hours once a week, and then go for a few beers afterwards. Every one of those guys became big Manic fans and attended all the home matches at the Olympic Stadium.

I was solely responsible for coaching the reserve side and scouting for new acquisitions; so, my days were a lot fuller than I had been used to. Much of my time was spent scouting, as so many recommendations came into my office, and I soon realise that only a tiny percentage of these youngsters had the ability required to make it in the game. I had an open-door policy and welcomed letters from amateurs, but I always sought recommendations from college coaches or well-informed journalists before inviting the prospect in for a trial. We were more or less starting from scratch and I did a lot of groundwork in a team of one.

The second-string all bought into my own vision of instilling a hardworking ethos and winning mentality into everything we did. Putting players through their paces at training and getting them fit was one thing, but how could I implement this 'winning mentality' into a young side who had been born into a vastly different soccer environment to the one I was used to?

I explained to the players that I had been brought up this way at Celtic, and that only a win was acceptable when I played there. It didn't matter if you played in an under-14s youth side or the first team - the aim was always the same. They had heard of the Glasgow club's exploits, and I got them to realise that 'the Celtic way' was to accept nothing but the best - and that was to win at all costs. Everything we did was in preparation of winning the next game. I made those boys believe that, not only would they be pushing for the Manic's first-team, but that they could be international-standard players if they worked hard enough. I got a fantastic response.

I had some useful players in that reserve side, including: Elvis Comrie, an England-born 22-year-old striker; Canadian Charlie Falzon (20), who played in midfield; Chris Chueden (21), a Canadian striker who I picked up on a free; Mike Uremovic (30), another free agent who added some experience to our defence. I was able to set up trials at Inter Milan for two of our young Canadians - Mike Findlay and Mimmo Dell'Armi -

and I also sent Elvis Comrie and Greg Kern over to train with Celtic and Leeds United, so I was always looking to develop the players we had, even if this ultimately meant that Montreal could lose them to bigger and more auspicious clubs.

It was amusing to witness the reaction of the boys who had the experience of training with these famous clubs. They were bursting with enthusiasm upon their return, and couldn't wait to get on the training field to show us how much they had improved. They left America as boys and came back as men.

Some of these players had the potential to really make a name for themselves in the game. From this group alone, Comrie became a full American internationalist and Falzon, Chuden and Kern all went on to represent Canada.

Charlie Falzon described me at the time as, "A strict disciplinarian, who emphasizes fitness. We're in better shape than the first team."

When young Elvis Comrie returned from his trial with Celtic, he commented "It's as if I never left Scotland. Andy emphasizes exactly the same things that the Celtic coaches do. He also tries to instil that phenomenal pride in playing the game right."

Roger Samson was right behind me in terms of developing a youth structure at Montreal in the British mould, and a Manic III team was mooted for 1983. My plan was to develop a group of 16-17-year-olds, who would play in Quebec's top amateur league. I then wanted Manic IV, V and VI sides right down to pre-teen kids. Samson commented at the time, "Our eventual goal is to build the club from the ground up, to have our home-grown players come up through the ranks and go into the first team. I want to avoid going elsewhere, especially to Europe, to look for players."

Another layer to this structure was the setting-up of coaching camps for Canadian youngsters, which was something else I implemented. We took on 100 kids for a week's coaching at a time. If they didn't finish the week as potential Manic players then we at least aimed to make them supporters of the club, as they were sent home with club-branded videos, t-shirts and signed footballs.

I sold the entire youth concept to Roger Samson by describing how Celtic developed players back home. I explained that youngsters learned all about the traditions of the club from their early teens, and that the line-up who had just clinched the Scottish Premier League title included eight home-grown players. Samson was immediately sold on the idea.

The General Manager wholeheartedly supported my vision, and he fully expected that our unique structure would allow the Montreal Manic to grow into the most successful team in the North American Soccer League. There was no pressure on me, as Samson boldly proclaimed to the press, "The future of the Manic is in Andy Lynch's hands."

I felt comfortable under such loft aspirations, because I knew that my organised, hard-working, and winning ethics and mentality would bear fruit. Le Manic II won our first 20 matches in-a-row.

"I remember when I first arrived in Philadelphia," I explained to the local *Sunday Express*. "I had never played in North America before, so I didn't know what to expect. But what I saw was unbelievable. They had so many kids with such great potential, with no place to put them all."

My efforts in setting up a youth structure for the Montreal Manic, coupled with my reserve team's exploits on the field, meant that my stock has risen considerably with the Molson Breweries executives. Having led the Manic to the play-offs in two consecutive seasons, Eddie Firmani was sensationally fired on 30th September 1982. Eddie was very much his own man and his demise was said to be due to conflicts with Roger Samson, no doubt over plans to completely restructure the Manic playing pool. I had no time to consider the possible ramifications of this bold decision, because I was appointed the Head Coach of the first-team the following day.

My focus on youth development (as opposed to the purchase of highly paid ready-made imports) had clearly suited the Molson Breweries manifesto for the future of the Montreal Manic. The Molson Chairman, Morgan McCammon, had already sanctioned a deal with the NASL President, Howard Samuels, and the Canadian Soccer Association, that promised to transform Canadian soccer on an international scale.

An announcement was made that Montreal Manic would become 'Team Canada' at the beginning of the 1984 season. The aim was that this would be a team entirely based of Canadians, and we would build a side capable of playing alongside one another at club and international level. The theory was that if the squad could work together on a full-time basis, then the international side (comprising of the same players) would flourish in time for the 1986 World Cup finals in Mexico.

The concept had already been introduced in relation to 'Team America,' who were inaugurated into the NASL for the 1983 season, and I honestly believed that it was a forward-thinking and achievable idea.

In addition to being the Manic's Head Coach (with Romanian, Pierre Mindru, as my assistant), I was also named as Canada's Assistant Coach to national Manager, Tony Waiters, to oversee preparations for the 1986 World Cup. This would ensure that the transition from club to country would be seamless for the squad we would have at Team Canada. Once Team Canada were officially born, I would also take over as Head Coach of the Canadian national side.

"At the moment, we have half-a-dozen big-name foreign players," I explained to Alan Davidson of the *Evening Times*. "They'll be replaced by the cream of Canadians, from the Olympic side right through to the professionals. Everything is being geared towards making a real impact at the next World Cup."

I had gone from being a reserve-team coach to the assistant coach of the Canadian national side in one fell swoop. These were exciting times, and I had to start my preparations immediately. The first thing I did was buy myself an A4 notebook, and I went about listing all the contacts that I thought could assist me in my role. This list included figures whom I felt I might have to call on for advice or recommendations. I listed them in alphabetical order with their accompanying phone numbers and addresses, and pulled together hundreds of names from a lifetime in football. Some of the football men included: Roy Aitken, Tommy Burns, Jim Craig, Frank Connor, Johannes Edvaldsson, Sean Fallon, Bobby Lennox, Danny McGrain, Billy McNeill, Jock Stein and Jock Wallace. There were also a host of American-based contacts on the list such as Tom Fleck, departing boss Eddie Firmani, and Canadian-based Scot, Tony Taylor. Tony helped me out almost immediately by supplying a number of potential trialists, who were added to a short-list at the back of my journal.

Following the Montreal Manic's announcement, some of my other football contacts sent their best wishes via electronic telegram. The first message I received was from the boss of a country who would be Canada's first opponents following my announcement:

"Congratulations on your appointment. I wish you every success, and hope to see you this summer.

"I remember Andy as a regular outside-left with Heart of Midlothian F.C. and when he was transferred to Celtic for $115,000. Injuries held up his progress when he joined the club, and he never regained his progressive play as a forward.

"A move to the defensive role at left full-back seemed to suit him, and he developed into a dependable player who could attack from deep positions. His enthusiasm was a factor in him soon gaining the honour of being made club captain, which was important to a club like Celtic. A senior player with control over other senior professionals, while also having time for the younger players, is essential.

"In my opinion, Andy will be an asset to Le Manic and to soccer, as he always had been as a player."

Jock Stein, Scotland Team Manager.

"I would like to extend a personal welcome to you as you join the coaching ranks. You already have earned a good reputation in the Canadian soccer community as a potentially good coach.

"This is a very good opportunity for yourself and the SCA. I am personally looking forward to working with you. I have gotten to know you in the past few months and am impressed by your enthusiasm and honesty.

"Good luck and, again, welcome to the coaching ranks."

Tony Waiters, Head Coach, Canadian National Soccer Team.

"My heartiest congratulations to Andy Lynch on his appointment as Head Coach of Montreal Manic. He has earned the respect of the Montreal players and the obvious confidence from the club management. Look forward to seeing you both in Montreal and at our magnificent new stadium here in Vancouver.

Best of luck… except against the Whitecaps."

John Giles, Head Coach, Vancouver Whitecaps.

"My congratulations to you on your appointment as Head Coach of the Montreal Soccer Club, and for the association with Canada's National Team. I hope this signals the launching of a long and successful career. I am looking forward to our paths crossing in both characters - The NASL and National Team Associations. Good luck."

Alkis Panagoulias, Head Coach, USA.

Having analysed the squad in preparation for our opening league game against Tampa Bay Rowdies at our own Olympic Stadium on 24th April 1983, I decided that we definitely lacked some much-needed experience throughout the squad.

The difficulty we had in recruiting new players was that we could only offer a one-year deal to non-Canadians, as we had one eye on the transformation to Team Canada.

With this in mind, we lost key players in the shape of Mozambique-born goalkeeper Victor Nogueira; Dutch defender Bob Vosmaer and England cap Gordon Hill, who both signed for Chigaco Sting; Trinidadian defender, Hayden Knight, left for Team America in Washington; Nigerian forward Thompson Usiyan moved to Tulsa Roughnecks; and Irish midfielder Fran O'Brien was the biggest loss when he was sold for $100,000 to Johnny Giles' Vancouver Whitecaps.

We embarked on a pre-season soccer camp to Fiji, and I felt no pressure in making the transition to Head Coach. During my time as reserve team boss, I had been cut-off to a certain degree from the players who had been my ex-team-mates, and so I had no problems in making bold decisions for the good of the squad.

I had a heart-to-heart with England internationalist, Tony Towers, and explained that he would need to improve his performances or find himself a new club. I explained to him that he had not applied himself enough in training, and that it was time for him to move on. Tony reacted splendidly, and attacked the training as if he was a young pro again. I could see him getting fitter and hungrier by the day, and I ended up keeping him as my captain for my sole season in charge.

In the absence of Fran O'Brien, I expected big things from Belfast boy Brian Quinn. Brian was a midfielder who started off at Everton before moving Stateside. He was forever asking about my memories of Celtic, and he had a cheeky charm that I instantly warmed to. Instead of calling me "gaffer," he would often call me "Kipper," knowing that to have been my nickname at Celtic Park. He was one of only a few players who would get away with that because he was such a likeable guy. He became a hugely important player for us, and I told him that he had all the attributes to be a future captain. Brian went on to play almost 50 games for the American national side, and captained them on a number of occasions.

John McGrane was a Scottish / Canadian defender, whom I urged to be more offensive in the coming season. I wanted him to overlap in the best traditions of Celtic Football Club, as I explained at the time to The Gazette, "I know that the players all appreciate what we're attempting to do in an attacking sense. It's a good feeling to play this style of soccer. It's what the fans want too, isn't it? I mean, they're paying their money."

I demanded a big performance throughout the campaign from our veteran Yugoslavian international Dragan Vujovic. He had all the attributes to be a top-class player but his fitness and temperament hadn't been up to scratch. I worked on that with him because I knew how valuable he could be for us, especially in a partnership with top-scorer Alan Willey. At 6'1", the ex-Titograd striker had scored 20 goals in 58 games over two season, but was suspended for the previous campaign's play-offs after spitting on an official.

"I don't know if there is anyone better in one-on-one situations," I explained during pre-season. My musings were to be prophetic by the time the play-offs came around. "He's going to pull fans right out of the stands. He can frustrate the other team to death. Actually, sometimes he frustrates me to death too."

Even with the Team Canada transformation looming large, I did get a tip-off from a Scottish journalist about the availability of an overseas player whom I would still have signed in a heart-beat. Alan Davidson of the *Evening Times* explained that my ex-team mate Kenny Dalglish had stalled on signing a new contract at Liverpool, and that he may become available.

I spoke with Roger Samson, and explained that we should try and get Kenny over to Montreal during the English pre-season. The General Manager loved the idea and the club were more than prepared to bring the Scotland legend and the rest of his family over for six to eight weeks. We would pick up his wages, and his family could enjoy a relaxing holiday.

With everything agreed at our end, I contacted Kenny and pitched him my offer. Unfortunately for us (and the rest of the NASL), negotiations with Liverpool had taken a turn for the better and he was close to re-signing for the Anfield side. "It would have been difficult having to call you gaffer anyway, Kipper," came Kenny's typical parting comment.

I am certain his arrival would have captured the imagination of the supporters more than the two Scotsmen we did manage to bring in from the Golden Bay Earthquakes. Mike Hewitt was a 33-year-old Dundonian goalkeeper, and Gerry Gray was tough little Glasgow-born midfielder. Algerian international goalkeeper, Medhi Cerbah, was also brought in for a trial. My assistant (who was an ex-Romanian international goalie) raved about him, but I saw enough in one training session to know that he simply didn't have the height required for the NASL.

Regardless of what I did in the transfer market, we had lost the confidence of our previously vast fan base following Molson Breweries' premature announcement that they had offered its two-year-old NASL franchise to the Canadian Soccer Association (CSA). I felt that they had been hasty in announcing the deal before the Manic's final term, and our season-ticket sales dropped by more than 50% compared to the figures of 1982.

Despite having attracted average crowds of around 22,000 for two seasons in succession, the balance sheets didn't fill Molson Breweries with confidence and the company lost $2.7 million in 1982 alone.

Team Canada became a distraction to my squad, and it frustrated me at the time: "It's a brave man or a foolish one who can speculate about the future and neglects something more important right now. I refuse to be interested in Team Canada now.

"All my efforts are being concentrated on this season. It's important to us and I really believe we can do well. I'm not willing to risk what we want to do by being preoccupied thinking about Team Canada. And I'm not willing to risk the obligation I've made to the foreign players for this season, those guys who won't be around after the season. They're going to play for me and I've got to give them my maximum effort. They will not have the feeling that somebody is overlooking them and doesn't care."

Quick to smell blood, a new Canadian Professional Soccer League side was formed and bankrolled by Labbatt Brewery in an effort to prise away our legions of fans. They targeted the large Italian fan base that had hitherto supported the Manic, and even went as far as calling themselves Inter Montreal in a nod to the Milanese club. Furthermore, they appointed an ex-Inter Milan player as their Head Coach. You've guessed it - Eddie Firmani!

I was unconcerned with these developments, as I had enough to contend with on my own doorstep. "We want to make the play-offs," I explained. "We want to play entertaining soccer. I think the fans will enjoy this new team that I'm building."

When it came around, we defeated the Rowdies 3-1 in front of our smallest opening day crowd in the club's three-year history. We sold just 6,460 tickets, which was dwarfed by the 22,697 who came out to see our 1982 opener. This was a drastic decline, and time would tell that it would be the decimation of attendances which ultimately caused the entire league to collapse.

With season-ticket sales and attendances at an all-time low, the Team Canada backlash, the upsurge in support for Inter Montreal, and the loss of most of our biggest names, the Manic owners made a panic buy. There was no doubt that the purchase of 26-year-old French internationalist midfielder, Jean-Francois Larios, was aimed at garnering support from the French-speaking Montreal natives. The motivation to sign the player was all totally fine by me, as long the guy could play.

Larios had been a top player for Saint-Etienne and had been part of France's 1982 World Cup squad. His international career stalled after a much-publicised fall-out with Michel Platini, but on first glance this silky footballer may well have been an inspired signing.

He looked the part: 6'3" tall, dark flowing locks, superstar looks, an omnipresent cigarette perched on his bottom lip. There was just one small detail that concerned me gravely from day one. Larios displayed a distinct limp, as he was recovering from a serious knee operation that had prevented him from making a single appearance for former club Atletico Madrid.

He hobbled out for the first day of training, and I thought, "No chance." But we had already signed him on a $150,000 five-month contract, which made him the highest-paid player in the club's history. He certainly had a great track record, but I needed players to shed blood, sweat and tears for the Manic, and I knew I wasn't about to get that from this cult French icon.

I could see that he was an outstanding footballer with the ball at his feet. He actually scored on his NASL debut in a resounding 6-1 win against the San Diego Sockers. He had incredible vision and passing ability but I couldn't get him fully fit, and actually felt sorry for him in the end because he needed to rest his knee. Larios disappeared to Neuchatel Xamax of Switzerland as quickly as he had arrived, and thereafter played on for another five years in the French leagues. Suffice to say, the Larios experiment failed to draw in the crowds.

I decided instead to bring in young Elvis Comrie, a promising player whom I had worked closely with in the reserves for an entire season. Elvis repaid me almost immediately, as we enjoyed an impressive 4-1 victory against the Tulsa Roughnecks on 11th May 1983. I was thrilled that he had made the step-up, as that had allowed us to enjoy the fruits of our labour from the Manic II concept. Meanwhile, the Team Canada continued to be a white elephant in the room. Our attendances faltered, with the lowest crowd in our history (5,280) showing up to witness our resounding victory against Tulsa.

Keen to re-ignite interest in the Manic, an international exhibition match was arranged against English First Division side Nottingham Forest at the Olympic Stadium on 27th May 1983. This was the first and last time I had an opportunity to meet with Forest's legendary manager, Brian Clough. It's a meeting I am unlikely to ever forget.

Ian Wallace was a prolific Scottish striker, who had been an instant success after signing for the East Midlands club from Coventry City for over £1 million in 1980. The ex-Dumbarton forward was out of favour by the time of our friendly, and I asked him the day before our encounter if he fancied coming to play in the NASL for a few months to get him some much-needed game time.

This would be much the same as the deal we had made to Kenny Dalglish, whereby Montreal would pick up Ian's wages, and fly his family over for the duration of his stay. The striker was keen, but he made it clear that his manager would want to make something from the transaction.

On the day of the match, I finally met with Brian Clough, and described the proposal we had for Ian Wallace. After I had explained how this would benefit his player in getting him back to full sharpness for the season ahead, Clough responded, "Yes, but what's the deal?" I hesitated for a moment, in case I had missed something, and then explained the proposal at length again. "Yes, but what's the deal?" came his identical response. The penny dropped.

I left the two-time European Cup-winning manager without an answer to his deliberately ambiguous question, and rejoined my team to prepare for the game, which we lost 4-3.

After the match, I discussed the matter with Roger Samson, who asked if this was the normal way to conduct transfer deals in Britain. "Should we give him what he wants?" asked Roger rather naively. "No. We won't get involved in deals like that," came my instant retort.

Ian Wallace later approached me before Forest left the Olympic Stadium. "Well, was I right about Cloughie?" he asked. "I'm afraid so, wee man. It's a pity because it would have been a good move for everyone concerned." And it would have been, but not on those terms.

By the time that Canada's three-game international soccer series against Scotland arrived in June, my Manic side had won four league games and lost an alarming nine. Although our forward, Dale Mitchell, and midfielder, Gerry Gray, played against my home country, my main focus was on turning around Montreal's fortunes.

The matches came at a bad time for me, as we were midway through a league campaign, but I met up with my old boss Jock Stein during the international series and, although he wasn't a man for showing it, I could tell that he was impressed with what I had achieved so far in my coaching career. I was now a manager in my own right, he was still the "Boss."

Once the distraction of the international matches was out of the way, I went about trying to shore up our sieve-like defence. It concerned me that we were liable to collapse when things weren't going our way. New York Cosmos had destroyed us 6-0, and Golden Bay Earthquakes embarrassed us 7-1 in games on the road much to my chagrin. When asked by the baying press pack about the latter result, I described our defence as "diabolical."

Some quarters of the media were quick to jump on the Inter versus Manic off-the-field battle of Montreal, which they also believed we were losing by a landslide. Inter had gone out and purchased ex-Manic stars Gordon Hill and Bob Vosmaer, as well as Mimmo Dell-Arme in a further effort to rub salt in our wounds.

However, by July of 1983, our Inter counterparts folded for financial reasons amidst concerns that the Canadian Professional Soccer League would quickly go the same way. They lasted just eight games, and had banked on attracting an average crowd of 10,000 to break even. By the time that Inter Montreal closed their gates for the final time, they had failed to average even half that figure.

The press had attempted to create a circus out of the rivalry between the two Montreal soccer sides, but it was a minor sideshow as far as I was concerned. My entire focus had always been on our NASL season, and achieving a play-off spot.

My protégé, Elvis Comrie continued to impress, and I was thrilled to see one of my Manic II kids making the grade, as he scored 10 goals in the first half of our league season to become top-goalscorer. "I owe Andy Lynch a lot," explained Elvis to *The Gazette*. "Every time I set foot on the field I owe it to him, and to myself, to give my best. He's kept me in line. He doesn't always have to say anything to me. Sometimes during a game I just look towards the bench, see him, and I know what I have to do."

Remarkably, our first win on the road came four months into the league season, where a 55th minute Dragan Vujovic penalty was enough to defeat the Vancouver Whitecaps - Fran O'Brien and all - by a single goal. The victory was played out to the second largest crowd in the Whitecaps' history, but many of the 56,255 fans were undoubtedly there to see another post-match Beach Boys show.

The performance of North Vancouver referee David Roach was disgraceful, as he unfairly sent off three of our players (Tony Towers, Gerry Gray and Frantz Mathieu). Thankfully I was able to display a level of restraint when speaking to the American Sun after the match, "The referee was a disaster," I explained. "The fact that he's an official from Vancouver is a disaster in itself. It's the kind of thing that makes the league look like a joke. When is this league going to get some competent officials?"

I went one further when we played Chicago Sting in Montreal. With just 11 minutes left to play, and with us 2-1 up, I instructed my players to leave the field in protest of the poor refereeing decisions of Bob Evans. The ref awarded back-to-back penalties to the Sting and both were missed. I got the feeling that he was going to get them to retake the penalty until they scored, and so I took drastic action. It was only the second time in the 16-year history of the NASL that a game had been abandoned!

Thankfully, the next time we faced the Chicago Sting, I didn't force the match to be abandoned. Despite all of our early-season problems, I knew that in time we would get stronger, and an impressive final-day 4-0 defeat of the Sting secured us a place in the play-offs against Soccer Bowl holders, the New York Cosmos. "To put it honestly, nobody wants to play them," I admitted on the eve of our first game of the best-of-three quarter-final series at Giants Stadium. "A few weeks ago, I wouldn't have fancied our chances against them. Now, you never know what can happen."

The team spirit that we managed to build throughout such a tricky season saw us rendered fearless in the changing room of the Giants Stadium as we prepared for the play-off series opener. I had largely invested my trust in the players I had at my disposal at the beginning of the Manic's final campaign, and they paid me back ten-fold. We went on to shock the American sporting world with an emphatic 4-2 defeat of the mighty New York Cosmos.

We refused to buckle after going behind to a 40th minute Giorgio

Chinaglia opener, and went in at the break level thanks to a Tony Towers equaliser. Tony had been on his way out of the club altogether, but he had shown a fantastic attitude in getting back to his best after I advised him of my intentions to ship him out at the beginning of the season.

Brian Quinn had enjoyed a magnificent season after emerging from Fran O'Brien's shadow, and he scored a brace for us on this most memorable of evenings. The reliable and prolific Alan Willey also got on the score-sheet, and Eddie Gettemeier saved a Chinaglia penalty before Yugoslavian international midfielder, Vladislav Bogicevic, scored a consolation goal with five minutes remaining (the former Red Star Belgrade star had played against Celtic during our 1977 Australian tour, and he was a fantastic player).

"Every man on the field had the game of his life," I declared after the historical victory. "It was as if 11 players had become one. To be blunt about it, the Cosmos were shell-shocked.

"They'll throw everything they've got at us next time (in Montreal), and if the slightest degree of complacency takes hold of our team, we've had it. I look at this period as half-time because we don't want to go back there. I think by winning that game, we've taken a big step into the final."

The first game of the play-off series must rate as the second best 4-2 victory I have ever enjoyed in my football career. I wasn't being coy in my post-match interview however, as we still had a huge battle on our hands in the home leg on 12th September 1983.

As the game ended scoreless after extra time, we went into the shoot-out in front of a season-high of 20,726 - the Montreal faithful had returned to their first love, for one night at least.

We were tied 2-2 with the Cosmos after five kicks each, and so we entered sudden death. Giorgio Chinaglia, Franz Beckenbauer, Vladislav Bogicevic and Roberto Cabanas had all missed their attempts and now all we needed was one goal. I turned around to big Dragan Vuyovic, who was lying on the pitch with his socks rolled down and the laces of his boots undone. I knew he was exhausted but sometimes he had to have his ego massaged to get him moving.

"What are you doing with your boots off?" I asked Dragan impatiently.

"Coach," he groaned. "I can't do this. I need to recover. Leave me here."

"Tie your laces Dragan, you're up next," I ordered. And then I crouched down to have a word in his ear, and put my arm around his shoulder. "Get on your feet Dragan. You're the best player on this pitch, and that's why I've kept you for sudden death."

Dragan looked up at me, as the floodlights glistened in his eyes, "Shall I shoot or go round the 'keeper coach?"

"Just do what you do, Dragan," came my reply.

The referee's whistle sounds, and Dragan jogs with the ball from the 30-yard line. His socks are at his ankles, and he looks to be in no hurry.

"GET A MOVE ON, DRAGAN!" I'm screaming from the touchline to the big Yugoslav, as I wonder what on earth he's playing at.

He's moving in towards the goal almost in slow motion, as I look up at the countdown clock to see it strike the three second mark.

"MOOOOOOOOOOOOOOVE!" I scream, and I can barely contain myself as he finally takes the ball wide and directs a shot at goal...

Four seconds... The shot is on target and beats goalkeeper, Hubert Birkenmeir.

Five seconds... The ball is in the net.

You only get five seconds to score, and the capacity crowd has already erupted. I knew that the time was up before the ball crossed the line so I made a beeline to the fourth official on the touchline. The New York bench were also on their way to bend the young Italian official's ear so I quickly leant in and whispered, "Just listen. Listen to the crowd. If you disallow that goal there will be riots in this stadium tonight, and that will be on your head. The Cosmos' bench are on their way over, and will try to convince you otherwise, but don't disallow that goal."

At that point, the New York Cosmos' officials tried to shove me aside, and were all gesturing and shouting in the face of the referee's assistant, who ushered them all away. The goal stood.

The New York News reported: "At least one official was looking ominously at his watch. But before anybody could suggest nullifying the goal, Lynch was leading his players - and hundreds of fans - onto the field in a victory dance."

"A dynasty died last night at Olympic Stadium," proclaimed Ike Kuhns of the *Newark Star Ledger* the following day. "The Cosmos, rulers of the North American Soccer League for most of the past seven years, were eliminated from the 1983 playoffs by the Montreal Manic in a shootout, 1-0.

"Referee Peter Johnson at first signalled no score, but when the Manic players and some of the crowd of 20,726 rushed on to the filed to celebrate, the officials were intimidated into allowing the goal to stand."

The Cosmos' made an official protest against the winning shoot-out goal, and claimed that the ball crossed the line after the allotted five seconds ran out. NASL's Commissioner, Howard Samuels, reviewed the match tapes and ruled that the goal should stand, as it could have been scored "anywhere between 4.9 and 5.1 seconds."

The New York Cosmos had been the pride of the NASL but they released a scathing statement which questioned the credibility of the league. The great Giorgio Chinaglia retired from the game after our victory, and Franz Beckenbauer hinted that he may have played his final match for the Cosmos, "It would be a big disappointment if Warner Communications gave up the team. The Cosmos still have a good name in the world game. It would be a big disappointment for the whole soccer world and the NASL, but I don't think they will give it up."

Warner Brothers had reportedly become budget-conscious due to the recent dwindling attendances. Their own season ticket sales had peaked at 20,000 in 1979 but dropped to around half of that figure for the 1983 season in what the *New York News* called, "The post-Pele depression."

With eight Canadians in my starting line-up, I had managed to mastermind the Cosmos' earliest elimination from the play-offs since 1976. The Cosmos' dynasty was crumbling, and the infighting that began in the aftermath of our most unexpected victory created tremors throughout the already-fragile NASL that would shake the league to its very core.

Following the greatest upset in NASL history, *Montreal Gazette* journalist Tim Burke made the following comparison, "Lynch is emerging as the best motivator in Montreal since Toe Blake..."

In Canadian circles, Toe Blake is akin to sporting royalty on account of his coaching exploits in the National Hockey League; so, such lofty claims were high praise indeed for a relative newcomer.

We still had a semi-final to play, and I looked to push the underdog boundaries even further towards a Soccer Bowl victory for Montreal in the next round.

Against all the odds, my unfashionable side had scaled the heights and toppled the giants of the North American Soccer League. However, within a matter of weeks my American dream would all be over...

CHAPTER SIXTEEN
PARADISE REVISITED

The heights we scaled by defeating the mighty Cosmos in a shoot-out in the Soccer Bowl play-offs were going to be tough to beat. The shock victory was undoubtedly the peak of Montreal Manic's short existence, and it was going to take a huge effort to top it in the next knock-out round.

We faced the Tulsa Roughnecks in the semi-final, virtue of their quarter-final defeat of the Vancouver Whitecaps. The Whitecaps' publicist Jack Leonard (seething at his side's inability to progress closer to the Soccer Bowl final in their home-town) described our two victories against the Cosmos, and appearance in the semis, as "Incomprehensible."

It was a classic underdog story, and some quarters of the press even dared to question whether Molson Breweries would ditch plans to convert the Manic into Team Canada after all. Success had given birth to uncertainty, as no-one expected us to do so well. However the owners would be more concerned with the state of the season's balance sheet, which had plummeted to $4 million in the red.

Another shoot-out decided our fate in the first game of our best-of-three in front of 10,625 at Tulsa's Skelly Stadium. The pendulum swung in favour of our opponents on that occasion however, as we succumbed to a 2-1 defeat. Going into the home leg, I was still confident that we could overcome Tulsa on our own patch to set up a third match. Although we managed to draw the series level by winning 1-0, it was clear that we had already enjoyed our moment in the limelight, as we went down to the eventual winners of the 1983 Soccer Bowl by a convincing scoreline of 3-1 in the final match.

It was a round too far after our remarkable achievements against the New York Cosmos, but I was still hugely proud of my group of players. They had faced uncertainty and adversity throughout the season (ever since Molson Breweries announced their decision to fold the franchise to replace it with Team Canada) but we were still one game away from the Soccer Bowl final. Despite all the behind-the-scenes politics and drama, I was far more interested in the eleven players on the field of play. Their performances in turning things around in the second half of our league campaign filled me with confidence for the season ahead.

My rise in the NASL had been nothing short of meteoric. I had quickly gone from being a player in 1980, to coaching the Manic's reserve side two years later. My appointment as the head coach at the Olympic Stadium the following season felt like a natural progression, and my assistant coach role with the Canadian national side was a yet another feather in my cap.

Moe Sperber was a regular writer for the local sports-pages, and I got to know him pretty well during my three years playing and coaching in the NASL. In the aftermath of the phenomenal Cosmos victory, Moe had spoken to some of his contacts at the New York press, and they were of the opinion that the Cosmos were planning a move to prise me away from Montreal. That was the way the New Yorkers worked - They would back their champ until he was knocked out, and then they'd get behind the guy who took their crown. That man seemed to be me.

It is always flattering to hear of such interest, but I didn't have too much time to consider life in the Big Apple because the NASL announced that it was going to fold due to mounting debts (which had topped more than $25 million in 1983 alone).

Crowds had began to dip across the board following the retirement of Pele, and the TV deal with ABC was withdrawn in 1982. Despite this plunge in popularity, the New York Cosmos had remained as the jewel in the NASL's crown following the Brazilian legend's departure.

After Montreal had unceremoniously knocked the seemingly untouchable superstars out of the 1983 Soccer Bowl however, the crown had become one encrusted with thorns, as executives of the club's owners, Warner Brothers, and heads of the NASL came to very public blows. Many journalists theorised that the final nail in the league's coffin was hammered in when the countdown clock struck at around 5.1

seconds of the shoot-out to spell defeat against the hugely unfancied Montreal Manic.

Molson Breweries were a loyal corporation, and Roger Samson called me into his office to explain where the collapse of the NASL would leave me in the great scheme of things. He described a scenario whereby the indoor leagues would continue, but he didn't think the outdoor league would be restructured for another year. The Team Canada project was immediately scrapped; and Montreal Manic were dissolved.

"But we will be back, bigger and better!" came Roger's war cry, and I admired his positivity and enthusiasm. In the meantime, Molson Breweries offered me a job as their Sports Director, and they proposed that they moved me and my family to Toronto, where the children could attend English-speaking schools.

It was a good offer, and Tulsa Roughnecks had also given me an opportunity of a coaching position with their indoor team. After discussing the situation at length with my wife however, we decided to return to Scotland; I felt confident that I could progress with my coaching career once I got home.

The transition from Montreal to Glasgow would not have been too difficult for the children. They had already adapted to life in Philadelphia and Montreal, and they would be able to reintegrate into the schools system easily enough.

From a personal perspective, I felt that I had gained enough experience during my NASL coaching career that I would be able to return to the Scottish game in the dug-out. The response I was to receive from the Scottish football fraternity upon my return home however, would shock and disappoint me in equal measures.

Local sportswriter, Tim Burke, wrote my NASL football obituary: "Andy Lynch, the tough Glaswegian who came to the Manic in 1981 after serving as the grizzled defender-captain of the Glasgow Celtic, has returned to his hometown with his wife and four young children. Not much, if anything, was made of his departure. But few athletes who have ever come to this city acquitted themselves more honourably than Andy Lynch. In fact, I'd put the same stripe on him as I would on Toe Blake. Lynch was a tremendous soccer player and teacher, and an even more wonderful human being.

"When he took over a lame-duck team last season, nobody gave him or his remnants a hope of doing a thing in 1983. Yet the Manic somehow managed to squeeze into the play-offs. And then, thanks to the never-say-die outlook of Coach Lynch, they knocked off the talent-laden New York Cosmos in two straight. That was the great sports achievement of the year in Montreal. Lang may yir lum reek, Andy Lynch!"

***

"One of the most respected coaches on the crumbling North American soccer circuit is currently up for grabs in Scotland," wrote Jim Blair in the *Daily Record* upon my return to Glasgow. I threw down my own marker by proclaiming, "I've spent the last four years improving my knowledge of the game, and now feel confident and experienced enough to get into management."

I had maintained links with a few trusted Scottish journalists while I was over in North America, and used to provide Alan Davidson with a weekly feature called 'Andy Lynch in America' for the *Evening Times*. In turn, Alan was able to fill me in with developments at Celtic Park and within Scottish football in general. During one of our conversations, my trusted journalist urged me to apply for the Celtic job when Billy McNeill left the hot-seat for the first time in 1983. Alan's thinking was that I was in the correct mould for the Celtic board, as they had appointed ex-captains as managers with Jock Stein and the aforementioned Billy. I could see his point, as I had extensive knowledge of the Scottish game and the club. I had also gathered an unbelievable amount of experience in America and Canada, and had coached players from all over the world. The game was changing in Europe, and overseas players would soon become the norm in Britain. I already knew how to deal with a multi-cultural changing-room. I decided that I'd throw my hat in the ring.

By that point, I had been coaching for two seasons, and had a track record of developing youth players in the best traditions of Celtic Football Club. I also had international coaching experience, and was keen to embark on a management career in Scottish football. However, my gut feeling was that the Celtic job had come too early for me. Ideally I would have gained further experience elsewhere before taking on a position of such magnitude.

Desmond White was still the Chairman, so I called him up directly and advised him that I would be interested in the Celtic job. I explained briefly about the coaching role I had at that time, and Desmond thanked me for my call. I left him with my contact details, but it was the last time I ever spoke to him.

In my final season in Montreal, I was as fit as the players I was coaching. My preparation and diet had been completely transformed, so by the time I returned to Scotland as a 32-year-old, I felt in even better condition than I had been in when I left. I had long-since fully recovered from my illness, and genuinely felt that I could have played for another five years. However, I had the coaching bug and had progressed as a trainer and motivator season-on-season. All I needed now was to get myself back on the Scottish football ladder, and then I could build up my reputation like I had done in North America.

Jock Stein and I had spoken in the summer during Scotland's trip to play Canada, and so I decided to give him a call, and we agreed to get a catch up at the pub he owned at that time. As we sat down for a coffee, I explained my predicament to Jock. Without hesitation, my ex-gaffer said to me, "Andy, there are three Scottish First Division clubs looking for a manager at the moment. You won't get an interview for two of them, and you are unlikely to get an interview for the third one... This has nothing to do with your capabilities as a coach, but you'll be struggling to get a job in Scottish football where you come from..."

My mind raced back to my discussion with Jim Craig, where he was of the same opinion as our ex-manager about our job prospects in the Scottish game. I had returned to my home country having gained an outstanding coaching education. My achievements had made global news after I managed to develop and transform an infant and unfashionable club into a side that toppled a North American empire. The methods and techniques I had honed could be introduced into the Scottish game for the benefit of youth development, yet I was being told that I wasn't wanted.

I came crashing back down to earth. Were these prejudices still at large in Scottish football? Two Lisbon Lions had now told me they were, and I felt a sense of anger at this realisation. I wasn't angry at Jock Stein, who had been brutally honest. If anyone knew how the Scottish game worked then the national manager would. I was in a state of shell-shock as I thanked Jock for all his advice and made my way home. It was clear that I had a lot to consider.

My experiences told me that this prejudicial attitude wasn't just a problem in Scottish football, but in other areas of our society as well. My father had disclosed to me that he would never have progressed beyond the rank of Detective Sergeant in the Glasgow Police service due to his religion. He was told as much by colleagues who were progressing through the ranks, and rising through their associated pay-scales. If my background was going to hold me back in the country of my birth, then where would I go?

The less-than auspicious East Stirlinghshire were on the look-out for a new manager. I decided that I would start at the very bottom of the Scottish football ladder and build my way up. My CV was sent to the Scottish League Division Two side, and I was invited to attend an interview. This took place in a Stirling hotel, where the club had booked a bedroom for the day. Each of the candidates were taken into this room for their interview, and were thereafter sent on their merry way. As I waited, I spoke to a few of the others who were also there for an interview. One of them remarked that they ought to go home, as it would be no contest with me being there, and I would definitely get the job.

When my allocated slot arrived, I went into the bedroom and was offered a cup of tea. The East Stirlingshire Directors sat on the hotel room bed and asked me a number of questions. I explained how I had taken a brand new club to the brink of a major success with very little resources. I described how I had placed a huge emphasis on local talent, and that I had been able to develop them through hard work and instilling a winning mentality. I finished by telling the Directors that I fully believed I could implement all of these developments with their club. They shook my hand and thanked me for my time.

When the letter arrived from East Stirlingshire Football Club (who had finished second bottom of the Scottish football pyramid the previous season), I was told that I was "over-qualified for the position."

Receiving that letter of refusal was a pivotal moment in my football career. It all but ended any aspirations I ever had of coaching a professional club in Scotland again. I was completely disillusioned and disappointed in the game I had dedicated my life to. I seriously contemplated moving back to North America - the land of opportunity.

As the doors of Scottish football were slammed shut in my face, the doors of a local saloon were opened, and I was welcomed inside its dated interior. Not for a drink of condolence though, but to run my own business. I had a young family to support, and so I decided to get my entrepreneurial hat on and embark on a new career.

★★★

Many footballers moved into the pub game after their careers were over. It's hard work, but could be fulfilling if you were able to make the distinction between business and pleasure, and many Scottish footballers were unable to do that.

'Andy Lynch's Bar' was in Finnieston and I threw myself into my new venture to make a real go of it. I remember one afternoon not long after I had taken over, Jim Baxter came in for a drink. This was the man who had mesmerised me as a child at Ibrox many years before. Once a genius of the football field, Jim was now an ex-footballer who certainly enjoyed a wee refreshment.

"How are you doing, Andy?" asked this legend of Scottish football. "I heard you had taken over here, so I thought I'd pop in to see how you were."

"I'm glad you did, Jim," I answered truthfully. "What are you having?"

"Naw, naw, Andy," replied Jim in his broad Fife accent. "I didn't come in here for a free drink."

"This is your first drink in my pub," I insisted. "And I'm going to buy it for you, Jim."

I poured him a Bicardi and Coke, and he sat at the bar alone. He was very keen to stress that he hadn't come into the pub for free drink, and he genuinely meant that, but I wanted to be hospitable.

It was early afternoon, and there were only three other guys in the pub having a drink. A Celtic fan was doing a crossword, a Rangers fan was reading a book, and the third punter (who was a regular but wasn't into football) came over to Jim, who was still standing at the bar.

"Another pint Andy, and one for Jim," the regular ordered.

"That's very kind of you pal, but I'm fine just now. Thank you though," big Jim was trying his damnedest not to take advantage of the free booze.

"Listen Jim, I'm not even into football. But it would give me great pleasure to buy you a drink. Imagine what all the boys at the work will say tomorrow if I tell them I've bought the great Jim Baxter a drink," the regular was determined to claim his little bit of fame.

"Thank you. I'll have a Bicardi and Coke please," conceded Jim, who clearly didn't want to disappoint his fellow drinker.

Then the Celtic fan came up to the bar...

"Get this man a drink, Andy," came the predictable request.

"Naw, naw..."

"Jim, you're a wee bit different from the typical Rangers' players," the Celtic fan interjected. "You're alright, and I want to buy you a drink."

"Can you put this one on the till, Andy?" asked the former Ibrox maverick, as I poured the Celtic fan his pint.

Now, that was before the Rangers fan had gone to the bar for a top-up, and there would be no doubt that he would buy Jim his fourth drink of the afternoon. In that short space of time, I realised how difficult it must have been for someone like Jim Baxter. He didn't come into my boozer for free drink. However, every pub he went into in Glasgow would have played out the same sequence of events.

He tried his utmost to refuse those drinks, but the public in all their glory insisted that he take them. They may even have felt aggrieved if Jim hadn't taken their offer of more alcohol. I'm not blaming the public for Jim's demise, but it must have been difficult for him when his demons wanted the alcohol and his softer nature couldn't refuse his adoring public.

I made a go of it in the licensed trade, and ran two pubs over the space of a decade. When I took over my second bar - 'The Riverside Tavern' in the

Gorbals - the great Joe McBride paid me a visit. We were both ex-Celts from Govan who were now in the same business, as Joe owned a pub near Shawfield Stadium on Rutherglen Road. He came around to see how I was getting on, and to reassure me that if I got any kind of trouble then I just had to lift the phone to him. He knew the kind of aggravation that could arrive at a publicans door, and he assured me that he knew the right people to sort it out. "We're footballers, Andy," Joe reminded me. "Not boxers."

It was reassuring that I had the support there if I needed it (and thankfully I didn't), but I had bought my pubs wisely, taking care to purchase them in Celtic-friendly areas. Big Johannes Edvaldsson wasn't as careful with his geography.

Shuggie bought a pub in Bridgeton Cross, which must be the area most densely populated with Rangers fans in Scotland. I asked my ex-team mate what an earth he was thinking, to which he replied, "I knew the pub was on the market, so went to check it out with a friend of mine. When I was inside, I heard all the punters singing about King Billy, and I thought they meant Billy McNeill!" Something, somewhere had clearly been lost in translation...

Running my own business gave me a great sense of satisfaction, but my undying passion was undoubtedly still in coaching and developing players. I was delighted therefore to be invited by Alf Galustian and Charlie Cooke to participate as an international guest coach at the Lake Placid Summer Soccer Camp in America.

★★★

Wiel Coerver had been a hugely influential Dutch Coach, who won the UEFA Cup with Feyenoord in 1974. He revolutionised individual skills development coaching techniques, which were picked up on by Alf and Charlie.

With Wiel's blessing, Coerver Coaching Courses were born in 1984, and over a million kids from all over the world have since attended these camps.

They had a stunning setting and magnificent facilities over in Lake Placid, where they rented a residential school which housed hundreds of kids at any one time, and my participation allowed me to continue coaching on an annual basis. I would spend between four to six weeks at Lake Placid, and I was even able to take my own kids out there to participate.

Alf Galustian had played professionally in his earlier days, but Scotsman Charlie Cooke had been one of the best players I had ever seen. He had starred as a winger for Dundee and Aberdeen in the 1960s before a big-money move to Chelsea. By the time that I played against Charlie, he was the 38-year-old player / coach of the Memphis Rogues, but he was still an incredible talent even then. I remember telling my team to shut down the coach if he made an appearance from the subs' bench, and they all looked at me as if to say, "That old guy?" Well, Charlie did come off the bench that day and orchestrated the pace of the game with a fabulous range of passing and movement that had the crowd in raptures of applause.

Alf was able to commercialise Wiel Coerver's concept, and put the coaching school on the world soccer map. Wiel would attend the courses, and I got the opportunity to meet him on a number of occasions.

The drills and techniques were all skills-based, and so Charlie was a great exponent of the methods. He would even devise his own drills and tweak some of the techniques. The cynics would claim that players would not be able to utilise the Coerver techniques during a game, but I would argue that this type of training was improving players' control, balance, dribbling ability and turning capabilities. Therefore their overall game was bound to improve.

Everything was done with a ball at your feet, which may sound obvious. However, a lot of professional football training was still geared towards physical conditioning, and Coerver was all about improving skills. About 20 years before these camps were set up, a similar mentality was introduced to Celtic Park by a coach who went on to achieve a thing or two in the game - Jock Stein.

Another of the guest coaches, whom I was privileged to spend some quality time with, was the legendary Sir Stanley Matthews. Stanley was 70 years-of-age when I met him at Lake Placid, and he had been a real football revolutionary throughout a lengthy career. I loved his company, and learned about some of his methods, and he explained that he fasted for 24 hours once a week. During that one day he would only drink water, and he explained that the process revitalised his body. He had always been very careful about what he ate, and he never drank alcohol or smoked. He had great foresight, and worked a lot of things out for himself in terms of fitness and nutrition at a time when there was far less focus on it in professional football. He explained that he used to go running on Blackpool's sands to strengthen his legs, and I instantly thought of Jock Wallace, who put us through our paces at Gullane Sands, and Bobby Lennox, who did the same in Saltcoats.

By the time that I met Stanley, he was still a fit and healthy man. He was a gentleman, who enjoyed a laugh like the rest of us, and I found him fascinating. I asked him if he had any regrets about his football career and he replied instantly that he stopped playing too soon. I thought he was kidding, because he had famously played until he was 50 years-of-age, but he was deadly serious and regretted not playing for even longer. He was very sincere and spoke highly of Scottish footballers, and stated that he had played with and against some "world class Jocks" in his time in English football. He had also spent a lot of time coaching in Africa and prophesised that the African nations would go on to regularly produce some incredible footballers.

I remember one year, John Motson came out with the BBC to film a Sir Stanley Matthews documentary, and they set up a mock football game involving Stanley, the other coaches, and some of the kids at the camp. I could see the undoubted ability that Stanley had, even at that age, as he dribbled around for the cameras.

Later on, once the cameras stopped rolling, we were sitting on a grassy verge on Lake Placid chatting away when Stanley started rubbing his knee. He explained that he had undergone surgery to have his cartilage removed five weeks previously. "I'm not 100% fit yet, Andy," explained this English icon. "You probably seen that during the game. I'm working the muscles every day, and I think I'll be back to full fitness in four or five weeks." At the age of 70, Sir Stanley Matthews was still analysing his performance in a bounce match with kids, and planning his return to full fitness. No wonder he was the greatest ever player in English footballing history.

The Coerver Coaching was thoroughly enjoyable, and I was delighted to be involved in helping to develop youngsters who had the same dreams and aspirations that I'd had as a kid. My coaching career would never truly continue in Britain (other than a fleeting appearance as Assistant Manager at Albion Rovers in the early 90s), but I did go on to experiment with soccer schools of my own in Scotland.

The Albion Rovers job came about at a time when another former Celtic left-back was in charge there - Tommy Gemmell. I realised early on that the club were a shambles, and weren't being run properly. This wasn't Tommy's fault, the problems emanated from the very top of the tree at Cliftonhill.

I made efforts to identify players who would have improved the side, only to be told that the board wouldn't even pay for their travelling expenses. It was so amateurish that it was impossible to progress in any way, and so I called it a day. It shocked me that senior clubs in Scottish football were still being operated so poorly, and I didn't want to be part of that.

★★★

Coaching kids gave me a lot of pleasure, and none more so than my own boys - Martin, Andrew and Simon. I didn't pressurise any of them to play football, but once they showed an interest I was keen to get a ball out with them. We had two small goal nets in our backyard, and we would play football for hours. There were many crunching tackles out in the garden, but they were normally dished out by my daughter, Nicola, who also took part in our games now and again. My eldest son, Martin, had followed in my footsteps and played for Queen's Park. He was a tough-tackling defender, who relished the physical side of the game. Andrew was the most skilful of my three boys and he had a great touch, but he wasn't interested enough in the game to take his talent any further. I thought that was a great shame, but each to their own. Then Simon came along, and he showed some real promise from a young age.

Whichever team Simon played for, be it for the school or boys' clubs, he was always a prolific goalscorer; he just had that knack, and he had an excellent temperament as well. He started playing for Celtic youths at the age of 15, and was coached by former Aberdeen and Celtic midfielder

Dom Sullivan. Simon progressed quickly through the ranks and into the reserves, where he was coached by Kenny McDowall and my old team-mate, Danny McGrain.

After signing professional forms at the beginning of the 1999/2000 season, Simon got his head down and worked hard, and the goals kept coming for him in the youth and reserve sides. I went to watch him regularly in the reserves, and he was always going to get on the score-sheet. His positional play was excellent and he had some pace, although he wasn't as quick as his dad.

Celtic had made a bold appointment at the beginning of the season with ex-Liverpool star John Barnes being named as the club's Head Coach. After spending millions of pounds on largely unsuccessful imports, his bright start collapsed and he was sacked during his debut term in the dug-out. Barnes was replaced on an interim basis by my old team-mates, Kenny Dalglish and Tommy Burns, and it was under these two Celtic greats that Simon made his first-team debut.

Tommy was instrumental in developing the youth programme at Celtic Park, and it was due to his insistence that Simon got his first opportunity in the top team at the tender age of just 17.

Celtic played Dundee United in the final league match of the season on 21st May 2000 and quite a few youngsters got a taste of the action that day. Simon made a dream debut by scoring the opener in the 52nd minute, and fellow youngster Mark Burchill made it 2-0 with 25 minutes left to play. What an arrival it was for Simon, as he was named man-of-the-match in the game that marked the return of Henrik Larsson following his horror leg-break.

I had now attended Celtic Park as a supporter, an opposing player, a Celtic player, and the father of a Celtic player. The sight of seeing my youngest son representing this club, as I had done before, was a very proud moment indeed.

I spoke to Tommy Burns afterwards, and he explained that Kenny wanted to play Paul Shields ahead of Simon. It had been due to Tommy's insistence that they started with the striker who went on to open the scoring.

It was a great start for Simon, and I felt confident that he would get more top-team action if Kenny and Tommy remained as the management team. They both knew the traditions of the club, having come through the ranks as youngsters themselves, and all credit to them for playing so many kids that day.

The return of Henrik Larsson was also a hugely memorable aspect of Simon's debut. The Swedish talisman had suffered a horrific leg-break against Lyon earlier in the season, and everyone associated with the club were delighted to see the unmistakeable sight of his flowing dreadlocks, as he ran back on to the pitch in the hoops.

Simon and I had discussed how certain players were able to get 'into the zone' in order to succeed on a consistent basis at the highest grade in professional sport. It is a level of composure and confidence that makes you feel bullet-proof on the field of play. It is as much about mentality as physicality, and I had managed to tap into this frame of mind on the day of the 1977 Scottish Cup final, where I felt no nerves whatsoever.

The one player whom I believed mastered this mental fine-tuning in my day was Kenny Dalglish. His level of performance was such that he must have been able to mentally prepare himself so well on a daily basis. Simon cited Henrik Larsson as being the figure he noticed it with throughout his career. These two players were switched on during every training session and more consistently than anyone else during competitive matches. When a player manages to tap into that mind-frame, it can set them apart from their contemporaries and take their performance to a whole new standard.

No matter how well prepared Simon was the following season, his opportunities were going to be limited after the arrival of Martin O'Neill. The Northern Irishman was given a blank cheque book by the Celtic board, and he wasn't scared to use it. In came big-money buys Chris Sutton, John Hartson, Joos Valgaeren, Alan Thompson and Neil Lennon, and young players like Simon were pushed further back in the pecking order.

I can't say that I didn't enjoy watching Celtic during this period. The Larsson era (as I like to call it) was terrific for the supporters, but it was clear that Martin O'Neill was not going to build a Celtic side from within. Tommy Burns wanted to develop our youth players in the finest traditions of the club, and introduce them gradually into the first-team. However, O'Neill wanted players who could step into his first-team immediately, and he did this by purchasing ready-made (and hugely expensive) names right out of the English Premier League. He got instant results, so it was difficult for anyone to criticise his methods.

With O'Neill's side 4-0 up from the UEFA Cup first round first leg, Simon started against Jeunesse Esch in the return match at Celtic Park. After an hour, he collided with the opponent's goalie, Van Riffwifck, and suffered a stress fracture of the pelvic bone, which put him out for the remainder of that season.

I knew the frustrations that this long period on the side-lines would have caused Simon, but he continued to work hard behind the scenes, as Martin O'Neill's side swept their way to a domestic treble.

The following season saw another memorable performance by Simon, as he made his way back into the first-team against my former side Hearts at Tynecastle. O'Neill rested many of his first-team players for the upcoming Scottish Cup final against Rangers, and both Simon and Shaun Maloney scored braces in a 4-1 victory. In the last minute, and with both youngsters keen to grab their hat-trick, Simon and Shaun had a bit of an argument over who should take a penalty-kick. Shaun won the tete-a-tete and promptly hit the post from the spot.

Simon had a year left on his contract, and I was looking after his affairs because he didn't have an agent at the time. I arranged to go in and see Martin O'Neill to discuss Simon's future. When I went into O'Neill's office, the Celtic Manager seemed to be busying himself with other matters rather than focussing on the other person in the room. I felt that he was uneasy in my company because he had great difficult in actually giving me any kind of eye-contact. I found it all a bit strange.

"What are your feelings on Simon's progress, Martin?" I started the ball rolling.

"Well, he's done really well, but I'm not going to be going out of my way to play any youngsters," replied O'Neill. "I'm not here to bring young players through, I'm here to win trophies."

I'm not going to say that Martin O'Neill's approach was wrong because he garnered an excellent level of success, but it wasn't in keeping with the traditions of the club. He didn't even try to hide the fact that bleeding youngsters into his side wouldn't be a priority for him.

Following the Tynecastle fixture, the press contacted me for my thoughts on the match and Simon's performance. I had made efforts not to be too involved in that side of things, as it may have appeared too over-bearing on Simon, but I decided to speak to them on this occasion.

"It was great that the young players were finally given a chance at the end of the season," I announced. "I hope to see them getting more opportunities in the first-team in the coming seasons. After all, that's always been Celtic's way, and it's got to be the way going forward for the club."

Years later, a good friend of mine at the Celtic View, Stephen Sullivan, asked me, "Here Andy, did you ever make up with Martin O'Neill?" I was absolutely bemused by Stephen's question, and asked him what he was on about. Apparently, O'Neill had been furious at my comments in the newspaper, and he had gone up to Celtic's media room to ask the staff about me. What I had said in the papers wasn't even thinly-veiled criticism - it was my opinion on his approach to youth development. For some reason, Martin O'Neill failed to accept that I was entitled to that.

Listen, I'm not saying for a second that Simon should have played ahead of Chris Sutton or John Hartson. But giving a youngster one or two games a year does not aid his development.

As a Celtic supporter, I know that Martin O'Neill built a strong Celtic side, and he brought success to the club, but in the same breath he was given an unprecedented level of spending power in order to deliver that success.

Almost inevitably, Simon was transferred out of Celtic Park in 2003 and joined Craig Brown's Preston North End. Former Celt, Tosh McKinlay, was Simon's agent at the time, and there was an opportunity for Simon to sign for Bobby Williamson's Hibs. Looking back now, a transfer to another Scottish club would have been a better move because Simon needed first-team football at that stage of his career and he stood a good chance of getting that at Easter Road.

He scored on his Preston debut but I was slightly alarmed that Craig Brown gave Simon a "one for the future" tag after his first game. Sure enough, a few injured players returned to full fitness, and Simon was way back down the pecking order for a first-team berth.

Simon admitted himself that he struggled with the physicality of the English Championship, and he was loaned out to Blackpool and Stockport County in an effort to get some playing time.

Eventually Craig Brown was sacked (Simon always spoke highly of the ex-Scotland manager), and he was replaced by Billy Davies. Again, Simon rated him as a coach and he was a highly popular figure around the Preston squad, but his siege mentality seemed to hold back his progress.

As I mentioned before, I knew that the move down south wasn't right for Simon. He wasn't happy down there, and it was difficult for me as his father to see him going through those difficult times. During my rocky few years at Celtic Park, I had experienced some lows as a result of the injuries I had suffered. I was going into work every day, and wasn't allowed to do my job for a season-and-a-half. That would eventually get to anyone in their role. Add to that the additional high-profile nature of a footballer's role, the intensely high level of pressure to perform and get results, and it is a mine-field.

I knew what Simon was going through, but not a thing had changed in the world of football in the 30 years since my own struggles. There was no support mechanisms, and no counselling. Eventually, Simon called me one night to tell me that he wanted to come home.

Jim Duffy then brought Simon back up to Scotland and Dundee, and we began to see a completely different player again. I knew Jim (again we had played together in Celtic's reserves at the end of my career), and he was the perfect coach for Simon, who went on to score 18 goals in his solitary season at Dens Park.

Incredibly, Jim Duffy was sacked as his Dundee side were perched at the top of the Scottish First Division. The arrival of Alan Kernaghan resulted in a slow decline in the side's performance, and they began to gradually slide down the league.

This downward spiral led to Simon's move in 2006 to Brisbane Roar of Australia's A-League. After a blistering start, he earned himself a two-year deal under Israeli / Australian Coach, Miron Bleiberg.

★★★

I also moved out to Brisbane, and took on a coaching job with Sunshine Coast Fire in 2008. They played in the semi-professional Queensland State League, and I had to initially coach the squad the very fundamentals of ball control. They were a good bunch of lads, but I had a job on my hands. We trained three nights a week and I implemented some of the basic Coerver Coaching methods I had used years earlier to train kids in Lake Placid. After initially struggling to adapt to the ball drills, the squad responded well to my intensive training regime, and we won the championship in my only season there.

Surrounded by family, and enjoying the climate, I was content with how life had panned out for me. I was also delighted that Simon's career was back on track over in Australia. It didn't surprise me when he eventually retired in his late 20s through choice though. He wanted to do things away from the game, and went on to indulge in his thirst for study and passion for music.

I had enjoyed being back in my natural role as a soccer coach, but any aspirations I had to get involved in top-flight football again had long since evaporated. This should really have been the closing chapter of my football journey...

But then, completely out of the blue, I received a telephone call from an old agent I knew in Montreal, and my life was turned upside down. It was time to go back on the road again...

CHAPTER SEVENTEEN
THE BILLION DOLLAR BUYER'S CLUB

"When the piles of gold begin to grow... That's when the trouble starts."

Howard, 'The Treasure of the Sierra Madre' (1948)

★★★

Have you ever wondered what it entails to purchase an English Premier League football club?

Back in 2010, I was at the centre of an astonishing bid to buy one of English football's most celebrated institutions in a deal worth a mooted £400 million. We took negotiations right up to the edge of completion, and I stood to be a major player in the running of the club had it all gone through. But how did I get involved in such a gigantic deal? I sometimes ask myself that same question.

I was enjoying life over in Australia, when I received an unexpected phone-call from an agent I had known from my time in Montreal. I considered him as something of a bull-shitter, like most agents I've ever dealt with. Anyway, this agent (and I cannot reveal his name on account of a disclosure agreement I signed around about this time) was keen to make me a proposition.

"I'm working on something that you might be interested in," said the man from Montreal invitingly.

"Go on then," I implored.

"I'm representing the Sharjah royal family from the United Arab Emirates," began the caller, much to my mild curiosity. "The sheikh is looking to purchase a football team for his 12-year-old son's birthday. You know that

I know nothing about football; so, I'm asking you to be involved. You're the football expert, Andy."

I was astonished. In what sort of world did you buy an established football club for a 12-year-old boy?

I had to ask more questions about the origins of the deal, and he explained that the Canadian management company that he represented (Gameday) had been working alongside a cash-rich regime, who were determined to purchase a top-flight English football club.

I was to be appointed as the Football Advisor, in order for there to be a middle-man during negotiations who could actually speak the club's language. I stood to make a vast sum of money by getting involved. Naturally intrigued, I agreed to fly out to Montreal (at his expense, I made sure) to find out more of the finer details.

Once I touched down in Montreal, I was driven to the agent's offices, where I finally asked the all-important question, "So, what football club are we talking about here?"

"Liverpool," came his almost incidental reply. (I almost fell off my chair). "They're a good team aren't they? They're the ones who wear the red uniforms, right?"

This is not an exaggeration; the agent knew less than zero about the beautiful game.

He then introduced me to a Syrian businessman called Yahya Kirdi, who had been sent over from the United Arab Emirates to represent the Sarjah royal family. It was Kirdi's role to set up the deal with Liverpool's joint owners, George Gillett (whom he had already met), and Tom Hicks.

One problem was that Kirdi spoke less-than-impeccable English. Another was that the Syrian businessman was less-than-impressive on a personal business level. Apparently he only owned some minor companies in Dubai, but he represented one of the wealthiest and most powerful families in the Gulf States.

The agent was openly disrespectful towards Kirdi, and constantly spoke down to him in a curt manner. I felt that was unfair, as it became clear that much of what the Syrian wanted out of the deal was to get his family over to Montreal as immigrants. I rather think the agent had promised to assist him in securing Canadian citizenship, and in return the agent would get a substantial cut of the Liverpool pie.

Liverpool were carrying debts of around £250 million, and Barclays Capital had been tasked in April 2010 by the Royal Bank of Scotland to find a buyer, and oversee the sale of the club. Two offers were apparently in the works: A Chinese government-backed bid, and this package being put together by one of the UAE's ruling families, headed by Yahya Kirdi.

And, somehow, I had become involved in this complicated jigsaw puzzle.

"So, where do I fit in?" I asked the man from Montreal.

"The Liverpool Football Club don't know me, and they don't know who that guy is either (he pointed at Kirdi). You will be our football consultant, Andy. You're the football expert, and you will be the figure-head who deals with the football people in England."

Kirdi was clearly out of his element, and probably his depth too, and I felt like I had to do most of the talking for him. His English was poor but we still managed to communicate. He showed me respect because somehow he knew all about my career at Celtic, and revealed that he had played a bit of football himself in his younger days.

Throughout the negotiations, I would be the football consultant. Once the deal was concluded, I would be involved in the day-to-day running of the football club. "You can be the Chairman if that's what you want to do," explained the agent. "Once the deal is done, I'll be out of here."

The deal (and the figures were staggering) was that our party would invest £400 million of the Sharjah royal family's fortune into taking control of Liverpool Football Club. This would wipe out a near £250 million debt, remove Gillett and Hicks, and we would still have some 'change' to invest in the football team. The construction of a new stadium was also mentioned as being in the pipeline.

"Why Liverpool?" I asked the agent.

"I know the owner, no other reason," came the response, and I started to become suspicious. Who was he working for? I remembered that both Gillett and Hicks had owned National Hockey League (NHL) teams, and Gillett's were based in Montreal. I knew also that the agent had represented ice hockey players for years; so, it made some sense that he had joined the dots on this deal.

"Would you not be better off buying Celtic?" I asked, and I was deadly serious. "You would pick them up for a fraction of that price; they don't need a new stadium, and they don't have debts of that magnitude," I added.

The agent explained that money was no object, but he told me to go ahead and see if my ex-club were interested.

I immediately phoned Celtic Park, and spoke to the receptionist there. Being careful not to sound as though I was trying to wind them up, I was careful to explain in detail who I was, and that I had a close association as a player with the club over a number of years. The receptionist was left with a request for the powers-that-be to call me back as a matter of urgency. Almost needless to say, that call never arrived.

Who's to say what might have happened had the £400 million cheque made its way to the East End of Glasgow?

While back in Montreal, I was introduced to George Gillett and Tom Hicks over dinner. We all went for a meal in a beautiful and private restaurant, and it gave me a chance to get to know these globally successful entrepreneurs.

I got on well with the little guy - George Gillett - and he seemed very inquisitive; so, I decided to engage him in one-to-one conversation rather than open myself up to the whole group. Then, to my surprise, he asked me a question in a way that made all the dinner guests stop talking and focus on the pair of us.

"Andy, can you tell me why we get so many players at Liverpool who get these annoying hamstring injuries? I'm more of a hockey man - you know how great my team are because you lived in Montreal - but I'm not up on soccer much. I've been wondering about these injuries for a while now. Do you have any ideas what might be causing them?"

He had put me right on the spot in front of everyone around the table. No one else had really spoken to me during the meal, but it was now all eyes on me. I composed myself, and then recited my story about my first day of training at Philadelphia Fury, and how the physio had explained that the lack of preparation by British players caused poor flexibility, which inevitably resulted in far more muscle injuries.

Gillett was nodding all the way through my explanation, and he seemed suitably impressed with my knowledge of a sport he clearly had no real interest in beyond a balance sheet.

Meeting Gillett and Hicks confirmed to me that this was the real deal. The Montreal agent's lack of knowledge, and Kirdi's lack of interpersonal skills (including his command of English) had not filled me with confidence up to that point. Having met the Liverpool owners, I finally realised that this deal wasn't the stuff of fantasy.

I got the impression that the two Americans didn't get on with each other. They both had a level of wealth that exceeded the wildest dreams of most and, compared to the sheik's hapless representative, they were operating in a different league in terms of business acumen. However there was no doubt that they wanted to sell the club, and Kirdi had the backing to provide them with a nine-figure cheque.

With such vast sums of cash being touted, it was only a matter of time before the greed set in - if it had not done so already. The agent was taking another trip to the Middle East to meet the sheikh for a second time, but I wasn't asked to attend. I stressed that I should be introduced to the money-man if I was going to be his eyes and ears during boardroom discussions and negotiations with the bank, but I was told that I only had to deal with the Liverpool side of the deal. His obvious reluctance to take me over and introduce me cast some doubt and more suspicion in my mind regarding the whole deal. As it happened, he went over to ask the sheikh for more expenses and returned with a six-figure sum and a brand new Rolex watch. I smelt a rat.

Our next trip was to Liverpool itself, and I was very impressed with their excellent Melwood training facility. The Academy Director was Frank McParland, whose reputation was on the rise. I asked him if he would do anything differently if we took over, and advised him that I would do everything I could to assist him with Liverpool's youth programme if the bid was successful.

I was also introduced the club's Chief Executive, Ian Ayre, who came across as an all-round decent individual, and who explained to me that the club sold more replica jerseys in Asia than any other football side in the world. It was clear to me that Liverpool were operating in a different stratosphere to any club I had ever been involved with.

We were invited to attend the Liverpool versus Stoke City game as guests of Gillett and Hicks, and I remember being introduced to Steven Gerrard at half-time in the guests' room. Upon hearing that I was an ex-Celtic player, the Liverpool midfielder was quick to explain to me that he had a great love of the Glasgow club. Steven went on to explain that he had a framed Celtic jersey at home, and that it had the name of 'Lynch' on the back of it. At that point I realised that my son, Simon, had been thrilled to swap jerseys with Steven after the Ronnie Moran Testimonial match at Anfield a few years before. I explained this to the Liverpool captain, who seemed happy to stand and chat about my former team.

I was presented to the press as being the spokesperson for the potential buyers of Liverpool Football Club, and this resulted in a huge amount of media interest in the story.

"Everyone knows Liverpool aren't the force that they once were, so this is just what they need at this time," I told the press. "I've been to Anfield on business recently, and am acting as the go-between in the takeover deal."

Everywhere we went, we were chauffeur-driven. I remember we were based in London when we visited Liverpool, and we were driven from our hotel in the capital to the stadium in Liverpool. We had regular meetings in London, Montreal, Dubai and Liverpool, and stayed in the most prestigious of hotels in each city. Tens of thousands of pounds were being haemorrhaged but Gillett and Hicks weren't spending a penny of their own cash. The American owners didn't seem to mind burning money mainly because it wasn't theirs; it was Liverpool's. Gillett and Hicks were pushing the boat out in an effort to finalise the deal. Accordingly, it didn't surprise me when those loyal Liverpool fans began a revolt against their co-owners to get them out of the club.

Kirdi and I went over to Dubai so that he could finally introduce me to the Sheikh. The Syrian explained to me that the new owner would bank-roll the purchase and running of the club, but he wouldn't want to be involved in the day-to-day operation. That would all be down to me, as I would be his representative at Liverpool F.C. The responsibility of such a role was huge, but I wasn't overawed by it, and I started planning the types of people I would bring into the club to assist me.

The sheikh had his own football club over in Dubai, and he took us to watch them train. I could have gone over their to coach his side and earned myself a fortune, but I had invested so much time in this takeover deal that I wanted to see it through.

He came across as a well-educated, polite and surprisingly humble man, and he was keen to learn more about Liverpool. I explained to him that Liverpool were similar to my old side, Celtic, in so many ways, because the passionate support raised the clubs to a different level from most other clubs. I described how the passion these supporters displayed was unrivalled and that they would worship him if he was able to rescue their club because they lived for their football. The sheikh enjoyed gaining an insight into his investment, shook my hand warmly, and thanked me for all my ongoing efforts.

Before we left Dubai, Kirdi made a point of asking me who the best manager in Europe was. I told him that, in my opinion, it was Jose Mourinho.

"Will we go for him?" asked Kirdi excitedly.

"Yahya, we haven't concluded the deal yet," I cautioned. "Wait until we buy the club before you start worrying about things like that."

If the deal had gone through, I know they would have gone for Mourinho, because they trusted my judgement on football matters, and they had unthinkable wealth.

Once I returned home to Glasgow after our Dubai trip, I decided that I better start putting plans in place. I wanted to build a team of trusted aides who could go into Liverpool with me. The first guy I contacted was a friend of mine who worked as the Head of Media for Celtic - Tony Hamilton.

Tony and I met for a coffee in the city, and I described how the deal with Liverpool was moving in the right direction. If it went through, I would need to employ professional and loyal individuals, who could help steer this great club back to the top. I told Tony that we could double his wages, and asked him to consider joining me if things worked out with Liverpool. His sense of loyalty was one of the main reasons that I asked Tony to join my team, but it was this core value that may have prevented him from leaving his beloved Celtic. I had planted a seed with Tony and told him it wouldn't be long before I got back to him.

The next stop was London, where I was to meet three executives of the Royal Bank of Scotland. Kirdi and an accountant came down with me. The accountant was one of the Montreal agent's men, and I remember he said to me crudely, "Can you believe that he (Kirdi) represents one of the richest people in the world?"

I must admit, I had asked myself that same question a few times already.

When we got sat around the table with the banking executives, Kirdi was staring out of the window, and the accountant was taking notes. With no-one else to focus on, the executives started firing financial questions directly at me. I thought I was the football guy?

We were there to verify that Gillett and Hicks were paying the interest on the debt, which was around £2.5 million a week, and the bank supplied us with all the relevant accountancy figures that we needed confirmed at that time. The bank was desperate for the deal to go through because they had allowed the financial mess to escalate, and someone's neck was surely up for the guillotine.

Meanwhile, Gillett and Hicks had fashioned the perfect scenario. They had bought the club with someone else's money, milked it for as much as they could, lived like the millionaires that they were, and it didn't cost them a penny. Now they were about to walk away from the shambles with a profit.

On the fateful day of the deal, Yahya Kirdi and the Montreal agent's accountant went to the Royal Bank of Scotland with the official bid of £400 million and the proof of funds. Everyone else involved in the deal were waiting by the phone for confirmation.

Enter King Rat.

The Montreal agent, who had dragged me into this deal in the first place, had a foot in both camps and that was muddying the waters. All of a sudden the deal stalled, and the sellers failed to conclude and ratify the sale.

We were told there was some kind of legal hitch, and we were to all go home for the time being. Once the deal was concluded, we would be informed.

I phoned Kirdi, who was on his way back to Dubai incredulous with rage. Before the deal had been concluded, Gillett and Hicks had asked for more money at the very last minute. Kirdi had spoken to the sheikh to seek advice, and he was told to tear up the offer and return home immediately. Not a penny more would be offered.

The deal was dead, and there was to be no second chance.

I packed my bags and returned to Glasgow, never to see the charlatan agent from Montreal again. It was clear to me that he had been in cahoots with Gillett and Hicks, and had fed them information on the buyer. Thinking they could increase their own profits, the Americans asked for more, and they snuffed out the sheikh's interest with their greed.

My experience with Liverpool Football Club gave me an incredible insight into the mind-blowing multi-billion-pound enterprise of English football and, had it not been for that deadly sin of greed, then the deal would have surely been concluded.

Having devoted months of my life to what had become a circus, I decided to retreat back to the sanctuary of my family, and the quiet life that it offered me.

Have you ever wondered what it entails to purchase an English Premier League football club?

The truth is even stranger than fiction.

EPILOGUE

The rail journey from Queen Street to Haymarket is a well-travelled path for me. It was in Scotland's capital where I made my first tentative steps as a professional footballer in 1969, when Johnny Harvey plucked me from junior football and almost immediately threw me into the Hearts first team.

As I sit in my carriage on the sun-blessed afternoon of 17th September 2016, I take a few moments to think back to those halcyon days of the late 1960s. I've been doing a lot of reflection over the last two years, as my life story slowly poured from the deepest recesses of my mind and on to the pages you see before you.

I'm travelling to Edinburgh to meet Paul John Dykes, who has worked with me in putting together my autobiography. We have enjoyed numerous writing and discussion sessions over the last couple of years in the Auld Reekie, Glasgow, and even in Spain - where we took a ten-day break for some inspiration over a glass or two of red wine and a few beers. Today will probably be our final meet before the book goes to press, and we are making the final photograph choices after sifting through hundreds of possibilities.

I am early (as always), and my writing companion joins me on George Street soon after with a huge folder of photos. As we go through the piles of images, Paul John asks me a few more questions about Hoops, Stars and Stripes…

Q.) You've been largely out of the game for quite a few years now Andy. What made you decide to put your memoirs together now?

A.) Writing my autobiography was always a possibility because I had enjoyed some marvellous success with Celtic, but I specifically wrote this with my grandchildren in mind. I wanted Sophie, Ajay, Josh, Erin, Sean, Amelia and

Maya to have a lasting document from their granddad, and what better way to do that than to write my life story?

I hope my four kids – Nicola, Martin, Andrew and Simon – enjoy the book too of course, and that they are still speaking to me after reading it!

Q.) How have you enjoyed the process of writing this book, and did anything surprise you as you were working on it?

A.) It has been an unusual experience at times because I really had to delve into the past in order to do the story justice. Sometimes retracing your steps doesn't always provide you with positive memories, and that is something I have had to deal with at certain stages of the process.

I hadn't looked at my old scrap-books for years. When I finally read through them again, and saw the quotes from my former manager Jock Stein, I felt very humbled that he always believed in me. During my time at Celtic, many players arrived and departed - Jock didn't waste any time if a player didn't measure up. But throughout all of my injury anguish, he showed great faith in me. For that I will be eternally grateful.

Q.) When you read over your achievements in the 1970s for Celtic, it must fill you with a great sense of satisfaction and pride, having supported the club your whole life?

A.) I've never taken my achievements at Celtic Park for granted, and I have always been immensely proud to have represented this special club. I think I enjoyed the good times even more due to the terrible disappointment of initially missing out on first-team football through injury. But having gone through my entire career with a fine tooth-comb to write this book, I can only say I am fairly satisfied with what I achieved in the game. This may surprise some readers but I think I could have done even better.

My injury problems held me back from showing the real me. I signed for Celtic as a highly-rated left-winger, and you don't lose that ability overnight. Circumstances resulted in me not playing in my original position, but I wanted the opportunity to realise the potential that Jock Stein identified when he signed me. I got another chance (at left-back), and a lot of players never got that. Those performances from 1975 onwards showed that I could still play, but I've always been over-critical of myself.

Even as a 12-year-old, I kept a diary of all my games and I mentioned this in my book. If I scored a hat-trick then I thought I should have scored five or six. I always wanted to improve and strived to be the best I could possibly be.

The prospect of me leaving Celtic having failed to achieve a first-team starting place was hellish for me. Again, I have Jock Stein to thank for having the patience and belief in me throughout my nightmare 18-months.

I never did work out the difference between having a desire to win or a fear of failure. I would say that I am more in the second category, but you tend to achieve the same results in any case; it's just that the source of motivation is different.

Q.) How difficult was it for you to leave the club, having scaled the heights in your last five years at Celtic?

A.) I can split my seven-year Celtic career into three different first-team squads: The Scottish Cup-winning team of 1975; The 1977 double-winners; and the 1979 league-winning side.

If you compare the 1975 team to the 1979 side, then you get an inkling of the level of turnover in personnel over a relatively short space of time.

It seemed to be that Celtic sides were quickly broken down and rebuilt during my time at the club. Not too many players remained at Celtic beyond the age of 30, and there was a real revolving-door transfer policy.

This may have been because we were constantly looking back at the Lisbon side. No matter what Celtic achieved, we always compared it to the success of 1967, and nothing was ever going to match that.

Eventually the time came when I wasn't picked for the first-team even though I was fit to play, and I quickly realised that it was time for me to move on too. I was sad to leave, but Celtic have never left me.

Q.) That attraction to Celtic certainly never leaves you. What is it about this club that makes it so special?

A.) Celtic have a very unique attraction, and I think it has a lot to do with their charitable origins and what the club stands for. There is no doubt that a lot of figures in the public eye wish to be associated with the good name the club has. Numerous film stars, musicians, and politicians have all had that affinity with Celtic, and they are not afraid to publicise it. I saw it during my time there in the 1970s.

I remember one such occasion, when Rod Stewart made his way into the home dressing-room after a match at Celtic Park. We were all thrilled to see him but I think Rod was just as excited to meet his Celtic heroes, specifically Jimmy Johnstone. One of the boys got a ball out and Rod started doing keepie-uppies in the changing room. Then he was handed a Celtic top and he promptly put that on as well. He explained that he had a gig in Birmingham that night, and his chauffeur was waiting in his Rolls Royce outside to take him to the airport.

I also recall being in the Celtic Park changing room one day when Sean Connery walked in with Jock Stein. He was showing his two sons around the stadium, and he introduced himself. I remember noticing how huge he was, but he was a pleasant big guy.

'What did you do at work today, Andy?'

'Just the usual, you know; I was chatting to James Bond...'

I was never really star-struck by that kind of thing though, because I was playing football every day with most of my heroes. And, in any case, these 'famous' people were all really down to earth.

Billy Connolly's exactly the same; just a really decent human being. I remember not long after I signed for Celtic I met Billy through a Priest I knew, Father Timmy McGlynn. Father Timmy and I would meet up for a coffee, and he was always fundraising for areas like Blackhill and Provanmill.

Father Timmy asked me to go along to one of his fund-raisers to hand out prizes to underprivileged children, and I was only too happy to assist him. When I arrived at the venue, the Priest explained that one of his old school-mates would also be joining us to help out. Just at that a Rolls Royce drew up, and out jumped Billy Connolly. They had been pals for years!

Of course, Billy wanted to chat to me about Celtic, and he was actually a wee bit nervous about getting up and speaking on stage believe it or not. He had given the people of Blackhill a hard time in one of his sketches, and he was worried that he might not get a great reception from them. I told him not to be daft, and that they would love him.

Sure enough, he got up on the stage and brought the house down with laughter.

I remember years later, I was out having a meal with my partner, Margaret, when Billy walked into the restaurant with his adult daughter. I wouldn't have bothered him, but he spotted me and came right up to chat. Once he sat down to eat, I heard him saying to his daughter, 'Do you not know who that guy is? That's Andy Lynch of Celtic'.

Imagine him saying that about me? He's the superstar!

Q.) You also noticed this affiliation to Celtic numerous times during your time in North America. Where did it all go wrong for the NASL?

A.) During my years playing and coaching in America and Canada, I really was impressed with the way they went about their business. The way they organized and managed to sell events amazed me sometimes, but they didn't focus enough attention on grass roots back in my day.

As I explained in this book, I was responsible for setting up the youth structure at Montreal Manic. Unfortunately, before we could see this through, the NASL folded in the early 1980s.

I've not been surprised at the game's progression since the league was re-launched back in the 1990s, and it seems to just get better and better. I still watch the American game now. Some of the matches are getting capacity crowds and we shouldn't really be surprised. If they have a weakness then they root it out and the Americans have always had the Midas touch when it comes to sport. So why not with soccer? They really love their football over there now and I can only see it going one way. I truly believe that the U.S.A. will win the World Cup within my lifetime.

Q.) During the writing of your autobiography, I got the opportunity to watch a couple of Celtic games with you in 2015. It was clear to me then that you haven't lost any of your passion for the club. How impressed have you been with the man who currently fills your left-back shorts, Kieran Tierney?

A.) With a club like Celtic, it's not a huge surprise that they can produce a quality young player like Kieran Tierney. You would expect that an exceptional player should be produced through the youth development system every couple of seasons. They certainly brought them through in droves when I played.

Kieran looks a calm player, who approaches the game as though he's been in the side for years. He looks like the type of natural performer who doesn't have to think too much about the game. He has been terrific, has a good temperament, decent balance, is decisive in the tackle and he knows when to overlap, which is so important for a Celtic full-back.

The philosophy of the coaches that brought me up was that a good young player would be put into the first team for maybe 10, 12 or 15 games and they would then be pulled back out again for a rest. This also allowed the player to observe the game from the sidelines before going back into the fray. It has all been going so well for Kieran and I am not suggesting that he is going to have a loss of form. If he was to drop out of the first team for a spell, the only problem I could foresee would be that there is nowhere for a young player in Scottish football to go to continue their development. That was where the Reserve League was paramount to our game when I played. Many of my contemporaries would agree that it was the perfect platform for young players who are simply too good for the youth level. It also allowed first-team players to come back from injury and play at a competitive standard, and those who were out of the picture had an opportunity to put themselves in the shop window. There was a really good blend there and we definitely miss the Reserve League in Scottish football.

It would also be a very positive message to the Celtic supporters if the club were to stand firm against any massive bids from down south for Kieran Tierney. The fans would be very grateful if the powers-that-be did all that they could to hold on to their young talents. There is a real affinity between the supporters and young players like Kieran, and this is because every Celtic fan in those stands has fantasised about playing for Celtic Football Club.

At that point, Paul John and I are interrupted by a stranger, who has approached us from the hotel bar. We are sitting in the corner of the room with a lifetime of photos strewn all over a couple of tables, and I realise that this middle-aged man is about to recall one of his memories from our collection of stills.

"Andy, I was at Hampden the day you scored that penalty kick against Rangers in 1977," he exclaims, as he shakes me by the hand. He then turns around to Paul John, "What a day it was. This man won us the Scottish Cup and I'll never forget it."

I accept this man's compliment and feel a genuine warmth in his demeanour and handshake, as he wishes us all the best and rejoins his friends at the bar. Celtic have probably played a huge part in that guy's life and I never take that for granted. As a player, maybe I made his weekend a bit more enjoyable a few times. Perhaps I gave him the bragging rights for a whole week at his work after an Old Firm victory. Either way, I have had conversations like that with literally hundreds of strangers all over the world.

But they are not strangers are they? They are part of this unique Celtic family. No matter where they are from, the one thing that binds them all together is this thing called Celtic. We have all been intoxicated by this magical club at some point in our lives; it is the seductive temptress who trips us up when we least expect it, and raises us to heights we never thought possible.

Celtic Football Club has given ordinary people extraordinary experiences and emotions for almost 130 years. It is a family of millions, and one that I am eternally proud to have represented.

Andy Lynch, 17th September 2016

ALSO FROM CQN BOOKS

THAT SEASON IN PARADISE - TEN MONTHS OF CELTIC HEAVEN

"That Season in Paradise' perfectly captures the greatest year in the history of Celtic Football Club. Alex Gordon's book takes me right back to that unforgettable campaign when I was delighted to be part of the Celtic team that won everything – including of course the European Cup. This makes me feel as though I'm back in the Celtic dressing room! Bertie Auld.
Published August 2016. Foreword by Sandro Mazzola. Price £15.99

CHARLIE GALLAGHER? WHAT A PLAYER!

Charlie Gallagher was a Celtic player over over a decade and his time in the Hoops was certainly eventful, touching the depths of despair and the ultimate triumph. He was much revered by the Celtic support, his football brain was much admired and he had the ability to spray passes that Celtic's fast running forwards would relish. Remembered for his role in the 1965 Scottish Cup Final and his delivery in the last minute against Vojvodina, Gallagher is the latest Lisbon Lion to have his book published by CQN.
Published March 2016. Forewords by Willie Wallace and Tommy Gemmell. Price £14.99

THE WINDS OF CHANGE - MANAGING CELTIC FC 1991-2005

Continuing the story of managing Celtic after Jock Stein which started in the acclaimed Caesar & The Assassin. Here the spotlight starts on Liam Brady and moves on to the subsequent appointments of Lou Macari, Tommy Burns, Wim Jansen, Dr Jozef Venglos, John Barnes, caretaker boss Kenny Dalglish and last but not least Martin O'Neill. This was the most turbulent, tumultuous, topsy-turvy period in the history of club. A time when Celtic teetered of the very brink of extinction, an age where they would come so close to achieving a second European trophy.
Published November 2015. Forewords by Billy McNeill and Davie Hay. Price £19.99

CAESAR & THE ASSASSIN - MANAGING CELTIC AFTER JOCK STEIN

This is a compelling and fascinating insight into life as a Celtic manager for two of the club's legends. During an extraordinary, tension-laden thirteen years, Billy McNeill and Davie Hay were entrusted to continue the unique tradition of one of the world' most famous and romantic football clubs. There were spectacular highs and heart breaking lows, unforgettable League Championship triumphs and dramatic near misses, breath-taking Cup Final wins laced with suspense and controversy. And European nights that for better or worse will live long in the memory. This is essential reading for Celtic supporters and is perhaps Alex Gordon's finest book.
Published in November 2014. Alex Gordon with Billy McNeill and Davie Hay. Price £18.99

These, along with all other CQN Books are available from **www.cqnbookstore.com**